NO OUTLAWS IN THE GENDER GALAXY

Chayanika Shah identifies as 'a self-defined atheist woman'. She is an optimist activist at heart, a physicist by training and a teacher by choice. She has worked in areas like politics of population control, communalism, feminist studies of science, and sexuality, which seem to have no connection with each other but which have come together of late to define her as a queer feminist.

Raj Merchant identifies their gender as a work in progress. They have worked in a variety of fields ranging from micro-finance to marketing to animal behaviour to engaging with queer feminist activism. Working on this research and book helped them greatly (re)shape their gender.

Shals Mahajan identifies as 'genderqueer'—but prefers being called '*nirale*'—and is a queer feminist activist and writer. Ze loves reading, cats, writing fiction and lounging around, and is roused from these exciting activities to work on gender, sexuality, communalism and other structural inequalities because of the rage they generate. Ze has also published a children's book, *Timmi in Tangles*.

Smriti Nevatia identifies as 'a feminist who prefers the pronoun *she* for herself'. She enjoys dark beers, dark chocolate and reading about the dark depths of humanity in crime fiction while studiously avoiding it in real life. She has worked in documentary filmmaking and as a film festival curator, and has published a few (very few) short stories, poems and essays.

NO OUTLAWS IN THE GENDER GALAXY

Chayanika Shah
Raj Merchant
Shals Mahajan
Smriti Nevatia

zubaan

ZUBAAN
128 B Shahpur Jat, 1st floor
NEW DELHI 110 049
Email: contact@zubaanbooks.com
Website: www.zubaanbooks.com

First published by Zubaan Publishers Pvt Ltd 2015

10 9 8 7 6 5 4 3 2 1
ISBN 978 93 84757 68 7

Zubaan is an independent feminist publishing house based in New Delhi with a strong academic and general list. It was set up as an imprint of India's first feminist publishing house, Kali for Women, and carries forward Kali's tradition of publishing world quality books to high editorial and production standards. *Zubaan* means tongue, voice, language, speech in Hindustani. Zubaan is working in the areas of the humanities, social sciences, as well as in fiction, general non-fiction, and books for children and young adults under its Young Zubaan imprint.

Printed at Raj Press, R-3 Inderpuri, New Delhi 110 012

Contents

List of Tables and Figures

Tables

Figures

Acknowledgements

As we approach the bittersweet end of an incredible journey—from the idea, to the research, to the first published report and sharing it with community, to the occasional paper in academic journals, and now this book—there are some heartfelt acknowledgements that we'd like to make.

It is difficult to articulate our feelings towards our respondents, mixed as they are in jostling measures of gratitude, love, awe, solidarity, fierce protectiveness, despair and immense hope. We salute your courage and generosity in sharing your lives, experiences and ideas so openly with us, and trusting our politics and persons with them. Both have been deeply enriched by these conversations.

The strength and conviction of what one feels, the commitment to live on one's own terms, the ability to love oneself and others despite everything, the *himmat* to take on the world and its ridiculous norms, the gall to be able to say, 'Just because everyone in the world says something, that does not make it right!'—this spirit that came through again and again gives us hope and spurs us on.

We send a huge shout-out to the other members of the original research team—Georgina Maddox, Hasina, Kranti, Meena Gopal, Meenu, Sabala and Shruti. Thank you for all the camaraderie, the hugs, the discussions that threatened to tear us apart but strengthened us, the endless rounds of tea and coffee (and other spirits).

A project of this magnitude would not have been possible without the generous support of our queer and feminist comrades and friends. To thank them all here is a task we find ourselves unequal to, since it is not just about the naming of names but also the innumerable ways in which they have been part of our individual and collective lives. We send you love and heartfelt thanks, and hope you know who you are and how important you are to us.

To all the comrades, activists, friends and readers who gave us feedback at different stages of the work, thank you. Amalina Kohli Dave and Aparna Joshi, thank you for reading our manuscripts and giving us detailed feedback. A huge thank you to Shweta Vachani and the wonderful team at Zubaan for their keenness to publish this and their patience thereafter.

And in the title of the book, we tip our nibs to Kate Bornstein, who started us as well as many others on our explorations and adventures with transfeminism.

A big cheer to all the members, past and present, of LABIA—A Queer Feminist LBT Collective. The work done by all of us over the last 20 years is no small part of who we are and what we bring to this writing. Thank you for forging the politics and persistence that motivated this research, the vigilant minds that do not let the least nuance escape nor hold anything so sacred that it cannot be questioned, and for constantly being open to dissent and discussion.

A very special thanks goes to all those around us who sustained us over the last few years: those who cooked for us in our homes and the places in Matunga where we landed at all hours to eat and drink; the animal familiars who either sat with us or whose memories warmed us as we wrote and rewrote, the trees and the squirrels and the birds who chirruped and distracted us when needed; our families, partners and friends who dealt with our endless meetings and inside jokes without frowning too much; and, of course, those who reminded us that this was important to finish, however long and arduous it felt.

This endeavour was essentially a collective one, guided by shared visions towards goals that were as personal as they were political. And we found this process to be fulfilling in a way that no singular activity can ever be. We were friends and comrades earlier, and are happy to note that these connections have only deepened over the last five years of working together so intensively.

However much we read, wrote and worked independently (and we did need to do that, in long, intense bouts), we returned to each other incessantly. From each of us, then, our biggest thanks are due to one another, co-writers and co-travellers on the journey that changed us all, as journeys do. We wouldn't have done it any other way, or wish for anyone of us to be different, other, more or less than who we were. Talking, listening, writing, arguing, late into the night in several cities and homes, we kept arriving at clarities and complexities and confusions, and visions and revisions—finally, through it all, at the book you hold in your hands.

Introduction and Context

As per the judgement of the Hon'ble Supreme Court of India, Transgender will be included as a third gender under the various scholarships/fellowships schemes of UGC.[1]

This was the text of a University Grants Commission notice published on 23 July 2014, one of the positive fallouts of the April 2014 Supreme Court judgement on transgender rights, and the court's instructions to all state agencies to implement changes within the scope of their work and policies.[2] However, in this single sentence lies the whole space of confusion, conflict and debate—about who is transgender, what the term 'third gender' means, and what all of this means for people marginalized on the basis of their gender identity or expression. At the same time, the debate does foreground the existence of genders beyond the binary, thus complicating the understanding of gender itself.

The language used by most people in popular media and even within state institutions themselves shows that 'transgender' and 'third gender' are both considered synonymous with hijras, aravanis, kinnars, eunuchs or other region-specific terms (henceforth referred to collectively as hijras). This is probably because hijras are the only visible gender-divergent socio-cultural community who have, over time, organized themselves in support networks. Yet, they have been denied basic citizenship rights—the right to identity and expression, access to education, health and livelihood, and so on. So far, apart from the token gesture of being given the obscure identity of 'other' by the passport authorities and the census, all such rights and access have been open to only two genders, 'men' and 'women'.

This is a very brief exposition of a rather complex question, but the conflation of transgender with third gender with hijra is one that exists all around us. The recent judgement and subsequent discussions, while very welcome and providing much needed space to transgender concerns and issues, have aided rather than altered this particular equation.

The crucial point here is that hijras are not the only transgender persons who have been denied their rights and marginalized on the basis of their gender identity and expression. There are many more who do not conform to the gender that they have been assigned, who face differing degrees of violence and exclusion, or are forced to live in ways that they do not wish to, often in silence and isolation. Their concerns and issues too need to be raised with as much urgency. This asks the question: What does 'transgender' mean and who, then, is transgender?

This question is necessary but it is not by itself sufficient. The assumption that the gender categories 'man' and 'woman' are self-evident, and questioning all others who challenge the norms that define these categories, is merely a fallout of the hegemonic understanding of gender itself. At the heart of this issue lies the 'naturalness' of the gender binary, the constructed 'naturalness' of a world made up of two sexes and two genders, and heterosexual desire as the only legitimate desire. The more crucial questions, then, are: How is gender understood and constructed in the world that we inhabit? How does it operate through the various socio-political-cultural structures around us? What does this mean for people who conform to, or diverge from, its strictly imposed norms?

The questioning of these norms, and the continuous breaking of them, have always happened, and the histories of the marginalized tell us that every norm has had to deal with dissent. However, the mainstream understandings do not shift nearly as much as those struggling for change desire. There are more histories to be discovered, more stories to be told, more voices to be heard—of those who dissent through their very lives. The need is to work not just for inclusion of these voices, but also for shifting the very way in which we think of gender and sexuality.

This book is part of these conversations and attempts. It follows from a research study that we did as LABIA to understand more about gender through the lives of queer individuals who had been assigned gender female at birth.[3] The details of the why, the who and the what of this study, and of this book, will come by and by, but to understand the context of the present enquiry, it is important to also locate ourselves, the authors of this book, and our politics by tracing our journey till this point.

Where We Began

The first time we had to answer the seemingly innocuous question, 'Why are you a woman?' was in 2001. A bunch of us were working on organizing a workshop on gender and sexuality for 'people like us', who were, from that particular point of view, friends and fellow feminists. Some identified as lesbian, some straight, all of us either part of organizing within the feminist or the LGBT movements, and interested in finding space and time to discuss our ideas and work on sexuality and gender.[4] This question, both in the preparations and later in the workshop, provoked some intense discussions, even some resentment. We were, after all, all of us feminists, and had struggled all our lives and in our work almost continuously with being and becoming women in our own right. We had broken several norms of society and often had had to fight tooth and nail to be able to be the way we wanted to be. In our lives, work and politics, we had intensely questioned social and cultural constructions of gender and sexuality. We understood patriarchies and the ways in which they operate, the construction of gender binaries and the imposition of norms, and the complex interactions of family, class, caste, gender and society in the creation and protection of gendered hierarchies and power.

Yet, this question, in the context that it was asked, shook us. The answer to why it did so lies not just in our personal journeys, but also in the twin contexts of feminist and LGBT organizing and politics of the country.

LABIA – A Queer Feminist LBT Collective, then Stree Sangam, started in 1995 as a collective of and for lesbian and bisexual women with two clear agendas: to support and network with other women like us and to together create safe spaces for women to talk and express themselves; and to work towards change in larger society along with other groups and movements. Gender and the imposition of gender norms were a large part of our discussions since the time we began. Several of us identified either 'butch' or as 'women who look different', and spoke of continuously facing violence or oppression because of the way we looked and dressed, and the way in which we were perceived by both men and women. Some of us found it easier to see ourselves as androgynous and some even spoke of 'our masculinities' though that was a contested space. It was clear even then that often, for some of us, gender-segregated women-only spaces were not necessarily safe. Some of us went to great lengths, in fact, to avoid travelling in, say, women's compartments on the local trains and such like.

The political and feminist space of 'being women' and of celebrating 'difference' was precisely that which gave us the strength and courage to fight our continuous gender battles. The women's movements in India, where most of us located ourselves, itself was one where the question of difference was a primary one. The category 'woman', and sisterhood, were not monolithic, and discussions around differences of caste, class, work, location and others took centre stage.[5] These discussions were often volatile and sexuality had been part of them since the 1990s.[6] Issues around inclusion and exclusion were very much part of these debates; only, they had not yet entered the arena of questioning the entity 'woman' itself.[7]

The 1990s were also an intense period of activism in lesbian and gay organizing. At one level, there was the growing work on HIV/AIDS, which spoke of sexual behaviours and focused on men who had sex with men (MSM), and within that framework started providing services and spaces for men. There were also many groups that formed around 'gay' identity in the metropolitan areas as well as an even smaller but vocal number of groups for lesbian and bisexual women. This history has been documented elsewhere and so we will not go into details here, but suffice it to say that this period also saw the beginnings of what would soon become the LGBT movement in the country.[8] It also saw the first coming together of the women's and human rights groups on LGBT issues, whether with the conferences and workshops in Mumbai or later in the formation of CALERI (Campaign for Lesbian Rights) in Delhi fuelled by the release and subsequent 'ban' of the film *Fire*.[9] Another crucial coming together of disparate groups was the arrest in July 2000 of HIV activists working with MSM in Lucknow, and the countrywide protests and campaigns around them.[10]

At that particular moment in history, though, the stress was much more on sexuality, and issues around gender were not being addressed as clearly. In fact, the first national meeting, in 1997, to talk of 'our' rights was called 'Strategies to Advance Lesbian, Gay and Bisexual Rights.[11] The work around issues of kothis had been growing in the 1990s and so some understanding of gender-transgressive behaviour and identity was also being formulated, though it largely used the language of 'sexual behaviours' and in the context of HIV/AIDS. By and large, though, the understanding of transgender was limited to our understanding of hijras, who were also being 'targeted' by the HIV interventions under the MSM umbrella, or to a few people who had done sex reassignment surgery.

Intense discussions on gender, gender transgression, the construction and deconstruction of the binary of gender, and the marginalization and violence people face because of this entered LGBT organizing only in the 2000s. Even then, it was a struggle and often transgender concerns (along with those of lesbians and bisexuals) had to fight for space. By the time the World Social Forum rolled in (January 2004), the Rainbow March there visibly addressed issues of gender with sexuality. Prior to that, the first international film festival in Bombay, Larzish (October 2003), was tagged as a festival of sexual and gender pluralities. This is not to say that the shift in politics was either smooth or universal, but that for a lot of people, and more importantly for groups, gender became as crucial an issue as sexuality.

Stree Sangam itself saw a transition, in 2002, from being a 'lesbian and bisexual women's group' to becoming LABIA, a queer and feminist collective of 'lesbian, transgender and bisexual women'. Our language was still quite uncertain, but in this period many transgender-identified persons joined various LBT organizations and many of us also found the words to voice our concerns in a manner that made more sense. Another important shift that happened in the early years of this century was the increasing use of the word 'queer' as both a politics as well as an identity. At one level, there was a realization that the terms lesbian, gay, bisexual and even transgender did not begin to encompass the lived realities and the multitude of identities that people lived with, and at another, a growing maturity of a politics that was invested in contesting the heteronormative constructs of both gender and sexuality.[12]

Locating Gender

One might say that, though destabilizing, the question 'What makes me a woman?' was very much part of this growing change in our collective politics and work. Today, some of us are able to answer this question with, 'Because that is how I feel.' But it has taken a long time for this simple thought to sink into our collective consciousness and it is still an ongoing process. At some level, this answer presupposes an innateness of gender identity, something that feminist thought had been deconstructing all along.

It was feminism that taught us that we were socialized into becoming women according to what society, family, law, religion and other such structures dictated. It was our experience of being treated like women that made us women. It was not our bodies, but our embodied experiences that made us women. So it was, and for some still is, difficult to wrap our heads and politics around the fact that many of those who are not socialized as women also feel like women. And the next logical step—that their lives and concerns were also as valid a concern of our work and movements as of those who were brought up as women—was even more difficult. Similarly difficult to grasp was the reality of those who may have been socialized as women but felt that they were 'men'. This took us to torturous debates around the belief that they were saying so to access 'male power and privilege'.

At the same time, those of us, to whom the question was addressed were also in search for a language to express ourselves. The language we have, much like every other thing, is extremely gendered, and again and again, it binds us into categories that we might otherwise be more able to defy. Some people have found the language of 'trapped in the wrong body' useful, but for many others it does not work. A few started speaking of their gender being wrong and used the language of gender dysphoria. Yet others kept trying to redefine 'woman' because they did not identify with being 'men' and did not quite know how to move beyond the binary identities of 'men' and 'women'.

In both the queer and the women's movements, these questions around gender were articulated from multiple locations as more and more people who questioned the gender binary in their lives and work began to speak up. But this did not mean that there was, or is till date, any uniformity to these articulations and to the identities being taken.

Hijras, for example, have not always felt comfortable organizing under the rubric of 'transgender', though alliances are continuously being built around different terms, and MSM has been one such troubled term. The specificity of hijras and the cultural space they occupy needs a different articulation, as does the experience of those assigned gender male at birth who do not see themselves as either men or hijras. There have also been internal and external contestations on who can legitimately occupy the 'trans' space since there are broad differences in our lived experiences and the kinds of marginalization we have faced. The realities of persons assigned gender female at birth are often overlooked in the larger queer movement when issues of transgender persons are being raised.

It is in these multiple contexts, then, that we located our study. On the one hand, there were these discussions on gender, and on the other, this invisibility of people's lived realities and beginnings of multiple articulations. This study aimed to fill this gap in our understanding, politics and our interventions.

The Last Five Years

Since we began our research to when we wrote the final words in this book, much has changed. As we conducted our interviews and wrote up the report of the study and worked on this book, we were witness to, and at times active participants in, many of the processes involved. As this is not the space to do a chronological or a comprehensive accounting of all that has happened, we mention a few events and discuss some trends.

Queer Organizing

We started our research in 2009 with the exuberance of the Delhi High Court judgement of July that year seeping through many of our lives.[13] It was much more than just a reading down of a legal anachronism that we inherited from the British, namely, Section 377 of the Indian Penal Code. The judgement decriminalized consensual sexual acts between adults in private by invoking the values of democracy, equality and freedom. In doing so, it gave us a language for the articulation of sexuality, morality and privacy within the framework of the Constitution.

As we were nearing the end of the process of this research, came the Supreme Court judgement of December 2013 that recriminalized consensual sexual acts 'against the order of nature' between adults.[14] This not only took back the victory over 377, but also clamped down on the larger possibilities the high court judgement had enabled for a new language to address issues of both sexuality and morality. Our protests after this judgement were as much about this loss as about 377, especially since we were also seeing the country moving further towards a right-wing ideology that wants to speak of these issues only in the narrow framework of culture, tradition and religion.

The cycle of good and bad judicial pronouncements continued with the same Supreme Court granting the verdict in April 2014 on transgender rights. This not only gave some relief to the visibly marginalized trans* communities in our society, but also granted recognition to the multitudes of trans* people who are not as visible.[15] This judgement acknowledged self-identification of gender by individuals; used the international language of 'sexual orientation and gender identity' to recognize persons identifying differently and for protection of their basic rights; and expanded the scope of 'freedom of expression' within the Constitution by extending it to gender expression as well.

Our journeys, punctuated by these judgements and judicial activism, passed through the rough and tough terrain of social change—in the lives of queer people of all kinds, in women's movements and queer organizing, in institutions of power that maintain heteronormative structures, and in society at large. The change has been rapid in some pockets, accelerated by the nominal legal victories. In some places it is barely noticeable, and in yet other situations it seems to benefit a few and not the vast majority.

Post 2009, in larger urban centres and in some smaller towns, many more groups and collectives have come up that want to talk of LGBT rights. These formations are beyond the initial few that came up either from within the women's movements spaces or those initiated in the course of HIV/AIDS work in different parts of the country. This is evident from the number of cities and towns that now regularly hold 'pride parades' and 'queer/ LGBT' events and festivals. There are many more urban social spaces available for those from the upper classes. A neo-liberal, more market-friendly economy has seen many LGBT businesses gain ground. The market for parties grows as there is a more confident set of younger people with control over their income in metropolitan cities.

This confidence stems partly from their own class and positions of privilege, but also from the increased number of conversations on issues of sexuality—whether in college campuses or in the media. All of this is the more visible, mainstream face of change. There is greater openness to a liberal acceptance of various ways of loving and being. The dominant framework here, however, is of globalization and neo-liberalization where identities are being emphasized, and individual choice and freedoms are articulated like never before. This kind of queer organizing has made LGBT a known term, one that people now use with greater ease. The realities of the various lives that are bracketed in this and other alphabetical abbreviations are, however, not equally visible and known.

Even LGBT social spaces are often segregated. Those opening up for urban gay and lesbian people are fairly open about excluding those that visibly transgress clear gender boundaries, as is evident in the dos and don'ts put out at these events. This internal transphobia is couched in the language of not wanting to hurt the sensibilities of the larger mainstream within which these exclusive islands try to exist. What makes for the spectacle at pride parades seems to come in the way of the neat assimilations aspired by and possible only for those that pass off as 'normal' and 'just like anyone else'.

This exclusion is not just symbolic. It also means that while terms like LGBTHKQIA... or queer are used, they do not really include all those that should find space under these vast umbrellas. The concerns and realities of each of the various groups are not foregrounded with the same urgency and commitments; hierarchies in issues and priorities do come into play. In this way, the marginalized create their own forms of marginalization until they start standing up for themselves and demanding a different politics at best, or more inclusive political organizing at the least.

One group that has started the process of self-organizing for rights and recognition from the state are the hijras. The April 2014

Supreme Court verdict is a result of this mobilization, as have been the various other measures like welfare boards and changes in official documents for transgender people instituted by the central and various state governments. Another marginalized group is that of queer persons assigned gender female at birth. Among these (who appear as LBT in the LGBT) too there are more faces and voices to speak for the L and the B, whereas those who identify as a gender other than female, which they were assigned at birth, are a minority voice. In the hegemonic conflation of 'transgender' with the socially visible class of hijras, these other trans* persons and their lived realities are becoming further invisibilized. Groups working specifically with LBT people have grown, but not rapidly enough. There definitely are more support spaces today than there were even in 2009, but they are far less than what are actually needed.

Women's Movements

These people and groups (of which we, the writers of this book and the researchers of this study, are an integral part) have often found political solidarity also among the women's movements and organizations in the country. This solidarity is based on the fact that these were the first spaces for political articulations on structures of gender and sexuality. The feminisms practised and evolving within these groups have continuously addressed their blind spots to the complexities of gender. In this work, and in political articulations over the years, there has been a constant effort to see the intersections of various structures of society, and to place gender and sexuality in this complex matrix of class, caste, religion, race, ethnicity, ability, nationality, etc.

While initially these groups only used the framework of heterosexuality for their work on sexuality, over the years we find that many have become more open to other aspects of sexuality. Several centres working on violence against women are now spaces where lesbian women can expect some sort of support. They are also attempting to be more inclusive in other ways, building solidarities through the complex terrains of caste, gender, sexuality and labour, while engaging with issues of sex work and prostitution.

Similarly, while discussions in these groups began with the simple understanding of gender in terms of men and women, over time they have moved beyond the binary. There is a beginning made in recognizing that marginalization because of gender also happens for those who transgress assigned genders or gender expressions. A reflection of this shift was seen in the campaign asking for reforms in the sexual assault laws. For the first time in 2013, there was an unanimous voice from the women's movements that recognized structured gendered violence on those not recognized as 'women' and hence asked for laws where the victim is gender neutral but the perpetrator is male. It has taken a long and nuanced shift in politics to arrive at this understanding of gendered, patriarchal power that extends even to those outside the traditionally understood 'woman'.

While this significant shift has been made, the opening up of 'women-only' spaces to those who transgress the gender binary still has to deal with many roadblocks. So the question, 'Who can be called a woman?' is still not easily asked, let alone answered. 'Woman' as a category has been questioned from many sites. It has, however, been very difficult, both to completely relinquish the notion that 'woman' is primarily someone who is assigned gender female at birth and to fully assimilate in this category all who self-identify as 'woman' irrespective of their gender assignment at birth. Alongside this, it has been equally baffling to include in the analysis the bewildering number of options that are becoming available beyond the binary.

Although the contemporary discourses around gender have been largely confined to the women's movements on the one hand and queer organizing on the other, there is a more recent third space—that of masculinity studies, which is nascent, but significant nonetheless for the potential it offers. While its interrogation of dominant masculinities has translated into a growing amount of community work with men and boys, conversations around trans-masculinities are yet to enter this discourse widely.

The State

Along with changing political understandings within the movements for change, there has been a growing engagement with the state. The demands have been for recognition of identities and validation of basic citizenship rights. The attempt is to make visible those invisibilized from the mainstream and marginalized in terms of the basic rights due to every person from the state, like access to education, livelihoods, shelter and health care. As with every marginalized and invisibilized group that attempts such negotiation, all these efforts lead to some 'legibility' being accorded to them by the state. And as has been well documented, every such legibility is accompanied by the imposition of methods of standardization and uniformity (Scott 1998).

This is what we see in the efforts that the state and its various arms are making in the context of 'according rights to transgenders'—a simplified and reductionist view of who this 'transgender' is or can be. In the process, the easy conflation of the transgender with the hijra gets further solidified. A few other trans* identities may be included only if they fit themselves into broad, predetermined categories. There is a danger implicit in these new formations and formulations: that unless the binary gender is consciously questioned in many more ways, 'man' and 'woman' could remain uncontested and closed categories, while a separate space is grudgingly accorded to some (but not necessarily all) non-normative identities. The manner in which the state and the mainstream media have interpreted the NALSA judgement thus far have not done anything to allay these fears. There is need for a constant questioning of the efforts to fit the multiple ways of being into yet another new straitjacketed category of transgender.

This study makes one such attempt. An attempt to not only complicate our understanding of gender beyond the binary, but also to learn ways of retaining the multiplicities and diversities so that the galaxies and the rainbows are maintained even as we negotiate the solid, bleak and stark hegemonic binary gender system.

About the Book

In the course of the study, we interviewed 50 people who were assigned gender female at birth and identified as queer in some way. Many of these respondents did not identify with their given gender. While the details of arriving at this and the study questions are discussed at length along with the process of the research, in the methodology, it is important to acknowledge what each one of our participants gave us. This study was possible and has reached this stage due to their trust in us and their faith in this process, which made it possible for us to together revisit parts of their lives that were often painful, difficult and private. Most crucially, the courage with which they live their lives transformed this study as well as our understanding.

We have long known that the gender binary is shaped by families, education systems, media, religion and socio-political institutions such as the state and law, and even the medical system. We have also known that these institutions collude in perpetuating a gender structure that is deeply rooted in patri-archy. While attesting to these truths, our study further unravelled another layer of the gender structure and the insidiousness of heteronormativity.

We found families and schools to be spaces where the lifelong process of being punished for behaviours that do not fall within heteronormative boundaries are first encountered. Thus, individuals learn very early what is expected in terms of appearance and behaviour for their assigned gender. In this manner, these narrow and binary definitions of sex and gender roles are learned, taught and modelled in society. In later life, workspaces and public spaces also operate in ways that privilege gender normativity—remaining most accessible to persons who conform to norms of gender and sexuality.

These gender rules are communicated through social institutions and internalized through social interactions and relationships. Such a binary understanding of gender further acts in conjunction with structures related to race, class, caste and ability to create hierarchies of privilege, giving people unequal access and opportunity to education, livelihood and public spaces. This leaves no space for the realities of gender non-conforming lives in contemporary discourse. Thus, a whole range of experiences and identities is made invisible.

Our effort has been to understand not just various gender identities, but gender itself in all its nuance and complexity. Our respondents have challenged the gender binary in multiple and varied ways, some more overtly than others, but almost always subversively. Even though individuals manage to live in ways that are distinct and unique, the enforcement of the gender binary is so compelling that the institutions and systems remain seemingly impervious to such disruptions and challenges.

This book, therefore, explores how gender plays out in each of these public and private spaces as seen through our respondents' individual narratives and diverse lived realities. By looking at each institution independently, we hope to understand the specific ways in which binary gender norms are woven into each one of these. At the same time, our respondents' lives illustrate for us the myriad ways in which spaces can be created within these unrelenting structures. We also use these structures as a framework to explore the multiple ways in which interlocking systems of heteronormativity, casteism, class and ableism are enmeshed within patriarchy to create exclusion, marginalization, pathologization and violence.

Chapter one elucidates the scope and design of the study, as well as the methodology used to collect and analyse information. Chapter two gives demographic details about the respondents. Chapter three brings into focus the multiple ways in which our respondents name their genders and give meanings to these names. Chapters four to ten present our respondents' interactions with the institutions of family, education, work and public space, as well as their relationships with others and the self. We end each chapter with suggested short-term and long-term interventions that could work towards dismantling systemic oppression and challenging hierarchies around gender. The final chapter, keeping the testimonies of our respondents in mind, is an interrogation of gender itself, and how it can be envisioned or revisioned to be just and egalitarian.

A Note on Language

Languages mirror their time and place. Some may be more gendered than others, or less—Bengali, for instance, is entirely devoid of gendered pronouns, while English has 'he', 'she' and all their variants, and Hindi and French are among those that ascribe a masculine or feminine gender not only to humans but to all inanimate objects as well. Yet the norms and values of different societies tend to be deeply embedded in the language they use for everyday communication, so in societies based on the system of binary gender—as most human societies are—it is difficult to have conversations or to write more than a few sentences without bringing gender into sharp focus. With gendered languages this involves creative sleights of tongue or convoluted formulations. And with seemingly gender-free languages, proper names are almost always gendered even if pronouns are not and they certainly have words for boy, girl, man, woman.

In either case, it is absurdly difficult to sustain a conversation or a piece of writing without mentioning the gender of the people we are speaking or writing about. As listeners or readers in such a situation, we begin to experience the same restlessness that comes into play when we are unable to read the gender of a person we encounter: we demand to know if we are speaking of a boy or a girl, of a woman or a man. Once the gender has been made clear, we are relieved and can continue talking or reading with something 'basic' out of the way.

Just as binary gender defines our societies and, therefore, our linguistic expression, so too is heteronormativity as deeply embedded in our articulations as in our socio-cultural structures. Our languages, then, become tools that we use—deliberately as well as unknowingly—to enforce the gender binary and reinforce hierarchies of power and systems of oppression.

The words used for those marginalized—both by the binary gender and heteronormativity—that do find currency are often terms of abuse, ridicule or contempt. Thus, besides such persons being treated badly, the terms used for them, like hijra or kinnar, are often used in everyday language to indicate a lack of masculinity when applied to cismen. While this is true for the more widely recognized identities, the invisibility that other trans* communities experience is also reflected in our languages. At one level, trans* persons face the uphill task of speaking of themselves in terms and pronouns that feel comfortable for them, which varies according to the languages they have access to. At another, because of their visible but not clearly identifiable differences, they are targeted or spoken of in terms that vary from place to place and region to region. Sometimes, variations on existing words like man, boy, girl, brother, *bhaiya*, woman, etc. are used, and sometimes new vocabulary enters for a while through specific incidents. After the film *Fire*, for example, in small towns of Maharashtra, those who were read as 'women' and were visibly gender-transgressive, were often called 'Fire'.

The individuals and groups whose identities and expressions are marginalized because of the gaps in language try, then, to create new words or reclaim terms of abuse (like 'queer' has been reclaimed over time) or borrow from other languages to speak of themselves. LGBT is a good example of such borrowing and coinage as the term is not only used in mainstream queer organizing in its campaigns and public interactions, but has also entered media discussions and popular vocabulary. While this is largely positive, it represents an effort to create clear, visible and identifiable categories, which often do not reflect the multiplicity of experiences and expressions that people live with.

The conflation of T or transgender with hijra, discussed earlier, is one such outcome.

L for lesbian is also vexed. Since most Indian languages do not have a popular term for women who love women, lesbian is a term that is used by most people in almost all languages. While this does give visibility to women who love women or women who desire women, it negates the historical presence of the terms, and hence such desires, in indigenous languages and cultures. The argument here is not for rejecting the borrowing of words from other languages and realities; it is for reclaiming of wilfully ignored histories.

The other problem with the way in which 'lesbian' has been used is that it has been a catch-all phrase to include all persons assigned female at birth who express non-normative gender or sexuality. The presence of trans* persons in groups and social spaces has challenged this in the last few years. They have rejected this term being used for them because they do not identify as 'woman'. They may or may not have had names to speak of their genders, but they definitely objected to being called 'women'. Today, there is a shared vocabulary that has grown over time, with various names like transman, FTM (female-to-male), genderqueer, intergender, agender and so on added along the way. People draw from this and choose names for themselves when they join a group or community that has access to this vocabulary. The discussion has moved to include these trans* identities within the T of the LGBT, and also to keep this T as broad-based as possible.

For many people who break the gender binary, there is no popular terminology to describe their realities in ways that feel affirmative, while access to discourses in other languages, such as English, is usually a matter of class privilege. It is in the groups and collectives that are working to evolve a more inclusive lexicon, then, that these gender non-conformists are able to find not just a community but also a language that lets them feel they finally belong. This discussion on names and naming is, hence, important and reflects a complicated process of creating identities that can be categorized while finding space to retain nuances of the differences of identities and expressions.

In this book, we use trans* as an umbrella term that speaks of everyone who does not identify with their assigned gender, without even attempting to formulate the many specific identities that people might use. Our respondents have used a multiplicity of terms to talk of their gender identities and expressions, and we have tried to document these as well as the meanings that they imbue to these names. It is important that any discourse on gender takes such diversity into account and that has been our attempt here. We have also tried to use pronouns in a way that reflect people's gender locations by drawing from existing transfeminist discourses.

Our language, including our use of specific terms and pronouns, is as much a part of our learning process as it is of the movements and discourses around us. Given that the vocabularies emerging from transfeminism, queer thought and activism in this historic moment are dynamic and self-reflective, our articulations too might, over time and discussions, change. We urge our readers to look at the appendix for an elaboration of the specific ways in which we have used some terms and pronouns.

And, finally, a few words about the language used in this book. We see our research strictly as an activist academic project contributing to existing work on theories of gender. This theorizing, in our understanding, is similar to Halberstam's (2011: 16): 'Some theory is goal-oriented in a practical and activist way; it is designed to inform political practice rather than to formulate abstract thoughts for the sake of some neutral philosophical project.' And, like Halberstam, we belong to the school of thought that allies itself with the 'subversive intellectual' who agrees to steal from the university, to 'abuse its hospitality' and to be 'in but not of it' (Moten and Harney 2004: 101).

In the light of this, the language and style that we used to write this book was of great concern for us. We wanted to be precise in how we said things, but we also did not want our language and style to alienate those not trained within the university system. While we definitely wanted our work to be accessible to those from whose lived realities it emerged, we also wanted it to draw on the rigour of academic writing. And in this endeavour our writing collective of four was a boon. While each of us has a grounding in different academic disciplines, none of us is strictly part of the academia in the present. This interdisciplinary character, and our common connections of activism, allowed us an informed freedom from the use of rigid academic conventions so as to evolve our own ways of writing.

In this writing, we have chosen to introduce and posit ideas that our respondents spoke about in their own voices. Our analysis consistently flows from the voices of our respondents. Alongside this, we have freed ourselves from the oftentimes tedious style of referencing demanded by academic writing. This is certainly not to say that every idea or thought that we write about is new and has not been said before. It also does not mean that we have independently arrived at everything on our own without help from all the others who have written before us. We use this space to recognize the contributions to our work of all the people we have read and whom we have acknowledged in our bibliography. And we also wish to acknowledge equally the many discussions, conversations and writing that do not get formally published or acknowledged in academic referenced writing but have contributed immensely to our understanding and this book.

Happy reading!

Notes

1. This notice was published on the University Grants Commission website, http://www.ugc.ac.in/pdfnews/9200827_2.pdf (accessed 12 October 2014).
2. *National Legal Services Authority vs Union of India and Ors*, AIR 2014 SC 1863. (Referred to as the NALSA judgement.)
3. LABIA published a report of this study titled 'Breaking the Binary: Understanding Concerns and Realities of Queer Persons Assigned Gender Female at Birth across a Spectrum of Lived Gender Identities'

in English in 2013 and in Hindi in 2014. Both versions are available for download at http://www.labiacollective.org.

4. LGBT stands for lesbian, gay, bisexual and transgender. In the Indian context, there are several other identities like hijra, kothi, queer, intersex and asexual, represented as HKQIA and sometimes added to LGBT in different combinations to indicate the multitude of recognized identities.

5. The Indian women's movements have been documented quite extensively, but for a brief history of the autonomous movements, please refer to Mehta (2008).

6. For an insider perspective on the relationship of the feminist movement with queer issues, please refer to Shah (2005).

7. Also see Mahajan (2008).

8. There were many publications that documented this history, but are not accessible in the electronic domain. In print, refer to CALERI (1999) and Mahajan (2003).

9. *Fire* portrayed two Hindu women, married to brothers, who share a middle-class home in Delhi. Oppressed and unhappy in their respective marriages, the women become sexually intimate. Hindu right-wing groups, dismayed as much by the film's questioning of patriarchy as by its depiction of a lesbian relationship, disrupted screenings and vandalized cinema halls. After this, the film was pulled off screen despite having been passed by a censor board till the high court passed an order to resume screening. See Asmi and Bina (1999).

10. For details of this incident and other organising efforts of the 1990s refer to Fernandez (2002).

11. This meeting was organized by the Forum against Oppression of Women, Stree Sangam/LABIA, Human Rights Law Network and Counsel Club on 7 to 9 November 1997.

12. For more discussion, see Narrain (2003, 2004).

13. *Naz Foundation vs Govt of NCT and Ors*, CriLJ 2010 DHC 94. For a detailed analysis of this judgement, refer to Narrain and Eldridge (2009).

14. *Suresh Kumar Kaushal and Anr vs Naz Foundation and Ors*, AIR 2014 SC 563. Articles reviewing this judgement and other campaign material related to the legal battle are well documented at the Orinam website (http://www.orinam.net), which is also a good bilingual resource in Tamil and English on marginalized sexualities and genders.

15. Refer to the appendix for an explanation of trans* and a few other terms used in this book.

1

Method and Process

This study has been as much about exploring gender as it has been about exploring the process of a collective project; a project that had no principal investigators but did have a collective of 11 diverse and strongly grounded people working in cohesion. It has been as much an exercise in collective action and research as one of traversing the tricky terrain of the gender system in society.

We begin this section with a few words on who we, the researchers, are and then trace our journeys, both intellectual and actual, in doing this study. As with most planned but flexible and not custom-made journeys, we changed our paths, sometimes even our mode of moving, assisted by what we were learning from the landscape around us. What has been constant in these negotiations and decisions is our commitment to the basic questions with which we began this work and to the broader queer feminist politics to which we all subscribe.

We, the Research Team

One of the crucial contributions of feminist research is towards challenging the notion of the 'objectivity' of 'neutral' researchers in the research process. The work of feminists like Sandra Harding (1987), Donna Haraway (1988), Nancy Harstock (1998) and others has made it almost imperative to state the location and subjectivity of the researchers, and not invisibilize them under the garb of objectivity. As Shulamit Reinharz (1992: 263) says in her section on 'Involvement of the Researcher as a Person' in her review of feminist research methods:

> I conclude from this section that the connection between the researcher's experience and the research project remains a matter of contention between feminist researchers. I, for one, feel most satisfied by a stance that acknowledges the researcher's position right up front, and that does not think of objectivity and subjectivity as warring with each other, but rather as serving each other. I have feminist distrust for research reports that include no statement about the researcher's experience.

Since we identify with this school of thought, when we speak of how we did the research we want to talk about who this 'we' are as much as we want to talk about the process through which we arrived at the way in which the data collection and analysis was finally done.

The 11 members of the research team have many common connections and yet many diverse locations. We are all part of a voluntary feminist collective in the city of Mumbai, through which we have been actively engaged with the autonomous women's movements in the country.[1] Nine of us are also a part of LABIA and have been involved with queer organizing in the city and the country. Thus, we have a shared political background within which we have located our research.

Individually, we all identify 'queer', although each one of us may do so in a different way. Our gender locations are also mixed. We are all assigned gender female at birth and have at some point shared the political location of 'woman'. Being deeply entrenched in feminist politics, we have interrogated the social construction of 'woman' and redefined it in many ways in our personal lives. For some of us, such redefinition was enough to let us feel a comfort with ourselves and our lives. But for others it had been an uneasy acceptance of the identity 'woman'—more political than personal.

Queer organizing and politics, along with engagements with other kinds of marginalization around gender and sexuality, have complicated our personal understanding of the binary gender system, and so we find today that while for some of us 'woman' still is the chosen identity, for others it is not. None of us identifies as 'man', but we believe (and this research further confirms our understanding) that there are many other gender locations, and some of us choose from among those over 'man' or 'woman'. Those of us who say we are 'woman' are also complicating that identification in different ways.

While the team comes from varied religious backgrounds, most of us are from privileged positions of caste and class. Professionally, we come from very varied settings and we have tried to make this our strength in this study, just as we have done in our political campaigns. Some of us are trained in social science research and others in the natural sciences; some in the humanities and literature, while others in diverse fields like social work, journalism and management. Some have years of experience of informal education and self-help trainings; others of organizing around issues of women and other types of marginalization.

Our experience of working together has been in the contexts of campaigning and activism through LABIA and the Forum against Oppression of Women (FAOW), and so we have a shared culture of collective functioning. A formal study of this nature in such a large team, however, was a unique experiment for us. We were all equivalent if not equal members in the research process. There was no core team or any specialized task that only a few people did. This team of 11 researchers worked together till the coding and initial analysis of the transcripts was done. Subsequently, the detailed analysis, and the writing of this book, the reports and of papers based on the research was taken up by a group of four members of the team. This was decided on the basis of the availability and inclination of the individuals.

Given that this is a study of people like us, it is informed by our own individual experiences as well as by LABIA's intense and varied experience of working with LBT persons. We are aware of the advantages that we have in doing this study. Our collective knowledge and our own lives have informed us a great deal in figuring out how to ask the questions and in deciphering which are the questions important enough to ask.

It is a situation similar to that described by a disability rights activist and scholar:

> Working together, we decided to research a book which covered the range of issues in a coherent and fairly comprehensive way. This involved drawing up a loose schedule of areas to be explored in interviews with as many disabled people as possible. We looked at what little was already available, and we brainstormed from our own experience: we felt that our own lives and feelings were very relevant to the process. Rather than trying to achieve some spurious objectivity or distance, we acted as key informants and research participants. (Shakespeare 1997: 181)

At the outset, we broadly knew that we were going to talk to LBT persons. Since they are very much a part of the social and political community that we inhabit, access to them has relatively been easy. Years of knowing each other or being around in the same circles made it easier to win the trust of the people we approached for the study. At the same time, this put a huge responsibility on us as researchers: we are aware that we are treading the fine path between being 'insiders' to the community that we are studying and maintaining the 'outsider' status necessary to the process of research.

Being insiders helps cover a lot of the ground that someone not as familiar with it may have had to grapple with. However, this position also carries the risk of well-entrenched, preconceived notions making us deaf to some things we actually hear from the respondents. While we are clear that this is an issue before all researchers, our particularly partisan position made us very conscious of it. But we have tried to use our subjective locations to the advantage of the study.

In a sense, what helped us maintain this balance were several factors—our realizations of the multiple forms of marginalization that many people encounter in their lives, our recognition of the relative privileges that some of us had (making our experiences very different from those of many of our respondents), our bafflement with the lived realities of people that we were meeting as part of our work, and our commitment to the process of finding a way to talk about the subject in all its complexities without simplifying or unnecessary generalizing.

The fact that we did this study as a collective, that we are a diverse group of 11 researchers who have a common understanding and yet finely nuanced differences, has also helped in keeping this study an open-ended multidimensional exploration.

Designing the Study

Like any research, this one too went through some shifts. As we read and discussed more, the method and who we studied were continuously refined. These were important shifts since they helped us understand the complexity in the terrain of gender and enabled us to get a very diverse set of responses that took this understanding further.

Initial Ideas

Our first proposal, when we started thinking about the study, clearly stated that:

> This research will focus on the trans identity and politics as it is emerging in India today, with specific reference to transpersons who seek to connect with other queer women. This includes all those who identify as FTM (with or without medical/surgical intervention), transmen, transwomen who connect with queer women's spaces (as opposed to gay spaces), people who do not use the term 'trans' but do not see themselves as women attracted to other women... the list cannot be exhaustive, since the language of challenging binary gender is still a growing one, and identities and terms are still emerging.
>
> This study will, through exhaustive interviews and focused group discussions with individuals and collectives, aim to bring the specific concerns and articulations of such transpersons into

the queer movement. The more specific aim is to arrive at detailed strategies and interventions that the queer movements need to take up to foreground the issues of people, who have, till date, received very little attention or visibility.

We had begun with the idea of looking at the lives of trans* persons who connect with other queer women, and this included transwomen. As we started concretizing our research questions, we realized that we were taking on too many varied lived experiences. The life experiences of those brought up to be 'women' tend to be very distinct from those of persons brought up to be 'men'. Moreover, in a society where there is a visible community of hijras and a very strong culture around being hijra, transwomen or persons assigned gender male at birth had a very different lived experience from those assigned gender female at birth. In the growing LGBT organizing in the country, the section of people whose lives and concerns were not being foregrounded were trans* persons who were assigned gender female at birth (PAGFB). And so we decided to make them the focus of our research.

Accordingly, we named the study 'Understanding Lives and Concerns of Transpersons across a Spectrum of Identities Loosely Clustered under FTM'. We identified the main concerns, which spanned people's lives from childhood to the present, and also involved their complex interactions with very intimate spaces and relationships (familial, sexual and other such intimacies) as well as public spaces. We were interested in seeing how gender was understood, social structures negotiated, how people accessed queer spaces, and also what they expected from these spaces and from society.

The Method

We initially thought that we would start with a quantitative questionnaire administered to 60 to 80 individuals all over the country and follow up with qualitative interviews with 15 to 20 individuals who would be selected keeping in mind the diversity of situation, location and experience. Hence, we formulated a draft questionnaire and tested it on one potential respondent.

This first experience was an eye-opener. Though quantitative, the questionnaire elicited long answers. It was impossible, we realized, to get anything substantial on intimate concerns around gender through a quantitative tool. What we needed was to understand each and every experience in the light of the omnipresent binary system. Since the binary system is so deeply entrenched in language, which is our only means of communication, and considering that there has been so little conversation or shared knowledge about the lived realities of people who are 'transpersons across a spectrum of identities loosely clustered under FTM', it was clearly impossible to gain any insights through short answers. It became apparent that using a quantitative tool would lead us to a very stereotypical, non-nuanced naming and understanding of gender. Hence, we decided that we needed to change our methodology.

Our idea now was to do qualitative interviews with 50 respondents, whom we would access through our political and social spaces. We also planned to do focused group discussions with LBT groups (groups primarily working with lesbian and bisexual women and trans* persons) to get a sense of each group's collective understanding around issues of gender, and also to get some ideas on how they looked at their own present and future work on gender.

For the qualitative interviews, we decided to use the guided life history narrative method. Since all 11 of us were going to be conducting the interviews, we worked collectively towards creating a fairly detailed interview guide to ensure uniformity in the nature of the data collected. At every meeting, we found this guide growing in size, both in depth and in breadth. We added sections to include more and more aspects of people's lives that we felt might be significant—growing up, school and college education, intimate relationships, work and migration stories, interactions in public spaces, experiences of the body, sex, the health system, mental health, questions around marriage, religion… the list kept growing. Within each section too, the questions kept increasing in number.

So Who Will We Talk To?

Alongside this, we started discussions about how to choose our respondents and what would be the universe from which we would choose them. This became a point of extensive debate and discussion. The study aimed to understand the nature and degree of discomfort that some PAGFB have with their birth-assigned gender and also the ways in which they negotiate around this. The question before us was: how are we to *know* who is discomfited, and in what way, by their assigned gender? We had three options before us. One was to contact people whom we ourselves perceived as transgressing gender norms; the second was to ask people to self-identify. The third, a radically different option, was to assume that every person has something to tell us about their discomfort with and negotiations around their assigned gender, and so open up the study to include all PAGFB.

Since we were approaching known groups and networks for the study, the first or second option, or both in conjunction with each other, were easily possible. But we were dissatisfied with these choices. There was no certainty, but there was a sense that many people who might not say they were trans* might still have things to tell us about gender. What if some were not identifying as trans* because they were not yet used to the language? Wouldn't we, then, miss out on the realities of all such people? If we looked at people who already identified as trans*, then would we not start getting very boxed-in answers?

The third option meant redefining our study in some ways, because here we were changing something fundamental. Up until now, we had focused on hearing from and about only those who explicitly transgressed the binary system. We were now moving towards the premise that to understand what lay beyond the binary, we needed to look beyond the transgressions.

We spent many hours trying to understand the implications of all these choices and trying to make the 'right' decision. We read, we discussed, we talked about our lives and the lived experiences of our own gender and sexuality. We went back and forth on this over many meetings.

There were questions and doubts for every side of the decision. If we chose option three, we feared that we were probably in danger of altering the study too much. Had we not begun with wanting to look at the lives and issues of people who transgressed? Would not the lives of those who identified as 'women' be very different from those who said that they did not identify as women? How could we have both kinds of people in the same sample? Was there not enough written already on the lives of 'women' and how they understand gender? What new thing would we get from there? And if we said 'persons assigned gender female at birth', would we not be expanding our universe too much?

On the other hand, we also felt that even if by making this choice we would change the study, that might be a good thing in the final analysis. We had a fairly clear sense that many people who might not use any 'trans*' terms for themselves might still have things to tell us about gender. What if some people were not identifying a certain way only because they were not familiar with the language? Wouldn't we then miss out on the realities of all such people? If we looked only at people who already identified in trans* terms, then would we not be predetermining our sample even before a shared understanding could emerge on who can be trans*?

Meanwhile, a fairly detailed draft of our interview guide was ready. Each of us decided to say whether we considered ourselves apt respondents for such an interview and whether our lives could contribute to such a study. We were surprised to discover that in our group, where most saw themselves as 'woman' politically or otherwise, there were many who said that in principle they thought they could be part of such a study. This self-identification as a suitable subject for the study was coming from people who did not identify with the original category of 'transpersons across a spectrum of identities loosely clustered under FTM'.

Defining the Parameters

We had now moved towards a common understanding of what exactly we were looking for, which was a little different from where we had begun. In the process, we realized that we had come to the study with differing notions around gender and about what constituted transgressions of the binary. This was not surprising, because prior to this exercise, we had had discussions among ourselves on these issues, though not as exhaustively. At this point, we renamed our study 'Breaking the Binary: Understanding Concerns and Realities of Female Assigned/Born Persons across a Spectrum of Lived Gender Realities'.

We finally broadened our sample to include all those who were assigned gender female at birth, but narrowed our universe by choosing our respondents only from among queer PAGFB, who identified as non-heteronormative in some way and allied with queer spaces or organizations. In our understanding, all such PAGFB are already challenging societal gender norms, either in terms of their sexual or gender identity, or both. The ways in which gender and sexuality are bound together under patriarchy means, in any case, that 'same-sex desire' becomes a violation of the gender norm too.

As a final round, the team did an exercise of conducting interviews on each other using the latest version of our interview guide. As mentioned earlier, since we were 'insiders', all of us qualified as respondents in keeping with our final decision. This exercise helped us test every part of the guide, gave us experience in conducting interviews together, tested our technology and helped us arrive at the final decisions. This trial round also warned us about the length of our interviews. Even when we were testing them on each other—people who were familiar with the questionnaire—we took anywhere between four to eight hours to complete an interview. This exercise helped us in finalizing the actual modalities of the interviews.

All set now, we conducted two pilots in Mumbai. They went off without any hitch and we were ready to begin with our interviews.

Selecting Our Respondents

We sent out letters to queer LBT groups—Sappho in Kolkata, Sahayatrika in Thrissur, LesBiT and WHAQ in Bangalore, Parma in Vadodara, Sangini in Delhi, and to Sampoorna, a global network of trans* Indians.[2] We followed up with phone calls and in person where feasible. We wanted the groups' help in reaching out to individuals who would participate in the study, and we also wanted to have group discussions with members from each organization. Besides this, we contacted individuals, especially in Delhi and Chennai, for help with other contacts through their social networks. In Mumbai and Pune, we relied on our connections as LABIA with other queer spaces and people. We also got in touch with some individuals from rural areas, whom we had met over the years and stayed in touch with, but who were not part of any of the groups.

We got helpful, supportive and wholehearted responses from most of these groups and individuals. It must be emphasized here that without their help, we could have never reached out to such a diverse group. We eventually managed to get a good sample of respondents fairly well distributed across the four geographical regions of the country.

There were some disappointments too. The call for participation in the study was put on the Sampoorna e-list, but it did not elicit any response from there. We did, however, get to do a group interview with Sampoorna. Parma wrote back, and told us in person and on the phone that they could not participate in this study as they were doing a similar one themselves. We did not hear back from Sangini—they did not respond to our emails and we were unable to talk to them over the phone.

We tried to get as diverse a sample as possible in each geographical location. We used purposive sampling to get variations across age, class, caste and religion. The number of people available for interview was not very large in every place; wherever we had more than the required number of people who fit any given criterion, we kept the selection random by picking lots.

The Interviews

Each interview was conducted by two members of the research team. In situations where the interviewers and the respondent did not speak a common language, we made arrangements for translators, taking into account the comfort and consent of the participant. Seven interviews were done with the help of translators.

Most people were interviewed in the cities where they lived, but in four cases we made it possible for the respondent to travel to another city for the interview. In three other cases, the interviews were conducted in other mutually convenient locations to which the respondents had travelled for their own reasons. The spaces used for the interviews were our own houses, respondents' homes, organizational spaces, other people's homes—basically where everyone was comfortable and we were assured of privacy. No interview was conducted in any public space, as we had realized in one of our pilots that these were not comfortable spaces for interviews that explore so many intimate aspects of people's lives. Most interviews were conducted in the course of a single day, with small breaks. Only in exceptional situations did we have to do an interview over two days.

The interviews broadly adhered to the guide, but took many different routes depending on the inclination of the respondents or interviewers. Sometimes we followed the sequence of the guide, but most people spoke first of what they felt were the most important parts of their lives. For some these were stories about growing up; for some it was about intimate relationships;

for others it was their specific passion or profession; and for yet others it was school, college, friends, or coming to organizations and meeting others like themselves. Often the interviews turned into conversations and we were able to go beyond the surface to understand what was being said with all its layers and nuances.

We did not go back to our interviewees to fill in any gaps, but when we sent back the transcripts, many of them added information and some deleted a few things. We are glad that we sent back the transcripts since several interviews came back with changes. This had been expected to some extent because while the interviews had created an atmosphere of easy conversation and safety, we realized people might not feel as confident about sharing sensitive information later. This was especially true with respect to identifying details or incidents to do with other people mentioned in the interview.

Besides the individual interviews, we also had focused group discussions in some cities with Sappho, Sahayatrika, LesBiT and Sampoorna. In these conversations we kept our questions fairly open ended and group specific. They came from our knowledge of the group, and some were also inspired by aspects of interviews that we had conducted with some of their members. They were based on our observations around how each of these organizations has used diverse strategies to deal with the question of gender and also of their interventions in the lives of people marginalized due to sexuality and/or gender.

Analysis and Writing

After completing our interviews and transcripts, the collective process of research went on. We met regularly and continued with our discussions, aided by different academic readings. We looked specifically at readings from trans* studies and queer studies to inform ourselves of how these debates and discussions have evolved in other contexts. Besides this, we looked at resources on feminist research methods to help us, especially with analysis while conducting qualitative research.

We recognize the intersubjectivity of such an open-ended interview process in which we as interviewers were as much a part of the meaning making and narrative as the person themselves. We understand the specificity of the stories told to the context in which they were told and the time at which they were narrated. Any generalizations from these texts and narratives has to be carefully done, with due recognition of the subjectivity of those involved and the contexts in which they were made. Life stories are very intricate, and we are aware that what can be obtained in a single interaction is finally just one layer of a complex life. Having said that, at the end of these 50 interviews, we do feel that the subjective positions from where we entered into these conversations were very crucial to the kind of data that we have been able to collect. The only way in which we as researchers can reciprocate the trust that our respondents showed in us in openly sharing details of their lives, in revisiting difficult parts of their lives and struggles, in facing up to parts of them that they might want hidden, is by implicating as much of our individual and collective selves in analysing these narratives as possible.

The initial team of 11, though, did not continue through this whole process of analysis and writing. After the final transcripts were vetted by the respondents and shared with the whole group, we met and did a sharing and discussion on the whole process, the interviews, our impressions and feelings, and also a preliminary analysis—and even devised a coding sheet. Thereafter, it was four of us, the writers of this book as well as the report published in April 2013, who continued with the long process of detailed analysis and writing.

As with the initial research, the writing and analysis too has been an experiment in collective functioning and has extended to well over four years. Some of us have done individual academic research in other areas, but this process has been unique, frustrating and extremely rewarding.

While we had devised a coding sheet to break up the interviews after the preliminary analysis, and while several interviews were thus coded, we found ourselves unable to use those codes. One of the challenges with the length, depth and extent of such life narrative interviews was their resistance to be thus codified. On reading and rereading them, and discussing them time and again, we discovered that the interviews guided us to a coding process that was nowhere as neat or defined as the earlier one, but much more comprehensive. We started talking in terms of areas of peoples lives, themes within them, and various trajectories that fit or defied any categorization.

The correlations and patterns that emerged were seldom cohesive, and we had to learn to write in the difference and dissonance into our analysis. First readings of interviews were often unable to capture their complexity, and sometimes narratives seemed to either fit easily into social and political notions of our lives or were too starkly in dissonance. But multiple readings led us to move away from these to more complex positions, which often challenged our understanding, both personal and political.

Gender, family, intimacies have all been at the centre of feminist discussions along with other concerns for the last several decades. These interviews added to these discussions and made us shift and negotiate our beliefs and politics. Perhaps what sustained all of us most in this long journey was the fact that each interview spoke of powerful and hard lives pushing continuously towards spaces, internal and external, where people could truly be themselves. These are not narratives of victimization, though there is immense trauma and violence, but narratives of affirmation and resolve, of deep desires to be able to live lives the way they want to. And this pushed us each time we felt overwhelmed by the pain and dissonance.

The interviews also triggered our own traumas and experiences of pain and grief, and also spoke starkly to the privileges we have had in our lives besides resonating with and challenging our collective and personal politics, and understandings of power and structures. In effect we have ended up writing as much about gender as we have about various social institutions that hold and perpetuate these structures of power.

There are few studies of this nature and focus around the world, and none in our context, so while other texts and lives, and our collective experiences have informed the writing, we have concentrated most on what we have learned from our respondents themselves. It has been a tightrope walk between writing about 50 lives without divulging their whole life stories, and making generalizations without losing the context.

Notes

1. The Forum against Oppression of Women (FAOW) is the oldest, non-funded, autonomous collective of women active in Mumbai, in existence since 1980. It has been involved in campaigns against sexual assault, domestic violence, communalism, reproductive technologies, sexuality, growth of right-wing politics in India and its impact on women, and many other such issues. It has worked towards supporting other autonomous women's groups, like those of Muslim women, tribal women, and lesbian and bisexual women, and has actively supported other struggles and movements, including those of workers, against the big dams and large development projects.

2. The first letters were sent in July 2009 and these were the only groups we knew of then that worked primarily with LBT people. All data collection was done between August 2009 and June 2010.

2

Profile of Respondents

Our endeavour was to talk to a wide cross-section of individuals across location, age group, caste, class and religion. These variations were critical, as we wanted to reach those living at the intersections of many marginalized identities.

Location

Most respondents were living in urban areas when we met them, primarily in Bangalore, Mumbai, Kolkata, Chennai, Delhi, Pune and Thrissur. We contacted them through queer groups and networks in these cities. The relatively large number of respondents from south India (see Table 2.1) is due to the existence of vibrant and active queer groups and networks in Bangalore and Chennai, and in Kerala. Only two respondents were still living in rural areas, one in Maharashtra and one in Jharkhand.

Table 2.1: Region-Wise Distribution of Respondents

Zone	Respondents
East	9
North	10
South	18
West	13
Total	50

Caste

Most of the respondents were from dominant castes. However, in each location, there was at least one individual belonging to a Scheduled Caste/Scheduled Tribe (SC/ST), Special Backward Class (SBC) or Other Backward Class (OBC) (Figure 2.1).

Figure 2.1: Distribution across Castes

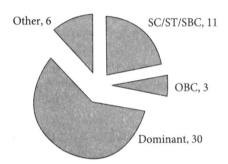

Other, 6
SC/ST/SBC, 11
OBC, 3
Dominant, 30

Class

We asked our respondents about the class background of their natal families while they were growing up. The categories were lower class, middle class and upper class (Figure 2.2). Answers were based on individual self-perception, which was influenced by relative exposure, geographical region and the rural or urban nature of the setting.

For example, two of our respondents saw their families as lower class, but one went to school because there was no food to eat at home, whereas the other was sent to a private school. This is the range that we glimpse in the lower-class category. There were similar variations in the other class categories. One respondent said his family was middle class despite his father being a daily-wage earner because his older brothers worked and brought home wages too, whereas another considered hir urban family lower middle class despite hir father working in their family-run industry.

Figure 2.2: Class Distribution of Natal Families

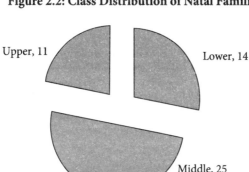

Upper, 11

Lower, 14

Middle, 25

An upper-class background also didn't necessarily mean having resources and privileges. One respondent was deprived of education because of problems with hir sexuality. Another respondent who hailed from a business family was unable to afford the education ze wanted due to family dynamics, and had to support hirself earning small sums of money playing cricket.

In Mumbai and Delhi most of our respondents came from the middle class and a few from the upper class. As we primarily used social networks to contact respondents in both these cities, this data suggests how class operates as an inhibiting factor in many of these spaces.[1]

Religious Background

Recognizing marginalization due to religion, we made explicit attempts to talk to individuals from the non-dominant religions, but were unable to do so. We also found that the make-up of queer groups seemed to be largely reflective of mainstream society (Table 2.2). In Mumbai, we tried to reach out to potential respondents from varied religious backgrounds, and succeeded to some degree. It is important to note that many individuals we spoke to do not currently practise the religions into which they were born. Some had changed their faith, some chose to believe in God but not in any specific religion, and some were atheist.

Table 2.2: Break-up According to Religious Background

Religious background	Respondents
Buddhist	1
Christian	3
Hindu	42
Jain	2
Muslim	1
Sarna	1
Total	**50**

Age

The youngest respondent in our study was 20 years old, the oldest 65. We had intended an even distribution of respondents across the age brackets of 20–25, 26–30, 30–35 and over 35, but the sample seems to lean towards younger people (Table 2.3). This could be due to the largely young membership of groups like Sappho and LesBiT.

Table 2.3: Distribution across Age Groups

Age group (years)	Respondents
20–25	13
26–30	12
30–35	16
>35	9
Total	**50**

Education

The variation in level of education was more or less similar across all locations (Figure 2.3). As discussed later, gender and sexuality played a significant role in many people's access to education.

Figure 2.3: Levels of Education

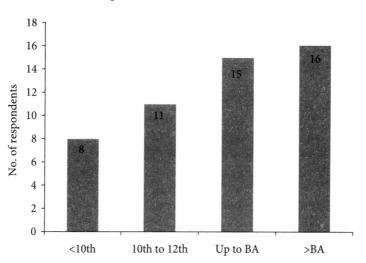

Current Gender Identification

Early on in the guided interviews, respondents were asked to state their current gender identification. To ensure that they felt safe and free to respond to this question frankly, we did not furnish any options. Hence, these were self-defined gender identities.

The answers varied. All those who clearly said that they identified as man or male were clubbed together under 'man'; those that said they were woman or female under 'woman'; and all others with variations on these under the category 'others'. Of our 50 respondents, 10 were 'man', 22 were 'woman' and 18—in different ways—were 'others' (Figure 2.4). Even for 'woman', people often had individual descriptors.

Since how people name and live their genders, and what meaning they make of it is one of the main areas of enquiry for this study, we have a much longer discussion on this in a later chapter.

Figure 2.4: Gender Identity Categorization

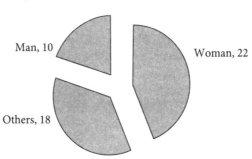

Man, 10

Woman, 22

Others, 18

Marriage

We asked our respondents about their marital status. Of those legally married to cismen, one was still married, one was separated, three were divorced and one had lost her husband. There were five people who considered themselves married to women. One individual was married to a non-cisman and two saw themselves as having been married to women from whom they were now separated. Seven of our respondents were parents to either adopted or biological children.

Migration

Twenty-five of our respondents had migrated from their native places. Of the 11 who grew up in rural areas, only two had not migrated. Migration was largely propelled by tensions around gender and/or sexuality. All respondents who had moved had done so from smaller towns or villages to metros or large cities, drawn by the relative anonymity of the latter or by the existence of support groups. Some people had moved to bigger cities/towns to pursue their education. This latter category was made up of individuals who all identified as 'woman' or whose identities we have categorized as 'others', and came from middle-class backgrounds. All the migrants spoke of the greater freedom the new place enabled, giving them a chance to express their gender and/or sexuality.

Current Income

Apart from class and caste disadvantages while growing up, the interviews showed how non-normative gender and sexuality become axes of further marginalization. It was in this context that we looked at the current income of our respondents to understand their class situation at the time of the interview (Figure 2.5).

As we see in Figure 2.5, there were 27 people earning less than Rs 10,000 a month, which qualifies as a lower-class income in the urban settings where most of them presently live. Of these, three were students, while another five were neither employed nor living with or being supported by their natal families—which meant they were being supported by queer groups, friends, partners and personal support networks. This figure of almost half of our respondents falling in the lower-class category is a stark indicator that they had not moved up in life. In fact, they seem to have moved downwards in terms of class.

Figure 2.5: Current Monthly Income

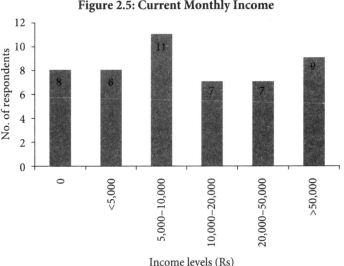

Income levels (Rs)

Respondents living in the cities of Mumbai and Delhi earned higher average incomes as compared to those in the rest of the country. This is due to two reasons: the cost of living is highest in these two metros; and the people we met here were largely from the middle and upper classes.

Note

1. In the interim, newer social spaces that have come up in both Mumbai and Delhi are being accessed by queer PAGFB from a wider range of socio-economic backgrounds.

3

A Gender of One's Own

We did this study to talk about gender, and talk we did. The stories and conversations began flowing with the very first question around current gender identity. From childhood experiences to the pangs of puberty; from a growing awareness of one's self and body to multiple meanderings in the realm of desire, love, sex and relationships; from the minutiae of hair length and turn of the collar to the complex arena of negotiating personal and public spaces; from finding words for oneself to creating spaces for an open exploration of consensual gender— our conversations traversed these paths of joy, pain, repression, violence, anger, silence, discovery, struggle, camaraderie, love, despair and hope with all our respondents.

Naming One's Gender

One of the first questions in the interview guide was an open-ended one on how respondents identified themselves. Almost everyone had a clear answer to this, though it might have been as long as a life history or just a word or phrase. Current gender identity was the one that our respondents were living, had arrived at and were articulating, using whatever language and terms they had access to.

Although all 50 respondents were PAGFB, their answers to the question were varied (Table 3.1). While several used the two available identities of 'man' and 'woman' (or their corresponding synonyms), several others articulated their gender identities in other terms. We have clubbed all those who clearly said that they identified as man or male under 'man', those that said they were woman or female under 'woman', and put all others with variations on these under the category 'others'. This third category of 'others' is a deliberate use of the plural, and not the singular 'other' as the latter implies just one more gender besides 'man' or 'woman'. As we have said earlier, we have also, throughout the book, used pronouns that correspond to the gender identities that respondents chose for themselves.

Thus, one of our very first findings underlined the vast gap between our respondents' assigned-at-birth gender and the names they chose to call themselves. The fact that 28 of the 50 people chose a gender identity different from the one they were assigned is very significant. More crucially, that 18 of these 50 chose names

Table 3.1: Respondents' Articulations of Their Current Gender Identities

Man (10)	Woman (22)	Others (18)
Man	Woman	Confused
Boy	Bisexual woman	Shifting from female to male
Male	Girl	Confused and variable
Male (but use	Female	Gender queer
FTM for others	Androgynous	FTM
to understand)	female	Other
	Woman with a	Androgynous
	difference	Fluid woman
		Do not articulate
		Society made me feel a woman but
		I have denied and challenged it
		Between transgender and lesbian
		50 per cent male and 50 per cent
		female
		Man but have come to terms with
		socially being seen as a woman
		Transgender
		Think as woman but am not sure
		Woman from outside but not fully
		a woman

not within the binary indicates that the normative genders were, for them, inadequate as positions from which to speak.

The names that our respondents used to identify with were not easy to classify in all instances as some seemed to use qualifiers along with the given categories of 'man' or 'woman'. In each of these cases, we used our sense of the person's gender as articulated in the whole of the interview to ascertain which category they fell most comfortably into. A respondent who identified as a 'woman with a difference' clearly saw herself as a woman, while simultaneously conveying her differences with social norms and expectations, whereas a respondent who identified as a 'fluid woman' did not see hirself as a woman but a person with a more fluid gender. A respondent who identified as 'FTM' was, at that point in hir life, not taking the identity of a man and thus was put into this category of 'others', while another said that he used 'FTM' only for those people who did not understand when he called himself a man and thus was placed in the category 'man'.

It is also important to note that while several respondents used terms that might suggest they were confused or uncertain about their gender, that would be misreading the case. This will become clearer as we read more about the lives and realities of the respondents, but suffice it to say here that 'confused' should be read as shorthand for not being able to articulate gender outside of the given categories of 'man' or 'woman', and may refer to the gaps in language rather than indicate a person's confusion about their own gender.

The Search for Meaning

As we said earlier, responses varied from single words or phrases to long narrative answers, emphasizing the difficult process of naming oneself when language itself is so normative. Arun said, 'Intergender, genderqueer. I am most comfortable with people calling me by my name.'[1] Monu said, 'To talk about my current identification I will have to tell my story from the beginning.

I would like to begin from the time when I was very young.' For yet others like Nidhi, hir partner's perception informs hir notion of hir gender—ze said, 'My girlfriend thinks me male in terms of gender, I consider myself lesbian in terms of sexuality.' This underscores the number of ways in which gender is named and constructed by individuals, sometimes rewriting societal norms, at other times just tweaking them a bit, and at yet others following them in a prescriptive sort of way.

Even when different people used the same terms to describe themselves, the meanings these had for each and the ways in which each person actually lived these were considerably varied. Thus 'man' or 'woman', which are the available gender categories, often meant very different things.

Twenty-two respondents identified as 'woman', which suggested a relative degree of consonance with their assigned gender. Yet, we found that even among them what this meant was far from standard. Hemlata said of herself:

> I am a woman sexually and naturally, but my living style is not what society expects of me. I am not like other women. I live on my own terms.... I have become so confident and fearless and my whole body language speaks for it, so that people are now scared of troubling me.... They think me to be a woman but a different kind of woman—a working woman, confident and liberated.

We may read in Hemlata's assertion a continuing of the feminist project of pushing boundaries and further liberating the category of 'woman'. At other places in her interview, as with our other 'woman'-identified respondents, there was also a 'queering' of this identity in a variety of ways, as we shall see in later chapters.

Rahul, 22, who identifies as 'boy', told us how he began to understand his gender:

> Once I went for a school picnic to a water park. Boys and girls wear different clothes in water parks. I sat by myself there and kept thinking and looking at everyone. That day I felt horrible about why I am not a boy. I didn't know then I was transgender.... I made a list about what girls do and what boys do.... Then I cut out things

I did not like to do. Most of the things that were struck off in that list were things which were girl things…. That's when I realized that though I have a girl's body, by soul I am a boy.

All our 'man'-identified respondents were able to express their gender through clothes and behaviour in public spaces, as well as in their interactions with others. The exception is Kirti, who is 41 years old, lives in the village to which his family moved when he was 14, and is forced by his conservative milieu to dress only in saris and be seen in public unambiguously as a woman. It is only in spaces with intimate partners that he is able to express his gender and have it affirmed; he was able to do this within the safe space of this interview as well. He said, 'I feel I am a man because my thoughts, feelings and gaze are like a man…. But in my village, any change is laughed at. So I cannot do anything.'

'Others' Define Their Selves

'Others', as can be seen from Table 3.1, is not a monolithic singular category, but a broad and diverse one, used to refer to all respondents who articulated their gender in terms other than 'man' or 'woman'.

One respondent with an intersex variation said that ze thought of hirself as a woman, but was unsure. While ze would have liked to identify as 'woman' due to societal scripts around what male or female bodies should look like, ze did not allow hirself to call hirself a woman. Similarly, another respondent saw hirself as 'woman from outside but not fully a woman' because people who live in the same area as hir said and believed that ze was not 'fully a woman' due to hir reproductive health issues. The weight of societal pressure and rules, then, greatly coloured the way some respondents chose to name themselves.

Prem identified as 'confused' due to rigid rules around dress and appearance. Ideally, ze would like to wear trousers and shirts, and have hir hair short, but was worried about hir future earning prospects due to strict norms around dress for PAGFB. 'Now, due to NGOs, we can cut hair and wear pant–shirt, but if we do not have this kind of support, then sometimes I feel that for jobs it might be better to keep our hair long and have the same gender appearance as society demands.' It was difficult for Prem to obtain access to language and words that capture the dissonances that ze felt, but hir naming was in consonance with how ze lived hir life.

Chandni said about hir gender, '[I] don't articulate it as something specifically. I take it as it comes.' Upon pondering on why ze felt unable to fix on a name or location, ze said, 'It's fluid, not carved in stone. I would use "gender fluid" along with "genderqueer"... [but on] a scale of 1 to 10, I would place myself at 5, right in the middle.' This strong critique of the binary was evident in other interviews as well. Bhargavi, who articulated hir gender as 'shifting from female to male', said, 'Sometimes just being a child is better. This gender has created all the confusion.'

The rules and norms around the gender binary are challenged not only by such articulations, but also by other very deliberate and specific ways of naming or identifying oneself. Sunny, who said that ze is '50 per cent male and 50 per cent female', expounded on hir intentional usage of that phrase. 'I avoid Hindi because of the gender confusion.... I have started slanting language to create a third kind of gender.... While writing English I have no issues using male/female gender.'

Evolving Identities, Not Rigid Compartments

As is evident from all the previous examples, naming one's gender was a conscious, careful and measured process. Some individuals have traversed long routes in arriving at their current gender identity, for some others it was something they knew very early in life, and some did not want to stay fixed in any static understanding of their own gender. How people named themselves also changed as they met other people and groups, and learnt newer names.

For some respondents, their sense of themselves was uncomplicated right from childhood, though at complete odds with their assigned gender. Sumit, who now identifies as 'transgender', said, 'If I look at my photos from childhood I see myself in boys' clothes only. I remember going to school also with boys; I would spend time with them, play with them, sit with them on the boys' benches, would stay away from girls actually.'

For others the internal conflicts began as puberty hit, bodies began to change and societal norms around gender began to be reinforced, with strictures being enforced by parents, teachers and other figures of authority. Jai, who identifies as 'man', said:

> After maturity I was stopped from playing with boys and I was angry with the rules imposed on me. When the body started developing, I did not like that at all and felt—why was this happening to me? I would tie a shawl tightly around my breasts every night and sleep, and would pray, 'Make me a man when I get up.'

We also realized that some people tended to use different terms for themselves at different points in the interview because they were using terms not in common currency.

It must be pointed out that some respondents might very possibly have chosen to call themselves differently if we had met them at an earlier point in their lives. This is true not just of all those who named themselves in terms outside the binary, but also for those who chose to call themselves 'man' or 'woman'. This means that while for some their sense of gender might have been certain from birth, they might have found the language and the articulation that worked for them later in life. For others it may mean that they have arrived at an understanding and articulation of their gender over a period of time. And for yet others this points to the fact that for them (as for most), gender itself was a journey and may have shifted over the course of their lives and with experience. The fact that a person's gender might not remain static in their lifetime clearly does not mean that it is a frivolous thing that changes depending on the mood of the moment. It does, however, indicate that it is both intrinsic and arrived at, and hence may change.

Alex, who called hirself 'between transgender and lesbian', talked about coming to terms with an ageing body, of having given up on the idea of surgery, of being less able now to pass as a man—and making small but significant adjustments like using women's toilets now where ze would have used men's loos earlier. Ze said:

> I don't think terms are so important. Every time you grow your identity changes. There was a time I really wanted a sex change.... If people ask me if I want to do a sex change, [if it's] 100 per cent successful I will do it, but if not, I am happy like this. I am comfortable in my space.

This flexibility and shifts in naming oneself were typical of most respondents who saw their own genders as outside the binary. Sandy said:

> In forms I fill 'female', but if there was an option I would fill 'other'... so when I have to renew my passport I would like to fill 'other'. The other reason that I fill 'female' is that I am not transgender.... But this binary does not work for me, neither F nor M feels applicable and right. I have never wanted to be male, not that it is wrong for others to want that. Given this, then, F is probably closer [to me], and also a lot of the challenges that I have faced have been because I have been placed in the F category, like, say, unequal pay.

Meghana identifies as 'androgynous', which could of course mean different things to different people, but also means different things for hirself at different times. It might be a catch-all term for all the inflections that no single word can express. As ze rued, 'Some days I feel that I have to change my clothes seven times. Some days nothing feels right, you just feel your gender is off. You cannot understand your own gender... hair is too long, too short, and those days are miserable.'

'How Many Genders Do You Think There Are?'

This somewhat unusual question was one of the last in our interview guide. It reflected a nascent research idea—that people challenging binary gender identities in their own lives might well have radical notions or speculations about the gender system itself. Several respondents were initially taken aback, as one might be when asked a trick question. Clearly, it was not always something that they had thought about already. Once they took it seriously and it became a question to be processed in the context of the entire life narratives they had just shared, we received a fascinating range of responses.

'Male and female are the two genders and there are many variations.'

'What I know of is three genders. Male, female and third gender. In third gender, there are five types of people. I don't know what they are—intersex, kothi, hijra, two more I don't know.'

'I don't know much about gender. But there are more genders than just male and female.'

'There may be many. There could be someone else different from me who might want to have a different name for herself/himself. But I think the number of people who are different is smaller, and so right now we should have only one category for all the others because that will also help them to unite and fight together.'

'Society has two genders. I don't know how many exist; 10 years from now, I don't know how many will exist, many more probably.'

'If given the space and acceptability, there will be many genders.'

'As many people there are in the world. Each person has their own degree of identity.'

'I do not think that you can count. Because it is like it is a fluid thing and it goes in many ways, and some people stop somewhere. It is a journey to find out what your gender is… so it cannot be fixed.'

'Infinite and none at all. I think it is infinite, but the exuberance is so large that then it becomes nothing.'

'Gender is a continuum, I don't get into the how many question. At one end of the spectrum there are people who seem to subscribe to the sex they were born in, in the middle you move away from that, and at the other end are people who want to change their bodies. And, of course, there are shades and shades.'

'I think there are countless genders.... Many times I have thought of it, that it is very much like *swaras* [tones]. In Indian music the variant *swara* can vary to whatever degree it wants to. So if you are sensitive enough, you can see many microtones between two tones. If you are not sensitive, you can see only two. And if you are sensitive then you may be able to see 60 or 80 or an infinite number of tones in between.'

This range of responses, from an uncertain belief in the binary and variations in it, to a complete reimagining of the system itself; from articulations of the need for political change to make gender openness possible to the demand for sensitivity to hear the difference—all of this tells us that not only are people naming themselves and living their genders in complex ways, but also continuously taking apart and reconstructing the structures themselves.

Living One's Gender

The naming of one's gender, then, is merely the visible tip of the iceberg, a crucial marker of the enormity of what gender comprises and how it is lived through a person's life. But it is an important and conscious marker nonetheless, and as we read further we will see how gender marks interactions and negotiations in everyday life. Naming oneself is a crucial link to living one's gender, and it was in listening carefully to these narratives of our respondents that we were able to see how intrinsically it is woven into the fabric of their lives. Defining oneself is not a singular act and happens not just in the articulation but in the living of it, and this is what we learned as we read and reread our interviews.

Living lives even slightly askew of the norms is hard, as the narratives of our respondents show time and again in different situations. Gender and sexuality also intersect with other kinds of marginalization and identities, affecting the lives of our respondents in severe ways. At the same time, these narratives also speak at length about the places where our respondents have been able to find support, camaraderie, understanding and space to be themselves.

The following chapters reveal how a questioning of rigid norms leads to more and more ease, which allows people to live and breathe in their own skins rather than suffocate inside somebody else's impossible boxes. We look into some of the complex processes by which our respondents arrived at how they name themselves; the nuances of living their self-ascribed genders in a world that not just assigned them genders but also a gendered life. We look intensively at the lives of our respondents from childhood to adulthood, their interactions with various structures and institutions of society, and their relationships with themselves and those close to them. In each of these circumstances their gender continuously interacts with other structures and norms. And in this interaction we find the complexity, the nuance and the creativity that is part of living gender both within and against the given norms.

Note

1. We extensively use our respondents' voices throughout this book. As expected, all names have been changed in keeping with the principles of confidentiality. As far as possible, all references to geographic location and other identifiers have also been generalized or removed.

4

The Early Years and Families

As we were completing our report 'Breaking the Binary', we heard that one of our 50 respondents, a very young male-identified person, had ended his life. He walked on to the train tracks and was lost to all of us forever. This despair that makes someone choose to end their life is something that became more real to us since we started talking to people for this study. Amidst the countless stories of courage and conviction to live life on one's own terms, we heard many a recounting of the various factors that make it difficult to go on.

One of the major sources of despair, unfortunately, is the inability to find adequate support from natal families, their inability to comprehend the lives and choices of their children or their active violence towards the children in their care. The hopelessness at this loss spills over into the other parts of their adult lives when they begin other intimacies and enter systems of care.

Birth or marriage are the only two socially and legally sanctioned ways of acquiring families. Despite not being one's families of choice, birth families are the primary support structures, especially in the initial years. Only six of our respondents were ever married to cismen. Of these, two were married very young and for them their in-laws were very much a part of their growing up as well. So, for most of our respondents family usually referred to the families in which they grew up.

Our respondents' lives indicate that these families remain significant even in later life. This study underlines that it is crucial to understand the engagement of the respondents with their families in order to be able to make sense of their lives. It also emphasizes the need to understand the dynamics of families, the violence and hierarchy inherent in them, and the need for urgent change in these structures. These families emerge as a critical site for intervention to alter society's opinions and structures around gender and sexuality.

Growing Up

Our respondents told many stories about growing up. Some of these were explicitly related to their gender and sexuality, but most often they were just stories of young people being raised up in very varied circumstances. The interviews showed that the influence and power of family can be pervasive, especially in one's formative years. Abuse, neglect, rejection of gender expression, prohibitions and punishment were common; stories of acceptance, love and support emerged more rarely. Only 16 of our 50 respondents had predominantly happy or reasonably happy memories of their natal families from their younger days.[1]

For some of the remaining 34, family circumstances overpowered the overall experience of growing up. These ranged from extreme poverty to other kinds of explicit marginalization, which had a major impact on the young in the family. For some the early years were all right, but things changed drastically at puberty and all kinds of restrictions started coming into play. But for almost half of the respondents the natal family, as they remembered from their earlier years, was a place of extreme violence and very limited support. The violence was physical, emotional, verbal, neglect—any or all of these. The perpetrators of the violence were fathers, brothers, mothers, extended families, family friends and, in a rare case or two, sisters.

Some of our respondents had come to groups seeking shelter from the violence unleashed on them from either their families or their partner's families. Thus, the stories of violence related to non-normative choices around gender and sexuality in their lives were expected. But even before this violence gained ground, the extent and pervasiveness of the other violence was astounding. Most often, what we recorded was the direct violence on our respondents, but it also seems that there are households that are spaces of conflict, of violence and contestations of power.

The stories of the fissures in the apparently comforting and nurturing space of the natal family were alarming. This is of concern because it could be the nature of any family, not necessarily one that is termed dysfunctional. The rarity of what one would think of as 'normal' is shocking and demands urgent attention. The study throws up very critical questions for us about the nature of the family as an institution and our respondents' voices call for a serious enquiry into this core institution of our society.

Family Circumstances

One of the important things that mediates the experience of childhood is the class of the family that one is born in. Privileges of class give people an edge because of the kind of skills, education and nutrition they can access, advantages that stay with them even in adulthood. On the other hand, being born in a poor family can lead to a cumulative cycle of deprivation, further exacerbated due to other forms of marginalization like those of caste or gender and sexuality. Hence, understanding the role that class plays in people's early lives is important to make sense of their lives in the present day.

As per Figure 2.2, 14 of our respondents said that they grew up in poor families. Since this was based on their own perception, there were many variations within it. For example, experiences of individuals who identified as poor ranged from a story of everyday hunger to that of a family that owned some land. Prem's first memory of childhood was of one evening when ze asked hir mother for food and she said, '"Today is salary day, let us wait for your father to come and then we will all have food.".… When he came, he was totally drunk and had spent all his salary on drinking. I remember there was a big fight at home.'

A result of this extreme poverty was that two of our respondents were married off to cismen at a very early age and they never went to school. Mala, who identifies as 'woman from outside but not fully a woman', faced immense violence from hir in-laws. Ze was used to working all day even in hir parental home as ze was the youngest and hir sisters had been married off early. In hir husband's house too ze worked all day and did not get enough to eat. A few years into hir marriage, hir brothers were killed in local political violence in their village. Mala said, 'My in-laws know I have no one so they use this against me. I am like an object that can be just thrown around. I am not considered as a human being.'

Other respondents said that they managed to go to school but were expected to do wage labour alongside. Sandhya's family were daily-wage earners, and ze was also forced to work in the fields when all ze wanted to do was study. Ze recalled, 'This was my routine. Go to school, then go to my mother's workplace and then come back home with her…. Sometimes my mother would also tell me not to go to school because there was a lot of work, but I would sneak out.'

Twenty-five of the respondents saw their natal families as middle class and 11 as upper class, though the variations are immense here as well. Santosh saw himself as middle class despite his father being a daily-wage earner because many of his brothers worked and brought home wages. Bhargavi identified as upper class because of hir perception of class relative to circumstances of others in hir town. And there were others who were upper class by any standard, like Geeta, whose early memories of discrimination were about her brothers getting horse-riding lessons while she could not.

Even though most of these middle- and upper-class families managed to provide some basic education to their children, in some cases class advantage did not necessarily mean easy access to higher education. Twenty-year-old Nidhi hailed from a business family, but due to family dynamics ze was unable to afford the education ze wanted and had to support hirself earning small sums of money by playing cricket. Another respondent, Falguni, who grew up as a single child in a middle-class household, said that she was forced to stop studying when she was 15 or 16:

> My father was depressed and quit his job. However, savings tided us through. My mom was struggling. They used to fight a lot, throw things around.... My mother got a minor heart attack.... My father didn't know what to do, he was no help.... I was in charge of my mother's care. So I started earning money from a young age.

As expected, most families that were from marginalized castes were also from the lower economic strata. Some of these respondents did get marginal access to education and jobs due to the possibility of access to reservations, but also carried the stigma of the caste that they were born in. Vasu hesitated to tell us his caste because he was from what he called the 'lowest caste' and was not sure if he could tell this to anyone. Schools were the spaces where this discrimination was felt the most as it was the only public space that children accessed outside of homes and neighbourhoods. Most respondents spoke of the experience of others not eating with them, not sitting next to them and other such indicators of the stigma that caste carried. No doubt, such separation and shunning left indelible marks on young minds and hearts.

Others were from mixed caste backgrounds and they bore the brunt of this from the dominant-caste side of the family. Jamuna, whose mother was born in a Brahmin household, said that when they visited her mother's family, they were not allowed to touch anything in the house as they were considered to be from a lower caste. She also spoke of her school where the Brahmin girls would constantly trouble the only three non-Brahmin students in the class, asking them their caste and complaining about the non-vegetarian food in their tiffins. Jamuna said that it did not affect her as she was brought up very differently by her parents and had other privileges, but this indicated that caste was constantly present in the milieu.

The cases of direct discrimination might not always have been articulated thus, but the systemic nature of class and caste oppression, and their constant presence in childhood and beyond, comes through in the interviews. Vimala, whose mother's family is Dalit, said that she was not troubled by people in her home state because

> they don't believe I am [from here].... If they thought I was, by now I would have been mauled and commented on.... Here a dark woman has a low status. It's related to low caste... and so a person like me, dressing up like this, staying out this late, is not imagined.

Juhi, who grew up in what ze called 'a very Brahmin neighbourhood', felt that caste was always present. In hir later years ze tried not to use hir caste surname, but to no avail:

> The way caste operates, the kind of language you speak, people know that you are Brahmin.... Even if you don't use your surname, you cannot get rid of the privilege.... The first time I rented a place from [a Brahmin]... as soon as I spoke to him, he knew.

Apart from the obvious marginalization and disadvantages of class and caste, there are many others that operate in ways that result in multiple disadvantages. A person from a tribal background spoke of the poverty and the presence of police violence in their area. Another spoke of the problem of looking racially different from others because she had migrated to another region of the country. One respondent told us of the multiple kinds of marginalization that he faced because of being from a Scheduled Tribe and as he was a disabled person assigned gender female at birth. Yet another respondent was adopted by a hijra mother and had a very different experience while growing up of living among hijras and spending time with sex workers.

The 'Normal' Family

The violence of marginalization in society is accompanied with a lot of neglect and violence within the family. Some of it seems to emanate from circumstances. For example, both Prem and Sandhya spoke of how their mothers were very violent towards them. 'My mother used to beat with whatever she could lay her hands on,' said Prem. Sandhya said hir mother 'used to beat a lot. She would run after me and hit me with whatever she could lay hands on.' Devi also told us how hir mother used to beat hir 'if I did not do housework. She would use sticks from the date tree. It would really hurt.'

These three came from very poor families. Their mothers were hard pressed to make ends meet and were very conscious of their 'daughters' taking responsibility for the housework. Some of this violence probably arose from the sheer desperation of their already tough lives. Sandhya and Prem's mothers supported them in later life through tough decisions. Sandhya's mother, who did not encourage hir to go to school, was the one who gave hir the initial monetary support so that ze could go to the city and continue with hir studies. In all the troubles that Prem has gone through in hir life, hir mother has been a constant support till date.

In other households, however, the violence and neglect that our respondents spoke of is in a way indicative of just how dysfunctional 'normal' families are. Unreasonable violence knew no boundaries of class or caste. It was as much a part of those who grew up in middle-class households as it was in poorer or upper-class families. Our respondents spoke of not only violence towards them, but also between parents and between other members of the family.

Domestic Violence

Priya, who grew up in a middle-class family, said:

> My father was violent towards my mother. The atmosphere at home had always been tense. My mother was too involved in what she was suffering…. There wasn't much emotional support, no love that I felt. I used to stay in my room or out. I hated coming home.

As she grew older, her younger brother started being violent towards her. She felt that he probably was learning from their father's behaviour. Their mother could never stand up for her. Later in life, when her brother's violence towards Priya became very intense, instead of asking him to stop or leave, her mother asked Priya to leave the house and stay away.

Another respondent started off about his childhood with this:

> [I] had tiffs with dad since I was 6. Saw the scuffle between [my] parents that killed my biological mom. I was at the window, he pushed her and she went down the stairs. I was too young to understand it could have been an accident, for me he had killed her. I stopped talking to him, our relationship was never too good.

This little child spent many years locked up in his room, refusing to communicate with his father till almost eight years later, when his father remarried, and his stepmother managed to win him over with her unconditional love and affection.

Others spoke of the violence from extended families. Nidhi said the following about the upper-class joint family ze grew up in:

> My parents were forcefully separated from each other. My mother and I were made to sleep in a room that had a dog in it. My father had to live and sleep in the kitchen, near the dishes. His mind was poisoned and he was told the child wasn't his... though he didn't say anything to my mother. Others treated her like a servant. For two years it was like this.

Things changed a bit when hir father had a fight with his brothers and moved out with Nidhi and hir mother.

Sandy had very painful memories of hir childhood. 'My mother tried to be a good supportive parent in a lot of adversity. She tried to be there for her children in the face of my father and his family, and also her own family, which was not great either.' Hir mother eventually left hir father, and thus the children had a safe home to go to when in trouble. She remarried and Sandy found support from hir stepfather. The memories of childhood, though, are best forgotten: 'I have left it behind and my greatest desire is to leave it as far behind as possible. I get irritated when it appears in my current life. If my sister finds someone from the past on Facebook, I do not want to know.'

Alpana, who has now lost both her parents, said of her childhood:

> We had a very disturbed family.... I was too young so I couldn't link things with each other, but I have many small impressions. [My father] was a different human being altogether when he was drunk—once I saw him standing on top of my mother, she was just 5 feet tall and he was 5'11. I used to be very sad. I guess so was my sis, but we never spoke about it. At times I was unable to speak at all. I'd hear my father saying they should take me to a doctor, but now I think it may have been a protest, that I won't talk if you guys carry on like this.

Witnessing violence in the home causes deep insecurities. But the scars of the violence that children themselves face are even more difficult to get rid of. Meghana, who comes from a middle-class family, had this to say:

> Both mom and dad beat us. Dad was particularly violent when he would beat us, like with a belt. Sometimes... it felt as if I had lost my hearing in one ear or had broken some teeth. It never really happened but it felt like that.... Another thing my parents used to do a lot was that at the end of a long night of crying and hitting and beating... they would take both of us sisters, open the main door of the house, and push us outside and close the door and say, now you go and live how you want and do this wherever you want, but not in our house, and we would stand outside for hours crying.

Similarly Neha, who grew up in an upper-class household, said:

> My mother had a tendency of being very violent. I have been punished, slapped, pulled by my hair, made to kneel outside the door, her threatening to heat and brand me by a hot *tava* spoon.... I lost trust in my parents from a very early age.

Vimala's story indicated that her family thought they were right to beat her:

> Because they destroyed my freedoms and my desires, I had to
> oppose them.... The first time was when this *tantrik* [traditional
> faith healer] told all of them that I was not an ordinary human
> being. He told them that since birth I have had a bad force within
> me, which is why I am against the family all the time.... Their
> belief was that they were saving me, but as far as I was concerned,
> they were destroying me.... Neighbours knew that such things
> happened in our house and were ready to intervene, and even came
> with a camera to inform the local press about it. That time I was
> just a child.

All this drove Vimala into depression. She could not even speak
about it to anyone. To 'cure' her, her family took her to a *tantrik*
in another village and left her there for seven days for treatment.
She recounted a gruesome experience of sexual assault there.
'The first day, having taken the medicine, I was lying down when
I felt a heavy weight on me.... When I opened my eyes with
difficulty... this man was lying on me and hugging me close to
him.' She pushed him away somehow and ran to an open ground
where she sat the whole day. When it was dark, she came back
and locked herself in her room. She could not sleep because the
doors of the house were old and weak.

> Those seven miserable days of my life were the most torturous
> and traumatic, and had made me mad. When my family members
> finally came... I refused to even go home and instead ran away.
> Then they caught me and took me home by force.... Nowadays we
> know it by the name of depression.

Sexual Abuse

Vimala could never tell her family of the experience of sexual
assault. Others spoke of similar experiences of sexual violence
in their childhood, which they could not share with anyone. Of
the people we spoke to at least 18 referred to sexual assault of
different kinds from close or extended family members in their
growing up years. Family friends, neighbours, teachers, uncles,
male cousins and sometimes fathers were the perpetrators.

Ujwala was one of the few who could tell her mother later in life about an older cousin's abuse. Her mother, however, did not do anything, saying, 'It happens in families.' Ujwala said, 'I am not emotionally scarred, but I do feel angry that he got away with it despite telling my mom.' When Priya was in the second standard, she was abused by a neighbour. She told her family, they took it up and the person had to leave the building. This, however, became the talk of the building and she says even now, when she is 27, 'sometimes they still come up and ask me if it really happened to me'. A subsequent abuse by a tutor was handled by stopping her going to him again. This kind of expected reactions was perhaps the reason that none of the others felt confident to report abuse even when it was evident that it was abuse.

Hemlata chose marriage as a means to get out of a house where she was repeatedly abused and her parents kept quiet. 'The first abuse was by my mother's friend who she was having an affair with…. Second, an activist from my father's NGO. Third, a tenant. But in all this, my parents never said anything. I lived in fear during these situations.' Others like Maushami managed to get out of it by moving to another city for education:

> There were many sexual abuses that happened to me all through my childhood. I went to a counsellor only when I came to this city. Otherwise I always accused myself of being overtly sexual. It is a big house, with open courtyards. During vacations, I used to be alone at home. I used to be always tense. My mother used to laugh at me locking all doors, windows, everything.

Not believing children or not being aware of the possibility of abuse seems to be a common thread for most families. Roma spoke of her inability to speak even though she was harassed by a stranger when she was 8:

> The first time I was molested, I was wearing trousers and shirt, I had short hair. My uncle, his wife and his kids were returning by auto after watching a film. My mother was there also. I was sitting in front next to the driver and the helper due to lack of space….

From the back my aunt was teasing me, 'Oh look at that, is that a boy or a girl?' And all the while the driver was touching me. The jokes she was making made it impossible for me to say something, to protest. All I had to do was scream, but I couldn't do that. It felt like something here was frozen.

This is not the only incident that she remembered:

I got badly molested by my uncle.... I don't know what would have happened if [my aunt] had not come back. I had to go to the bathroom to fix my clothes and hair and everything.... The sad thing is nobody in my family believed that the incident happened. They feel it is the fantasy of an insane mind. Only my mother believed me. My father was critically ill, my aunt was pregnant, so nobody took any action. It is a deep anger I carry in my heart. [Later] I had to go to my aunt's place and he did it again. Even my grandmother saw it, but said that he was just trying to wake me up. So now I am not afraid of these things.

Even today many did not want to talk about it. Arun tersely answered the question about non-consensual sexual experiences with, 'Yes I have been sexually abused, there was some touching and things and that too from someone part of my family but I do not want to talk about it.' Manjula also said, 'Was sexually abused at home when I was 12 or 13. Do not want to talk about this.'

There have been others who managed to not only deal with their trauma and make their own lives, but also stand up and question their abusers later:

As a child, I was abused by my father from the time I was 7 or 8, for two or three years.... My mother was oblivious and I was too small to talk to anyone about it.... Later as an adult I told my papa very clearly, looking him in the eye, that he had made a big mistake that had affected my whole life. By then I had lost my inhibitions and especially when he questioned my relationship, I told him, 'You are responsible for this and you don't have a right to say anything. Maybe I could have been with a man if not for your wrongdoings, so don't go too far. In deference to your age and because you are my father, I'm forgiving you. I'm a spiritual person and I don't want negativity in my life. But do not lecture me.' He said, 'Beta,

> I am extremely ashamed. I did not do it knowingly, I was so ill'....
> I told myself it's not just his fault but the fault of the whole system
> and so I was able to forgive him.... He was sick, you know, he was
> sick. I always questioned myself—whether I have also become sick,
> because of his sickness.... And I realized that that effect had long
> gone. Now I am living as I am, consciously and deliberately.

The Son Preference

Besides such overt violence, there were the other subtler ways
through which violence was perpetually present. Usually, the
family bears the onus of creating citizens that fit into the social
and cultural norms of the society and community to which it
belongs, and so many of its 'normal' practices are those that
allow it to blend in with the larger society. Discrimination against
PAGFB is one such thing that is built into the system of the
family. Some of our respondents spoke of the ways in which they
felt the discrimination even when they were really small and the
impact it had on their long-term attitude towards themselves.
This discrimination was felt more when there were brothers to
make direct comparison with.

Mala grew up in a rural area. Ze had two brothers and said
that hir father did not want daughters. 'My father wanted only
sons.... He was not happy that we were five girls. But he would
say that we will give the girls away to work to someone in the
colony.' Ze and hir sisters were married off very early in any case.

Devi, who grew up in a working-class family, said:

> My mother would cook meat.... Then would give the pieces to my
> brothers and father, and put water in the masala and serve me and
> herself. She would not eat it, but would not give any to me either.
> Then you know what my father used to do? He would use the
> darkness, fold a little piece of chapatti over the meat and quietly
> pass it on to me.

Saumya was also discriminated against at home. 'If my
brother was drinking milk and put the glass down... I was

expected to wash his glass, but not expected to take my sister's glass. He had the privilege of not doing housework because he is male.' In her world of play, however, she was Saumesh, the boss. 'Born in a family, where we are taught that a girl should get married, learn to cook, etc., I hated it…. So since childhood I identified myself as a boy. Maybe unconsciously. I did not like to be told that I am female.'

Sometimes extended families became the reason for discrimination. Jharna said that her parents were all right, but others in their joint family discriminated between her and her brother:

> I was healthier than my brother, so they would say, 'Why is she eating so many good things?' I used to feel very bad as a child about such things—they were not small issues for me…. Sometimes I feel that my past is still affecting me…. I've been trying all my life to get rid of that feeling of inferiority.

Sometimes brothers helped learn things that would otherwise be difficult to access. Santosh learnt to drive thanks to his brothers. But very often brothers became the ones to stop and control them as well. Sara grew up in a small town. She was closer in age to her brothers than her sister, and so played with them and their friends:

> I was really bullied by my brothers. If I didn't listen to their orders, they would not let me be a part of their group. Eventually, I stopped hanging around with them and started doing my own thing. I learned how to fly a kite by myself in the hot month of May….. Cut to a few months later… and I was competing with the boys in the other building and cutting their kites.

For Sumit, who today identifies as 'transgender', it was as if hir dreams and hir family's needs matched up to each other. Ze reminisced:

> If I look at my photos from childhood I see myself in boys' clothes only…. My family gives me only boys' gifts all the time. They have

never pressurized me into wearing anything against my wish....
Maybe it was because we were eight sisters and so my parents
looked at me as their son. Inside me I felt like a boy.

Sumit's father passed away when ze was quite young and since
then ze has been the 'man of the house', looking after hir mother,
hir father's business and all hir married sisters.

For respondents who grew up as an only child, their parents
were either overly protective or wanted to make their child
independent. Chandni said:

Things that would involve overnight trips, they were not keen on
me going too far.... If there's more than one child, then parents
have already gone through the experience at least once, and so
there's more freedom for the kids.... Every cut and every bruise was
made into this big drama.

On the other hand, Simran categorically stated:

They have always been very worried because I have been the only
child and without sibling support. They have been very conscious of
this and so have always asked me to go ahead, take risks in life, go
for it while they are there to support me if needed. They have been
wonderful.

It was somewhat heartening to see that many of our
respondents said that they always did everything boys did and
played with boys when they were very young. In fact, there are
quite a few stories of how family members encouraged this
behaviour when their children were young. For some it was an
expression of their own gender, while for others it was about not
being bound by norms of gendered behaviour. Depending on
whether the family lived in a rural or urban area, or had extended
families living with them or in close proximity, the norms were
altered. But for most people there was reasonable flexibility.
It was usually during puberty, however, that tolerance levels
dipped and the normative family took over. It is at that time that

gender norms were imposed and expected to be followed in a stricter manner.

The 'Normative' Family

Bhargavi, who grew up in a joint family in a small town, said:

> At 14, my breasts started developing…. Till then I was jolly with my cousins, but now I was told not to… play with boys or talk to them. The family expected me to follow the restrictions. I used to love riding the scooty, but I was not allowed to any more.

Kavi, who grew up with two brothers, her parents and an uncle, said that she did not see any bias in her family:

> My mother was liberal. I played with boys only. I liked aggressive games, football and cricket, not soft games…. At age 12, seeing my cricket talent, my uncle got me admitted to a cricket academy. There were only girls there…. [Yet] I had to stop in seven days as I was a girl and I needed to be protected—that's what my mother said. My brothers, who were 6 and 10 years older than me, also felt that way. I felt very sad as they said my prospects were very good…. I met a player from the state cricket team, and she said, 'It would be great if you join the team, but you won't.' I felt very bad, very, very bad. I die to play cricket.

For those not comfortable with their assigned gender, this was a very trying phase. On the one hand the body gave signals that were difficult to accept, and on the other the external restrictions grew. Monu, who identifies as 'man but have come to terms with being seen as a woman socially', said:

> I thought of myself as a boy. All my friends were boys…. But as I grew older, when I reached class six or seven and my body too started to develop, the boys who I used to play with started distancing themselves from me, saying that you are a girl. This was like a big stone dropping on my head—I was a boy, how had I suddenly become a girl? What should I do? It was a bad period for

> me. The family too started putting pressure, saying that 'you are a
> girl, you must let your hair grow'.... I also had to wear skirts and
> salwar kameezes.

This is the phase in which most families try to impose
norms around clothes and hair, and also control mobility and
other expression. Things that were possible for many people till
puberty became extremely difficult henceforth.

While Santosh lived at home, he had to do as his family
wanted. There were usually controls around dress and hair. Still,
he managed to wear a shirt instead of a blouse to school and
would change from the skirt into a *mundu* (a lower garment
usually worn by men in southern India) when he came home:

> My brother [closest to me in age] didn't like me dressing like this
> and he'd always fight with me.... When he went out his friends
> would make fun of him, asking why his sister was acting like a man,
> commenting, 'Look, your brother is walking down the street!' But I
> felt good when I heard that!

Santosh said that his parents would stop his brother from beating
him up, but as he grew older, the problems increased. 'I had
many male friends, which was no longer okay after my growing
up, in eighth or ninth standard. I was told not to hang out with
them, I'd get a bad name. Till then it had not been a problem.'
Even in the face of opposition and ridicule from neighbours,
Santosh was very clear about his own gender.

For Rahul, however, the dilemmas were more pronounced
because what he felt and what he saw around did not match,
and became even worse at puberty. It changed the very nature of
the person that he was. 'I used the masculine gender for myself.
Earlier they didn't mind me speaking in a tomboy way, but later
they started asking me why.... A time comes when you are made
to realize that you are a girl. That time came. I felt bizarre.' Rahul
waited eagerly to turn 18 because then he knew that he could do
what he wanted and no one could stop him. His family has never
understood and still cannot comprehend how he feels, but have

come around to some extent. He does not talk much to them and there isn't complete acceptance, but at least he has not had to leave home. Not everyone is as lucky.

Arun's choice of playing cricket and dressing as ze wanted led to immense violence from hir father:

> My father was a football player but still he did not like me playing [cricket]. Also people started saying, why is this person like this? This girl goes out in the morning and comes back at night? My family started saying, 'You cannot go.' [There was] a lot of resistance to my going, even house arrest, but I continued to go…. There were lot of pressures and also violence from my father's side. He would beat me and tear off my shirts. Then I would wear something else for a day or so and then again do what I liked. Then it would happen again…. My mother and others also thought that I needed to be corrected. At best, they would say, 'Do not beat, talk.' Father would beat, mother would not beat but say things, [like], 'Why are you here, go away.' Then I did not know where to go.

A neighbour finally guided Arun to a children's helpline. With help from people ze met through them, and the courage and exposure that ze got from being a good cricketer, Arun managed to chart a different course to hir life away from this family.

Marriage Pressures

As soon as 'daughters' hit puberty, apart from clothes and norms of when and where they can go and with whom, the next step to ensure 'good' behaviour is to get them married off as soon as possible. Six of our respondents were married to cismen at some point in their lives. All of them eventually got out of these marriages and lived a life of their choice, but after tremendous sorrow and pain caused to all concerned.

Kirti spoke of how he was forced by his father to get married:

> I told him no… I tried to tell him that I wanted to live my life on my own and that I hated marriage and I feel scared of men. They

told me that everyone has to get married and in the beginning everyone is scared.

He was already in a relationship with a woman when he was married off at 14. He was 15 when his daughter was born. He managed to stay at his parents' place for two years after that. 'I did not let [my husband] touch me. Then my son was born when I was about 19. That also by force.' Kirti managed to get out of the marriage after making false allegations against his husband, but was left with two children to look after.

Others were luckier and managed to escape. Anand fled from his small-town home to a big city when he was 17 to avoid marriage pressures. Though he had very little money, he knew where he wanted to go: a coaching class for entrance to an engineering college for which he had been selected. When he arrived, however, the class was closed for vacations: 'Those 10 days, let's not talk about [them]—they were horrible.' Somehow, he survived in an alien city with no one to turn to. He managed to work and study, and finished his education. His doggedness to pursue his dreams saved him from a forced marriage and also helped him understand his own gender and sexuality. He went back home much later and today his family respects his choices. But such success stories are few and far between.

Manjula, 36, managed to resist the pressure to get married and had many hilarious stories to share about the kind of boys hir parents made hir 'see'. 'Thirty-forty people from the age of 23 till as recently as two years ago. I have said no, but my parents have said always that it is our duty to show you. So meet them and then you can say no.' Hir mother was slightly unconventional but saw this as an obligation nonetheless. 'My father comes from a very different background, he does not understand anything about sexuality. It is very difficult for me to explain to him that I am interested in another woman.' Finally, ze spoke to them about hir relationships and that stopped the hunt for a suitable boy.

Some of our other respondents, however, could not deal with such pressures easily. The general spectre of forced marriage, either on them or their partners, forced many couples to leave their home and flee. Ranjana was in a relationship with another woman:

> My parents wanted me to get married, there was much pressure. They were waiting for me to finish my postgraduation…. We really had to take a decision then. First, we decided to kill ourselves…. We had decided to throw ourselves on to railway tracks. But it started raining and we didn't do it. We didn't know what to do with ourselves. We had no one to talk to.

Ranjana and her friend accidentally came across a newspaper article that helped them get in touch with individuals and groups who helped them out after they left their homes. This leaving was not easy:

> Later I got to know that my father had fainted when he realized that we had left…. When I called home a day later, he told me I should come back, I felt guilty, I actually was in two minds then, I thought we should go back. I told him, one day I'll come back, when I reach a stage in life where I feel very confident…. You will be proud of me.

She didn't meet them for seven long years, only heard their voices over the phone when she made blank calls. When she left home, Ranjana had been old enough to have completed her education and found a job as well as support. She became a confident, self-reliant person and was able to go back home. It was a happy reunion, but even then she could not talk of her relationship with her girlfriend who had been her sole family all those years.

Asserting Sexual Choices

Many of our respondents were aware of their sexuality and had also been in relationships with other PAGFB very early in life. Many a time, through schools and other means, families came to know of these relationships. Though eager to get their children married off, parents could not handle young people's assertion of their sexuality. Gender non-conformance was not considered a problem in childhood, but as soon as sexuality entered the picture, the scenario often changed completely. Immense controls were placed on communication, mobility and meeting people, which forced many individuals to run away.

Sam's life turned topsy-turvy after his flirtatious relationships with female classmates were brought into the open because one friend's parents complained and the school suspended him:

> I went home and told everyone that I was attracted to girls. My mother heard me and then beat me up badly with a stick. I bled, then I fainted.... After this there was house arrest. All my freedom was cut off.... I had a good arrangement for the music system. The day my mother came to know of my suspension, she broke everything and also burnt all my pant–shirts [and] T-shirts. She said, 'You think you become a man by wearing pants?' So she made me wear saris.... They made me learn how to cook. Till then I did not even know how to make coffee.... After my suspension, my mother never spoke to me directly. She would speak through someone else. And if there was no one, she would talk to the walls but not look at me. I was given a separate room, separate vessels for all those three months.

They also thought he was possessed by the ghost of a boy, and took him for exorcisms to every possible shrine. After a few months, Sam went back to school and fell into similar trouble. He was grounded again and was very lonely as he thought everyone was unhappy because of him. He also realized that they had plans to get him married without his consent. So he filled a bag with his brother's clothes and fled. It was a coincidence that he met some people from a supportive NGO, else Sam would have been yet another 17-year-old left to fend for themselves on the streets.

Kamal had support from his family, but his girlfriend was being pressurized to get married to a man chosen by her parents. She insisted that Kamal should marry her so that she was not forced into any other marriage. They found out about a free group marriage that was being organized somewhere and ran away to get married there. They informed her parents about this and her father filed a kidnapping case against Kamal. This became a huge media story because the local police leaked this information to the press. Another NGO got in touch with them and saved them just as they were losing all hope and thinking of committing suicide, frustrated by all the mud-slinging. Kamal's family were supportive even when the couple had run away and have subsequently accepted them both, but the girlfriend's family have still not completely reconciled to this relationship.

We heard many such stories of pressure from the partner's family or pressure on the partner to get married. In many such cases the couples ran away or made suicide pacts. There were stories of such pacts leading to the death of one partner or leading to outing both people in the school, neighbourhood or workplace, or in the media.

Whether parents or families actually act on their threats or not, the fear of the rejection is strong enough to push young people into actions that have long-lasting impact on their lives. Laxmi's parents were ready to get their only child married off to a relative. She protested and broke off the engagement because there were dowry demands. Then she went to a different city to study and fell in love with a Muslim boy. This was not tolerated and she was brought back, her studies discontinued and she was kept at home. While there, she fell in love with a woman next door. A common friend told Laxmi's mother about this and they were separated. 'Family restrictions were increasing. They would not allow me to go out of the house, I could not meet anyone; hence, B and I decided to leave the place.'

Neel has been in a long-term relationship with another woman. She did not talk at length about the problems they had gone through, but mentioned that her partner's parents had made a police complaint. Since that incident, she said, her family also have not completely approved. 'I was the pet in the family, that is why now all of the family is sad. I was always studious and good, now all that is changed.' She referred to her childhood as 'golden times', but 'now one feels terrible. But those were good times.' Her partner's family has not reconciled to this relationship. When they visit, some members speak to them and others do not.

If one's relationship with the family was bad, then running away was the preferred path. It was when the relationship was good that changes became difficult to deal with. Kanika was very close to hir parents, who, ze says, encouraged hir to be independent. This is why ze felt it necessary to come out to them. But this caused a lot of trouble at home:

> [My] parents get upset, angry, sometimes [my] mom cries, and seeing her crying haunts me tremendously. I feel I am guilty, so it is all emotional violence, and nobody ever asked me since puberty what my preferences are…. I wanted them to be more open and friendly with me regarding my gender and sexuality, but that didn't happen…. I was in a very bad situation because just a few weeks earlier my girlfriend also ended her relationship with me, so I was devastated and attempted suicide.

This conscious choice around sexuality and gender that goes against the grain of society thus adds another layer to the nature of violence, neglect and abuse that our respondents spoke of in their lives. Where familial relationships are not healthy, many people choose to move on and live on their own. The ability to survive and build a life for oneself in these circumstances then gets coloured by the privilege of education, class and caste, or lack of it.

The Violence of Silence

Given all of this, it is unsurprising that many of our respondents, about 18 out of 50, have completely hidden important parts of their lives from their families. For many of them, disclosure around their sexuality or gender is often not a choice at all. Very often, this means living relationships not just without ever talking about them, but also going through severe emotional and other stress without the families even being aware of it. This state of silence and indifference is not just alienating but also violent.

Aditi lost her father when she was just a toddler. She grew up primarily with her mother and her aunt. Her mother is very understanding and has been there for her throughout: 'The only person whom I really appreciate is my mother. She is not so educated, but she has never opposed me and always felt that her happiness lies in mine.' When her relationship of many years with the person she still refers to as 'the love of her life' broke up because the girlfriend decided to marry a cisman, Aditi was totally shattered and attempted suicide thrice. The last time she had written a note:

> My cousin saw the note and gave it to my aunt who showed it to my mother. I gave a wrong reason saying that I have tensions with my job. So my mother told me to give up the job, she could take care of me. She said she would not live if anything happened to me. So now I have given up the idea of dying. I live for my mother.

Aditi has still not been able to tell her the truth, though at some level she knows that her mother will accept it.

Some other queer people live in precarious and continuously negotiated spaces with partial disclosure and discussion. Yet others find partial acceptance because of the economic and other support that they provide within the family. Very often single LBT persons are the main support of their families, taking care of not just parents, but also other siblings and their families. And yet, their own lives and desires are ignored.

Sumit said ze sees hirself as a man and hir gender has full acceptance even in hir extended family. Yet, ze was sure that they would not accept hir relationships with women. 'I know that even if I have a girlfriend and she wants to live with me, they will not accept that. The way I am it is all right, but they will not accept her.' Ze added wistfully:

> They never ask me to get married. They do not worry about me getting old alone. They say that they will look after me, my sisters and brothers-in-law. My mother also does not worry who I will live with in future. Sometimes I have even asked them, 'Are you not worried about my future? Let at least a friend stay with me.'

Hir mother was all right with Sumit living with someone like hirself, 'but a girl in my life will most probably not be allowed to stay with me'.

In some cases there is a grudging acceptance of their sexuality or gender, but rarely does it transform into support that enables people to live with their partner like their heterosexual siblings do within the family space.

Family Support

We had a few stories of acceptance and they were a refreshing change in this otherwise dominant saga of violence, violation and abuse.

For instance, Alex said hir family has accepted hir gender and hir manner of dressing, but they still ask hir to wear a saree for the sake of society:

> Mom used to pray for me that I get a nice husband. Then I would glare at my mom and she would quickly change her prayer and say, 'I will pray for a nice girl!'… My family is very comfortable with my gender. If they see me dating a boy, they will be shocked.

This is one of the few families that made sure that there was a small house where ze could stay and interestingly, their worry was who would do the cooking for hir as Alex was not used to it at all.

Similarly, Sunny grew up thinking of hirself as a boy. Ze said that in hir childhood, 'I was not told anything when I did not do any housework, even now I am not told anything. Occasionally my family says to me, if boys are also doing housework these days, why don't you do some work?' Hir mother has a genuine worry:

> My mum is only scared of one thing, that I will be alone. She says, 'See your dad died, but I had a hope in my two kids. But when I die who do you have? You do not want to marry a guy. You do not want to have a sex change. A girl will not stay with you in this way, so how will you live alone?' I joke that I will have seven-eight wives, but actually I am scared about the future…. My relatives ask why, when she talks of marriage, she only talks of my sister and never

of me.... My mum cannot tell the truth, but she says, 'I am not interested in getting Sunny married, that's it!'

For Ujwala it has been a changing relationship that has helped her family come to terms with her sexuality and choices around it. Her parents used to be wary and controlling of her going out with boys late at night, but through constant dialogue with their children, they have been able to make a lot of changes in their thinking. The process was gradual. Her mother, in fact, now lives with Ujwala and her partner since her father passed away recently. 'Where my mother is concerned there is absolutely no question that my partner would not command the same respect as my sister's or brother's partners would. So at family occasions, she would be treated the same way as everyone else.'

As with Ujwala, for some others, there had been a sort of reconciliation and some sort of balance, over a period of time. Privileges of class and caste, of whether the family was in a rural or urban area, of whether the extended family were around and demanding conformity, or if there were other adults and friends who helped change outlooks—often these circumstances determined whether reconciliation was happy or difficult. Sometimes parents managed to show immense strength and courage in favour of their child even in the face of opposition from their other children.

Karthik's father is his role model and he grew up working with him, breaking stones in quarries. When Karthik got into a relationship with a woman, things were not easy. He and his girlfriend had to run away. After a few days of living in different places, when they came back to his village, there was a big crowd and a lot of media that made a spectacle of them:

> I had a fight with my brother. He was angry as this would cause problems and shame for them... now that the media was involved. I told him I have no problem with the way I am. I can live my life working so I can leave the house if it is a problem for you. My father said to my brother, 'It is my child and if my child wants to live as a man or a woman I have no problem. He can stay here. If anyone has a problem they can leave the house.' So my brother left the house.

The love story did not have a happy ending in spite of this because it was not acceptable to the girlfriend's family and neighbours. She was finally married off to a cisman. But the stand Karthik's father took gave him the courage to continue to lead his life on his terms.

Similarly, in Divakar's case, his brothers did not want him to have a share in the little property that their father has. But his father got his documents changed. 'It has been changed from two sons and three daughters to three sons and two daughters and my name is added as Divakar.'

For some of our respondents parents in fact offered an opportunity for new experiences and ways of living, the memory of which they cherish till date. Especially some fathers provided this access, which opened up a different world that probably made the internal gender negotiation a little easier, made it easier for young children to grow up into more balanced human beings.

Murali said of the times that ze spent with hir father:

> My father was a member of the Communist Party.... He often talked about the party with me. I took part in human chains, used to dress up with the symbol and shout out the slogans so party members too liked me and gave me a lot of attention and love.

Saran lost her father when she was 13. Her father took voluntary retirement from the army to spend time with the family and started a transport business. She had many fond memories of her time with him in his truck, making deliveries as part of his transport business:

> I used to love going with him on trips. I used to be his assistant, his cleaner.... I would put the log at the back of the wheel when [we were] stranded on the ghats, put my hand out and wait for directions. If we were stopping for meals at a dhaba, I would take the can to fill water, help dad to clean the windshield, manage his money for the toll, keep accounts for him, take papers for the octroi... there he never allowed me to go alone to the office.

Fathers like these were crucial because they stood up for their children, allowed them to experience life differently, do unusual jobs, and in the process made their children's differences easier to deal with. But in our study fathers were a mixed bunch. There are about 17 who were supportive in the long run. Ten respondents lost their fathers before they grew out of their teens. Two of these fathers had committed suicide. Of the remaining, there were many who were not really present for their children and yet they controlled their lives because they were considered heads of household by default. It is not surprising to note, then, that for our respondents the tensions around sexuality and gender were most often resolved when fathers were supportive or when they had died early.

Mothers were usually a much more constant presence in people's lives. Only two respondents spoke of their mothers' deaths when they were young. In both cases the fathers remarried. In our study mothers came across as either strong, independent people or dependent, weak figures. Disciplining children seemed to be a mother's task and this often also led to an iron fist being used against the child. No generalizations can be made on the basis of our sample, but on the whole mothers were more supportive in the long run. They may have been violent, but they also managed to help out and support their children in ways that were very sustaining.

The story around siblings is starker. Many more brothers were violent and restrictive as compared to those who were supportive, and this was true whether they were older or younger. Only two people spoke of brothers who were supportive. For the rest, they were at best irrelevant or else controlling and abusive. Sisters on the whole tended to be supportive, though there were a couple who had been antagonistic. Interestingly, some sisters played the role of 'ideal daughters' and yet were supportive of their siblings. In fact having a 'good sister' who met all the requirements of conforming to mainstream gender and sexuality sometimes took the pressure off our respondents.

Support from Others

Families are supposed to provide nurture and support, which ideally translates into an opportunity to live life on one's own terms. However, as we have seen in this whole chapter, this often remained a distant dream. When families were not even able to provide basic security and fulfil the needs of a growing child, others sometimes stepped in.

Some found support in the extended family network or from friends. Sometimes, as we have seen, extended families had been the perpetrators of discrimination and violence, but at times family members stepped in to provide the physical and emotional support that helped some of our respondents survive. As Jai said:

> After our mother passed away, our father was not with us, so our father's brother was looking after us. The system was that we would go to school in the morning; there would be nothing to eat, so we would just go. Then we would come back and this uncle would come back from work around 12 at night and then we would cook and have some food.

Later Jai and his sister were thrown out of their house by their alcoholic father when he remarried. They consumed poison in despair and were saved by this same uncle. Arun's grandmother and Neha's grandfather also stood by them when their parents were violent or negligent.

Yet others found people outside the family network. Juhi spoke of the various women neighbours who were there when ze grew up. 'Due to the communal living, especially because of the person my mother was, a dependent sort of person, I felt I had many mothers and never depended solely on my own.' These women helped and guided hir when hir mother could not, like telling hir about menstruation and so on.

For another respondent who was training in music, many hours of the day were spent with the guru who became the best friend:

> Very gentle, very nice, very funny, very humorous. Never shouted at me, never screamed at me…. I told him after six months that he

was making me do too many hours of work and also that because of that I could not spend time in school or play. Then we started going on walks or we would play cricket.... So in a sense he provided me the entertainment.... We would talk about everything and by the time I was 16 or 17, he was my best friend.

Even when faced with issues of gender and sexuality, the adults around who were like family sometimes became pillars of support. The aforementioned guru was a confidant after the suicide of the respondent's first girlfriend. In Sunny's case, it was hir mother's friend who introduced hir to queer groups and individuals, gave hir material to read and made hir comfortable in hir own chosen identity. Sometimes, the knowledge of others who were similar in the family and neighbourhood helped.

Vasu met a distant relative who was different and who eventually helped him meet queer groups and individuals:

I don't know how we shared our minds, but he began to say, actually, I am like a girl and feel that way. Then I too opened my mind and started to speak out. Then we would meet without anyone knowing.... I would cry a lot, thinking at least there is one person I can feel free with and share.

For Meghana the knowledge of hir aunt's lesbian relationship and life opened up new avenues for hir to validate hir own experiences.

The few people within the family who they could identify with made a world of difference for some respondents. Others found such space and support in the sports they played and the world they encountered through it, in their various other pursuits, or from the teachers they met or the queer groups that they finally encountered. We read many of these stories in the chapters that follow.

And then there was non-human support as well—in the animals that became part of their lives at some point or the other and in the communication they could manage with them. Divakar said that in the worst of times, when he could not really talk about what was happening to him, 'there was a cow. I used to talk to her and be with her.' Murali spoke of hir cat. 'If I did not feed the cat, it would not eat. It was a real comfort. It used to come and look at my face and say meow, as if it was asking me, what is the matter with you?'

Others found this space within their own fantasies and inner worlds. Ujwala said:

> I had this whole inner world. I remember wanting to learn the piano and we never had the money... [so] I had this fantasy that I had a piano. Once we had this huge mansion with rooms upstairs and my friends always believed that I had a piano. There was a whole life that went on inside me.

While Ujwala managed to convince her friends about her fantasy, Juhi lived hirs:

> I was a big bully. I used to use my grandfather's black cataract glasses, a toy gun and an *odhni* [stole/dupatta] and say I was a *daku* [bandit].... I had a gang of friends with me. I would catch some younger kid, wrap the *odhni* around the kid and make [it] my horse. I used to hang around in these clothes and with a lathi all day. I used to let go of the stick only at night, when it was time to sleep.

It is important to highlight each of these stories as even though they are few and far between, they are crucial in the isolated lives that people are leading.

Conclusion

The experiences of our respondents reiterate that families are extremely important, not just while growing up, but also in the impact they have on people's later lives. However, families by themselves are not spaces of love, support and nurture. In fact, we find that systemic violence and hierarchies are built into familial structures and spaces, and the nurture that people find in them often comes with control and strictures. This happened for many of our respondents even before they broke any norms of gender or sexuality. The nature of violence that our respondents reported is stunning—physical, sexual, emotional violence, and violence in the form of neglect and discrimination as well. Families stand out as violent spaces in general. Thus, we need to carefully study the structures and power hierarchies of families per se. This study provides a hard look at the reality of these families across class and caste.

When our respondents came to the point of expressing and exploring non-normative sexuality or gender, their families came down heavily as the primary reinforcers of societal and cultural norms. Often the violence escalated within the family even before any other social institution entered the picture, and when others like schools did, they often colluded with the family. Gender transgression tolerated thus far in little 'girls' was not allowed any longer. The making of the 'good' daughter is a very violent script. This is achieved through punishments, strictures and enforcements that leave a huge imprint on people's lives.

In the absence of any social security, families are not just the primary caretakers, but also the most important social resource a person has. In addition, they connect one with the larger community and society. Within these structures, parents, especially mothers, sometimes end up both as strict enforcers as well as supports at crucial junctures. Sometimes, though, that support is entirely lacking, leading to not just the taking away of immediate family support, but also of connected structures. Thus, respondents who moved away from home or were forced to run away found themselves completely alone without any of the social capital, which is otherwise available to migrants.

All PAGFB are not brought up to be economically self-reliant and opportunities to navigate the world with confidence are not given to them as they are to people assigned gender male at birth (PAGMB), who, since childhood, are encouraged to deal with the larger world with greater independence. This made it even more difficult for some of our respondents to resist the pressures to conform. And when some managed to run away, often out of desperation rather than with a well-thought-out plan, it was extremely difficult to survive.

Our respondents were among those who managed to eventually meet people like themselves and like us, which is why we know their stories today. But even then, it was hard for them to fill the gaps left by their own families, which had been absent all their lives. For many respondents this loss of family was not just a material loss, but also an emotional rift that was difficult to come to terms with. Yet, as we will see, some managed to create families of their own and others managed to reconnect with their natal families.

Through the remaining chapters of this book, as we speak of the various ways in which people create this sense of themselves and theirs, we wish to underline the importance of looking anew at families. Instead of being spaces that replicate the hierarchies and structures of society, we need to visualize them as truly safe spaces that allow their young to be different. Families need not only be those formed through birth or marriage, but they must be a haven in this world of inequality. Only then can the world be a place that people choose to live in rather than exit from, as one of our respondents was forced to do.

Note

1. Even amongst the 16 who had happy memories of growing up, five have had difficulties vis-à-vis their families once they were open about their choices around sexuality. Four of them ran away, of which two have had a full reconciliation subsequently. Of the remaining 11, six have chosen, mostly due to fear of non-acceptance, to not speak about their choices around desire to their families.

5

Experiences of Formal Education

The arena in which most of us spend a good part of our lives as children and young adults—that of formal education—shapes our later lives as crucially as the family does. Classmates and teachers, uniforms and subjects, rules and regulations, budding interests, early friendships and first romances: the long years in school and college are filled with interactions and influences that leave their mark on us no less firmly than our lives at home.

Education can be double-edged in many ways. Like other mainstream actors, it schools us in the binary, but it also gives us the tools and language to critique and question that binary. It is supposed to be the great leveller, bringing all who have access to it on to the same playing field. But it often ends up alienating, othering, punishing those who resist regulation; it can reinforce marginalization of caste, class, ability and gender. It is obviously of great importance for those who need to be able to achieve economic independence to live their lives the way they wish to, and all PAGFB come under that category. However, the ones who are the most in need of skills and qualifications that could stand them in good stead in later life are often those who fall through the cracks in the system.

And yet, as with every other aspect of this study, our respondents' experiences of formal education did not merely echo what we already knew or could guess. There were as many happy surprises as there were grim tales.

We asked how much people had studied and in what ways their studies may have been disrupted or enabled by gender and sexuality issues, as well as by class, caste and other factors.

Besides asking about each respondent's level of formal education, the questionnaire had a section exploring their experiences of school and college—affirmation and violence to do with gender expression or for other reasons; the roles played by teachers; subjects and activities that had a significant impact; early sexual attractions or relationships, and their consequences, including being outed.

These findings are intriguing, sometimes validating what we might expect, given our knowledge of the ways in which various kinds of marginalization tend to work, sometimes offering unexpected insights into the wide range of factors that may prove to be empowering in adverse circumstances. All these 'findings' need to be read, of course, in conjunction with other aspects of growing up: families, neighbourhoods and individual agency.

Nurture in Schools

As is usual for most people, some of our respondents loved school and others hated it. While many liked it well enough, eight of our respondents clearly preferred school because it afforded an escape from, or a contrast to, the oppressive atmosphere of the home. This does not imply that all other respondents had less oppressive homes; only that school was not necessarily a happier place for them. The oppressions were to do with grinding poverty, alienation from or neglect by parents or extended family, sexual abuse, a rigid discipline of dos and don'ts, too much housework, beatings and conflicts around non-normative gender expression—issues discussed in the previous chapter.

Maushami, who grew up feeling neglected by her parents, being sexually abused by an uncle and being made to do all the housework while her brother didn't have to lift a finger, adored school. She had many friends, enjoyed history, geography and literature, played every kind of sport. For Jai, home was a place of extreme poverty and hunger:

> If you are home, you have to starve, but in school there is the midday meal scheme, so that I liked. Second, I loved to study and

did it well, and third, I also liked to sing. I took part in many competitions and used to star in programmes. It was a mixed girls' and boys' school and I liked the girls.

Most of those for whom school became a haven were good at studies and/or sport, and so found much-needed affirmation from teachers and peers. Jharna also had a difficult home life that eroded her self-confidence, but her teachers and some subjects made up for it in many ways:

> I still remember one day I wrote something and my teachers were all happy, they picked me up and carried me to the staff room, saying, 'What you've written, such a small girl!' After that the whole thing changed for me; I got very special treatment in my school— that gave courage to live as I want…. Whatever I was missing in my house, I got slowly in my school.

One respondent lost his mother when he was very young. In his eyes, she seemed to have died because of a fight between his parents. He said:

> I had been a happy child, jumping around. Then I became a very sad-looking child. My teachers really went out of their way to make me feel okay—gave me chocolates, pencils, took me home to play with their kids…. After my mum's death, [my family] were going to take me out of this school. When the teachers found this out, they called my dad and said they'd make me take a scholarship test [and] if I passed I could stay on. At the age of six, I would sleep at 12, wake up at 4 and study! Studying in the games period, in the rickshaw to school and back, for the scholarship, so that I could stay on in that school.

Teachers seemed to have been crucial in many people's lives. In fact, they made things possible for many of our respondents. Kamal, disabled from an early age, might have missed out on education but for this incident:

> One day when it was raining very heavily, one of the teachers noticed me and asked why I was not coming to school. I told him

that I was interested in studying but my parents would not send me. Then the teacher very firmly spoke to my parents and asked them to send me to school, and if it was not possible, then he would make arrangements for me to stay in a hostel for the disabled.

Sandhya, who got to attend school only through sheer personal determination, recalled a teacher in hir 10th standard who encouraged hir. One night he came on a round to the village and to hir house, asking if ze had made a timetable for hir exam preparation. The determined child that Sandhya was, ze had done so and was also following it. 'My father came out and invited him in. I was a little unsure because the room was really small with vessels and animals all around but he said, "No problem my house is also like this."' Next day at the parent–teacher meeting, he praised Sandhya before everyone for having done what no other student had done. Ze narrated:

> On the annual day, when the 10th standard students taught the whole school, he made me the principal of the school…. Till then the most influential student would get this post and usually it used to be a boy or girl from the dominant caste…. That year it was decided that the student who gets the most marks would get the post.

Violence in Schools

The problem is that for every teacher who makes a positive difference to a child, there is a whole system that makes school and being in it very difficult for many others. Violence towards students is even now seen as part of pedagogy by many teachers. Many of our respondents spoke of the amount of beating, abusing and taunting that teachers resorted to. This harassment is important to note because, just like a good teacher can generate interest in a subject, a bad teacher can put the student off not only the subject, but school itself.

Hemlata said, 'I dislike English because the teacher beat me horribly and did not explain things well. Maths was my best subject… the teacher never beat me and he made me understand the subject with love… and he respected us as girls.' She said that she stayed in school and completed her 10th standard with much reluctance. The restrictions and punishments were the main reasons for this.

> We had a lot dos and don'ts…. We were also punished—I never did my homework and, hence, was invariably sent out of class…. Once they made me a *murga* [a form of punishment; literally, chicken] and beat me, after which I had a fever for three days.

She also had complaints against the boys in the school. 'Even the bigger boys used to beat and bully me. There was no space for my creativity.'

Prem liked school over home, but had a similar complaint against the male teachers:

> In school, we had to kneel… and were also beaten with sticks, especially on the hands…. We had no women teachers. Only men. The maths teacher had sexually abused almost all the girls in school. Whenever we went to show our notebooks, he would make us stand next to the table, put his hands near the crotch, pinching and scolding as to why we scored less.

Sam's mother had shifted him to a nearby school because she worried about his travelling to a more distant school as a 'young girl'. One of the maths teachers there used to harass girls. Sam recounted, 'He never did it to me. One day I told him, "Why do you have to come so close?" Then we all girls also complained… and he was suspended for a month.' Sam later had trouble in school because of his relationships with other girls and this teacher took his revenge. 'He hit me once so badly that he drew blood.'

Yet others had to negotiate their way around violence related to their class or caste locations, even when they were not particularly marginalized by those factors. Sandy recalled:

> My school was very classist… where everyone was classified based on the wealth of their fathers…. Not only the rest, but even my

friends would talk behind my back about me, ridicule me. The same way that Muslim children were othered. Whether it was class, religion, gender—we were all ridiculed and othered.

Jamuna, whose parents were college teachers and had married across caste boundaries, was 'technically' OBC and this had repercussions for her in school:

There were only three non-Brahmins in my class…. We were constantly being asked, 'What caste are you?' and my brother and I did not have a clue…. I didn't get along with the girls who were the toppers and [they] made complaints, like how I had brought non-vegetarian food. And so I was made to eat separately…. constantly things like this would happen.

For Jamuna such a casteist atmosphere did not do any long-term damage to her sense of self because she came from a home with caring parents whose own lives were the antithesis of all the prejudice and conservatism she encountered in school. But her experience flags for us the great harm such prejudice can do when it intersects with other kinds of marginalization like those of gender and sexuality, and is not countered with any reassurance within the family sphere.

Sandhya's story, mentioned earlier, revealed how schools perpetuate such caste prejudices. Vasu, for instance, not surprisingly, dropped out of school—the combination of poverty, caste and a gender transgression that was heavily strictured both at school and home proved too much to allow him to study further. He grew up in a very poor family and was beaten a lot since childhood by his father, mother, brother and uncle. Neither at home nor in school was he allowed to dress according to his own sense of his gender. 'I specifically hated the uniform, then they would insist on plaiting my hair…. And wear a dupatta. All that would make me a girl and I didn't like it.' He added: 'Yes I would like to be educated. When all of them talk, or when you talk, I don't understand anything. For instance, if I want to read what is in this paper, I really have to struggle.'

The Making of 'Good' Girls

Dominance by and acceptance of those with more social capital is an intrinsic part of the school system. Structured so as to produce good citizens, it does little to question the existing power structures—those of patriarchy not being an exception. While there has been a liberal discourse of equality for the last few decades, the emphasis on making 'good girls' out of PAGFB is part of the process of education. And though the discourse has changed curricular requirements, some subjects like needlework stay on to make the right kind of women.

Simran liked her schools, but, reflecting back on her convent education, she said, 'Now when I look back, I think education is all right, but what were they trying to teach us? Were they teaching us needlework? Were they finishing us to get married and become good wives or what?'

Chandni recalled hir battles with needlework. Ze had a time-bound exam in which

> they give you a square, you are supposed to fold it in, hem it down and tack a line around it. Then, we had to do lines of stitches with different colours.... I hadn't even managed to fold one side and the time was over.

Ze went home bawling and hir mother, concerned about this being included in deciding grades, made a complaint. Luckily, other mothers did so too and they were given re-exams.

The school uniform is another thing that not only emphasizes the difference between boys and girls, but also makes life more difficult for gender-transgressive PAGFB. Respondents who wanted to keep their hair short or wear trousers rather than skirts or shirts rather than blouses were more or less able to negotiate uniform regulations. But there were limits. Anand said:

> I continued with guys' clothes, though my hair was long, until eighth standard, when the teacher said, 'Now you have to wear the tunic.' She was very patient, explained why and I agreed. I don't think I had much of a choice.

The situation was less comfortable for others. Alex remembered hir rebellion around wearing a skirt on hir first day at boarding school when ze was 7, and this continued till later in life:

> Outside of school I wore pants, I dressed as a boy.... There was an English teacher who seemed to have left all her other work and decided to dedicate her time to making me wear skirts [*laughs*].... I would wear my skirt over my trousers and when that teacher objected I told her, 'You have told me to wear a skirt and you have not said don't wear pants, so I am wearing a skirt.' It was a horrible time when she made me wear skirts. It took up a lot of my mind space.

Even when schools were 'progressive' and did not have uniforms, they imposed norms of how girls and boys should dress. Neha went to one such school: 'My first day, I went wearing a short, tight top and short shorts, and the teachers called me and told me that I was wearing inappropriate clothes. I was... made to change at school.' She said that in this school there were unwritten rules around dressing according to gender and even 'boys were called [upon] when they wore jewellery or had long hair'. Before she came to this school, Neha had had a tough time in another school that she was forced to leave. As within the family, in school too the making of the good girl also meant an insistence on norms of 'morally good behaviour'. Neha loved her school till the sixth standard, but later

> it turned into a nightmare.... The boys wanted girlfriends and wanted me to do a lot of dirty work for them to meet the girls. The boys, of course, were not attracted to me, but we made out.... None of the girls were interested in getting physical. I was the only one as keen as the boys. Some girls found out and called me a slut... As I walked down the corridor, people would say, 'There goes the slut.' The entire school came to know about this. It became really difficult for me to be in that school then.... I lost my self-confidence. I became very bitter, nasty to friends in school.... It was also the same time that I ended up speaking with a close girl friend about how I feel for women and they went on calling me a lesbian.

> The whole class was told about this. At that age I didn't identify myself as a lesbian. I was only expressing a fantasy.... I was filled with self-hatred.... I wanted to get out of school.

Neha was targeted by her peers, but for many other respondents their expression of non-normative desires led to action against them by their girlfriends' parents in connivance with school authorities or even direct action by the school itself. Prem had bought an expensive gift for hir girlfriend in school. One day, ze was called to the principal's office by the girlfriend's mother. 'There she showed the gift that I had bought for [her daughter]. Knowing me and my family's background, the principal asked, "Have you ever bought a *banian* [vest] for your father?"' She made her daughter give back the gift to Prem in front of the whole class.

There are several other accounts of being outed in violent and disturbing ways. Nidhi, who spoke of how ze would wait eagerly for school, felt more comfortable in school than in hir violent joint family home, and was later forced to leave that same school because of a betrayal by hir peers and a vicious public outing in the school assembly:

> They called me up on stage. I was expecting to be announced captain again. However, my headmistress insulted me in front of everyone by saying, 'How can she be captain as she smooches girls?' I was very hurt.... I hadn't expected this at all.

In other incidents of being outed, the more overtly gender-transgressive person is the one who usually has to bear the brunt of stigma or punishment, or the burden of 'reform'. For instance, Sunny said about hir school, 'The vice-principal got after my case. She said she would not let me off and that I had to meet her every day until I started thinking of myself as a girl.' And then, when the respondent's furtive, abortive 'affair' with a girl in school became known:

> Things were put up on the noticeboard; we could not sit together. I was told, 'You did bad things with a Catholic girl.' I told the vice-

> principal about my desire to get a sex change. I told her I was a boy. But the restrictions became worse. She insisted that I wax my [legs] and wear short skirts.... Eventually, I left school; now I feel that I should have left school much earlier.

Sunny, who is upper class and urban, and had a supportive mother, went on to study privately and pass hir board exams, before opting for a skill-based diploma rather than a college degree.

Gender transgression and non-normative sexuality need to be recognized as often linked and overlapping rather than distinct categories. Not only is it almost impossible to understand sexuality minus gender, it is also evident that violence is not always triggered by sexuality alone; rather, a 'same-sex relationship' seems to bring the entire picture of transgression into sudden, sharp focus, so that what was tolerated before, perhaps because it was perceived to have a lower threat quotient, now becomes intolerable.

Dropping Out

Given the earlier discussion, it is important to note that five of our seven respondents who dropped out of school or failed their 10th standard finals identify as men. Of these, two were from middle-class families and three grew up poor; two were jobless when they spoke to us and one person was about to lose his job. Four had been or were employed by, or dependent on, the support groups through which we met, and their lack of education was obviously affecting their options, which were already limited by their transgressive gender expressions.

Sam's story is a case in point. His exchange of love letters with another girl was discovered by her father and, as Sam put it, 'all that about my sexuality, all about my attraction for girls, all came out at the same time. It was just one bomb that burst in my ninth standard.... Then after this there was house arrest. All my freedom was cut off.' When he rejoined school, the freedom he had once enjoyed there was gone as well. Sam was under total surveillance. 'Teachers would scold me that because of you the girls will get spoilt. I got a notice from the church too that I should not go there because I would spoil the girls there. They would become like me.' His friends, who were now a year ahead in school, stopped talking to him as well. Then he was suspended once more, again because of a girl, and that was the end of his schooling. Nowhere in his narration was there any mention of the girls with whom he had been involved being policed or punished by the school in quite the same way.

As a child, Jai loved school, always stood first in his class, enjoyed English and biology, was liked by his teachers and read books from the school library all the time. Yet, he failed his 10th standard final exams. His studies suffered because of the vitiated home atmosphere and his growing discomfort with his body and imposed gender. His story points to how, even when schools are supportive, they fail to provide a safety net for students to deal with the continuous violence outside. Currently unemployed, in debt, living with friends in the city, Jai said: 'I would like to study further and get a degree. I would like to study science and then do a computer course.'

We cannot assume that gender-based conflicts do not similarly affect any of those who identify as 'woman', or that all 'woman'-identified respondents are necessarily gender-normative. That would be to gloss over significant reasons that may have led some middle- and upper-class 'women'-identified persons to opt out of formal education despite economic means and family support, or to ignore the personal and political nuances that might lead some overtly gender-transgressive individuals to choose to identify as 'woman'. In other words, all self-identification along the gender axis needs both to be taken as the given as well as problematized with respect to each person's very complex lived reality.

One such person is Tuli, the only 'woman'-identified respondent who did not complete her school education. She chose not to study further when she failed her 10th standard exams. Tuli came from a middle-class family, which not only would have supported her in continuing with her education but was dismayed by her decision. She said:

> This caused a lot of trouble for me at home, I was beaten and scolded and cajoled, but I was stubborn. Even when my best friend said she'd stop being my friend if I didn't study further, I said so be it. I started working in my uncle's shop. She really tried to convince me, brought me her notes, but I refused.

Tuli did not offer an explanation for why she did badly in that final year of school, but the narrative of her school years provides a substantial clue: it had nothing to do with school or teachers or subjects, and everything to do with her vexed romantic relationships. These were all unarticulated attractions on her own part, but intense enough and troubled enough to cause her to change schools when one girl blamed her own poor results on Tuli's friendship with another, and to preoccupy all her waking hours and emotional energies. The situation was very likely made harder by the fact that all three girls who fancied her also saw her explicitly as male, and this at a time when she was struggling to come to terms with her own sexuality must have added to her confusion.

Access to College

A college education, not surprisingly, was accessed by many more middle-class respondents than by those from poor or upper-class backgrounds. It was also, less predictably, accessed by many more who identified as 'woman', all of whom had at least completed school, than by those who identified as 'man' or 'others'. Of those who did not identify as 'woman', seven had not managed to pass their 10th standard exams or even study that far. As Table 5.1 reveals, approximately 86 per cent 'women' and only 43 per cent 'men' and 'others' had studied beyond the 12th standard.

Looking at this in the light of individual narratives, we are led to speculate that while many queer women may be spurred towards higher education because of their strong need for

Table 5.1: Education Levels across Gender Identities

Education	Woman	Others	Man	Total
Less than 10th standard	1	2	5	8
10th to 12th standard	2	7	2	11
Up to a bachelor's degree	8	5	2	15
More than a bachelor's degree	11	4	1	16
Total	22	18	10	50

independence, for instance, in order to resist marriage pressures, people who are more obviously gender transgressive (and who probably have an equally pressing need for independence) appear to lack the same opportunities or access. The reasons for such a marked difference in higher education need to be better understood, and may be linked to other factors like economic deprivation, lack of family support and sexuality-related violence.

Twenty-eight of our 50 respondents were trans* persons, identifying either as 'man' or as other than 'woman'. If we look at the gender profile in terms of class, 15 of the 28 were middle or upper class, while 13 were poor. When read against the education profile, these numbers suggest a correlation between degree of gender transgression and lack of continuing access to education, even among more middle- and upper-class individuals who are not under that much pressure (other things being the same) to start earning a living right after school.

The stories of those few who did manage to go to college suggest that it was usually a liberating experience after the more constrained and controlling atmosphere in school, allowing them to come into their own. For many, it also meant leaving a restrictive home environment—whether to escape marriage pressures or simply because the colleges were elsewhere—and tasting complete freedom for the first time.

Alpana identifies as 'woman', but grew up being told she didn't behave like a girl. In school she was constantly ticked off about the way she talked or walked or stood. She could be herself in college with greater ease and made many friends, especially with the seniors and the boys in her batch. 'Even though I was more undisciplined and rowdy than I was in school, it was not [much of] an issue… maybe because there were many more bad boys than me!'

But being a woman in a very male environment took its toll on her—there was a great deal of discrimination during her internship, with tasks and expectations being gendered in a way that privileged her male colleagues while being dismissive of her. This may have been one among several reasons why Alpana never pursued the profession that had been her passion since her schooldays. She managed to turn her life around and recover the self-esteem and confidence that were damaged by her relationships as well as by her college experience, and today she is in a low-paying, part-time job that she likes very much, while doing a master's degree through correspondence. But the career she gave up continues to haunt her.

Sandy, who went through a brief, uncomfortable phase of trying to look feminine, spoke of how liberating going to a women's college was: 'That first day in college I went wearing a mini skirt; I saw women who looked like me. Butch, wearing pants and shirts, with short hair. And that was the last day I wore a skirt.' Sandy continued:

> In the absence of boys, the crazy politics of love, etc. was not there. In school the boyfriend you had was a status thing. Here people had boyfriends, but that was outside of college. Seeing women like me gave me the space to be myself.… I fell in love with this girl, in class 11, and for the first time I said something. It was a great feeling.

For the first time ze felt affirmed in hir sexuality, about which ze had had 'a non-speak policy for years'.

Laxmi grew up in semi-rural surroundings in a middle-class family. She had an older brother and she was made much of as the much-wanted only girl child; she remembers facing no discrimination or violence at home. Her early sexual relationships were with cismen and that became the problem. She was living away from home, in a city hostel, preparing for entrance exams for a professional degree, when 'my studies were discontinued because I got involved with a Muslim boy'. A chance at a profession was ruined for multiple reasons. When we met her she was unemployed and looking for a job.

On the whole, college seems to be a more open space, also because students are older and less under control of the teachers or authority. A few bad teachers, however, continued with their harassment and violence. Laxmi mentioned a teacher in her college who 'used to shout only at the girls. He never encouraged us, beat us and would call us all kinds of names.'

Divakar, a person with intersex variations, faced violence because, while he was doing his certificate course as Divya in a college, she started showing facial hair growth. Divya could not understand what was happening, but her classmates and friends started to keep their distance. Divakar recalled:

> I was treated very badly by the lecturers and the principal. They would throw away my assignments and insult me... they did not give me any internal marks.... Then they refused to give the certificate, saying that even if you get it, you are not going to use it. I went with my father to the secretary... we fought and then finally they gave the certificate.

Persevering against Odds

Gender—along with class, caste to an extent and sexuality-based violence—seems to play a direct or indirect role in the educational opportunities that people got. Some never get to go to school; for others it means dropping out of school or college in their need to start earning a living from an early age, and sometimes in their forced migration. Some are able to get back on track, in terms of access to education and better job prospects thereby, others are not.

There were a few noteworthy exceptions to this trend. Mala grew up in a very poor, rural, tribal household. There was no question of any schooling and when still very young, ze was married off to a man:

> I would go early morning to the river to fill water. I would see the sisters [nuns] with their bags passing by. They would see me, would

talk to me very sweetly. At home, the family used to talk to me very harshly and taunt me all the time because they said I wasn't beautiful.... I would go every morning just to meet [the nuns] and have them talk to me.

Hir husband told hir that they were home breakers and so ze kept away from them for a few days but then went back. The sisters asked if Mala wished to study:

I was so happy!... I used to go to their well to fill water and also learn my alphabets. I did not tell anyone.... I still remember that in six days I attended and learnt every step—and practised writing in the mud—straight stick, round circle, etc. I would also write on the wall.

When hir family members found out, they were so abusive 'that I decided not to see [the] sister anymore. The little that I had learnt had left an impression on my mind and I would practise in the mud and wipe it off.' Mala has since completed her school education and is looking forward to studying further. Ze lives with hir husband, and has a job that allows hir to live comfortably.

Two other respondents were propelled and able to access graduate and postgraduate studies in some senses *because* of their gender. Sandhya, 24, and studying for hir master's degree, came from such inimical circumstances that it was hardly even expected that ze would go to school. Being a person with intersex variations, ze always knew there was something different about hir. Although this difference troubled hir deeply, it became the driving force in hir life.

Since my childhood, my father has motivated me to do something.... Because we were very poor, I started feeling that... if I did not act on my own, then my life would just end right here. The other thing is that I was forced to go to the fields and work, and I would feel that it is all right if I come to the city and wash someone's vessels and study, but I cannot stay here in the village. This was the biggest reason [I left]. I used to tell myself that if you want to live, you will have to become somebody and that was a big motivation for me. Also, that if I am different, then I should do something different.

Ze managed to move to a bigger city. In spite of having no acquaintances, ze managed to survive doing wage labour and living in difficult conditions, with little or no support. Sandhya's persistence, hard work and will to study have brought hir to where ze is now—the first 'woman' from hir village to pursue a postgraduate degree and get a government job.

Anand's perseverance took another form:

> Two months before my class 12 ended, my dad had a paralysis attack.... People wanted to get the eldest daughter—me—married while he was alive... so that he could die after seeing his grandson or granddaughter. What rubbish it was. It was a shock to me because I was too much of a bookworm and I wanted to study further.... My mom was always very supportive—I studied in the best schools only because of her—but now she said nothing was in her hands, the extended family had taken over. I was hyper—always been hyper— ran away the day my exams got over.

Anand put himself through engineering college by earning money giving tuitions. He handled the college workload by taking pills to stay awake at nights. He was a star student and today is among the highest earners among our respondents. He not only charted the course of his life according to his own compass, but is also supporting his entire natal family financially at present.

Campuses and Subjects

However, college for Anand was not just about being a topper—it turned out to be in every way 'awesome':

> No dress code, I already had short hair and I could pass around like a guy guy! Teachers also used to be confused, shocked when they got to know my name.... And then the new first years came and you know how they look up to you, come and ask questions. And in my circle they said, 'What is this? New chicks—they have a crush

on you, they don't have a crush on us!' I said that's because I'm the coolest of you all. The girls had no clue.

Simran studied in another professional school that in its overall approach made a difference to her education:

> This is an amazing place. There are so many different worldviews and space to express all kinds of opinions. Conversation is not a joke; you are constantly debating on the ethics of everything.... It is a beautiful space because it is very open and allows you to experiment. So it allows you to move out of your own comfort zone and boundary, and experiment in a safe sort of space.

If it was not the campus as such, it was what they studied there that made a difference to some respondents. Evidently, specific subjects were—for many of the people we spoke to—as important in helping form their nascent worldviews or affirming them in the ways in which they wished to live and to love. At their best, these disciplines acted as agents of awareness and catalysts of change.

Literature was always Jharna's first love. Still a poet and writer, she read and wrote a lot from very early on, and says, 'Through literature I started understanding everything, what is social pressure, economic pressures.' And then in college she stumbled upon a very self-affirming subject and lecturer:

> One paper was 'Psychology of Sex'—they used to teach us about sexuality—what is sexuality, how it arises, what is the wider form of it. The teacher explained that homosexuality is a common thing and has been there since ancient times, it's not something to be afraid of. I got so much from her class.

For Kanika, sociology became hir window to the world:

> I fell in love with that subject. It helped me to know about myself.... I got a clear picture about... sex and gender. I did not have any problem about my sex and gender, though I know I cannot stick to any single gender.... After studying this discipline, I realized I am

not a sick person…. If anyone questions me now, I can give a logical answer…. Sociology is like my friend.

Conclusion

As is evident, school played a very influential part in the lives of most of our respondents. For some it was a refuge from an unhappy home; for others it always was an uncomfortable place. We find that it was largely stray encounters or chance opportunities that led to positive experiences, whether through a teacher or a subject that reaffirmed their sense of self. For yet others school began as a safe, much-loved haven, a place of escape from home, but became the most violent space as soon as their sexuality became known. Yet, more than half of our respondents were aware of their sexual desires and feelings at very early ages; school is clearly one of the sites where many young people tend to explore their sexuality.

It is crucial, then, for the education system to be more open and affirming when it comes to questions of both gender and sexuality. Our findings also support the wider, urgently felt need for sexuality education for teachers, administrators and schoolchildren. As one respondent said, 'Children in school should get education on sex, sexuality and gender. This should be included in the syllabus.' There is need for more active types of engagement that help make the school an affirmative location for young people's gender or sexuality rather than a place where they must control their explorations and expressions, or face constant monitoring, shaming and other kinds of violence.

Apart from a more open climate that enables non-moralistic discussions about sexuality, there needs also to be a de-emphasis on gender within the school structure. This does not mean that gender should be negated. There is still a need for gender-segregated schools as there are many parents who would deny education to their female children if coeducational institutions were the only possibility. The emphasis should be, rather, on deregulating gender. For example, uniform regulations make gender boundaries rigid and compel gender definition. Such a marker could be erased if there were a greater choice or leeway in the matter of skirts/trousers, blouses/shirts, etc.

We have already seen how several queer PAGFB were able to negotiate their way around these rules and regulations. The next step would be to transform that difficult personal battle, which defeats so many, into readily available choices for all, regardless of their birth-assigned sex or perceived gender. However, while most people might accept 'girls' in trousers, we are far from being as comfortable with 'boys'—or PAGMB—in skirts. Gender-transgressive PAGMB have it that much harder, as they face much more immediate stigma and opprobrium, and much greater levels of ridicule. There is a need to study and explore this issue further and to find ways of dealing with it.

Textbooks too need to be inclusive of different lived realities rather than presenting sanitized, homogenized, heteronormative accounts of culture, social realities, histories and families. Queer groups, child rights groups and educationists need to work together to ensure a modicum of openness in teaching and in textbooks. This would probably need an analysis of gender, sexuality and family in existing school textbooks, similar to the ongoing work on gender and communalism. Apart from textbooks, students should also have access to other kinds of books and materials that are more diverse and inclusive.

Finally, it needs to be said that we are not speaking about breaking the gender binary merely in order to set up another binary—of queer/non-queer PAGFB. Many of the issues faced by PAGFB are common, such as strictly enforced gender rules and regulations, restrictions that become more severe at the time of puberty, policing of sexuality, and being raised with cultural notions that mitigate against personal agency and economic independence. If families and the larger society are not about to change their attitudes in a hurry, it is really up to the institutions of formal education to do, more sensitively and more actively, what is their stated objective in any case: to educate and equip the 'girl child', indeed every child, with the learning, skills, opportunities and understanding they need to be self-sufficient in every way, and to fully realize their potential.

6

Sport and Other Passions

The roles in which their natal families cast most young PAGFB are often reinforced, as we have seen, by the rules that tend to shackle them in school. Both places define what is permitted and what is not. For some this could mean no more playing with boys in the neighbourhood after puberty; for others it might involve being forced by teachers to wear the skirts or pinafores they detest. In such closely monitored and strictly gendered environments, how and where do young people find ways of expressing their gender-transgressive selves—or even just releasing their pent-up frustrations?

Some of the pilot interviews, which helped us fine-tune our interview guide, suggested this as an area to be explored. Under the broad head of 'Interests/Hobbies/Sports', we included this curiously phrased question (emphasis added):

> Do you have any interests or hobbies *that made you comfortable with yourself?*

We were not merely asking respondents to list a few of their favourite things, but trying to find out if there were any activities or spaces they had while growing up, that helped them feel good about themselves and perhaps brought them some joy in the midst of all the difficulties associated either with being gender non-conforming or simply with being PAGFB in surroundings that discriminated against 'girls'.

We discovered that among our 50 respondents were kabaddi, carrom and cricket champs, trained singers and published poets, amateur actors and keen photographers. Many special areas of interest surfaced, which respondents may or may not have gone on to pursue professionally, but about which they had been—and in many cases were still—passionate. A number of these pursuits provided ways for people to arrive at a stronger sense of themselves and inhabit spaces they might not otherwise have been able to access.

Early Adventures

Exploring what they liked to do was part of the respondents' childhood and adolescence experiences of home and neighbourhood. Often in these explorations, while simply following the dictates of their hearts, they knowingly or unknowingly transgressed normative gender roles. Whether they were encouraged or punished depended on their specific circumstances, but the possibility of such explorations definitely contributed to making them who they are today.

Juhi was always being compared, to hir disadvantage, with hir sister—ridiculed for being fat and not as good at studies. While hir father let hir hang around with him and do 'boy'-type things, like going with him to the garage and learning how to clean the spark plug of his bike, ze recalled him beating hir for flying kites on the terrace with a boy instead of studying: 'It could have been because I was different, even though it wasn't articulated in that way.'

Sara echoed this sense of being different and unique, and also being constantly compared to her 'perfect' older sister. She was teased and taunted by relatives and peers for her 'tomboy' ways, but this in no way daunted her rebellious spirit:

> See, [the neighbourhood] is densely populated, Hindus live on one side and Muslims on the other.... Many services used to be in Hindu areas, with good teachers. We weren't allowed to go into that area.... There was a masjid close by where, once upon a time, they used to do *wazu* or ablutions. It was a huge place, with a 30-foot depth. This was converted into a swimming pool.... I used to get free entry there and [my brother] would have to be sweet to

me so that he could get a free entry with me... [I] used to wear my swimming costume under my salwar kameez... just remove my salwar kameez and... jump right into the pool.

Whether it is the mind that is kindled or the body that's engaged, whether it is music that moves one or acting that enthuses another, we found that the passions and pursuits of childhood and adolescence often seemed to answer a therapeutic need. They allayed social and personal anxieties, and helped people acquire self-confidence and a sense of worth.

Roma, who like several others spoke of abuse and ridicule from the extended family, was bullied by her peers in school as well. Her interest in sport was not encouraged by her parents and was scoffed at by others. She described how comic book characters, and other real and literary protagonists helped her form her own idea of the person she longed to be:

A combination of Nadia, Diana Palmer, my tutor, Black Mamba, Mrinalini from Tagore.... The image is one of a confident and upright person who can deal with situations, doesn't break apart, doesn't hesitate.... I took refuge from the real world in the comic world.... In that world there were no boundaries, no restrictions.

And as with several other respondents, Roma sought and found in animals the warmth and support her human environment repeatedly failed to provide. She lives today with her mother and 'a lot of pets. It's like a zoo. There is one dog, two turtles, two birds, one rabbit and four fish.'

From explorations at home and in the neighbourhood to more formally organized opportunities, our respondents pursued their passions wherever they could. Sport and other extracurricular activities were often first encountered in school as part of what was offered by the formal system of education, though not seen as integral to it given the focus on studies. Time spent after class on the playing fields or in libraries, dance or art classes and drama rehearsals also meant a kind of freedom and opportunity. Being able to travel away from home for tournaments or on camping trips served as breathing spaces for many and were legitimized for parents by virtue of the broadly supervised settings.

In most instances respondents chose their extracurricular activities themselves, sometimes with support but sometimes in the face of opposition, mainly familial. Clashes were usually to do with people wanting to access or continue with something that lay outside the formal sphere of school or college.

Of course, there were exceptions, like the parents who sent a child to learn something that the school perhaps did not teach. One person was trained in classical music from a very early age, a decision taken by the mother, and though the long hours and rigour were daunting, the child eventually found in music hir deepest fulfilment.

Sport and Outdoor Activities

Sport was the most popular thing to do. Since it is somewhat of a national obsession and there is some degree of formal training as well as a competitive tournament circuit, cricket was the most sought-after sport for seven respondents. Four of our respondents had been on teams that played competitively at the school, university, state and national levels. Simran even changed schools partly 'because of cricket.... This school... had the best all-girls' team. The girls I used to look up to at that point were all from this school and I wanted to play with them.' Only in the eastern region does football appear to have been as popular as cricket, if not more.

In a sample of 50, six achieving more than a moderate degree of success in sport seems high. It becomes even more significant when one notes that of these six, five come from poor or middle-class backgrounds and from families that did nothing to support them in their activities. Vasu was stigmatized due to his caste identity outside the home and constantly beaten by his parents and brothers and extended family for not wanting to 'dress like a girl' and for 'walking like a male'. Handball, high jump, long jump—these were the athletic interests he pursued despite all the disapproval. Then, when he was in the eighth standard, his father committed suicide, and Vasu was forced to drop out of school and start working. This meant the loss of a valuable space that had afforded some escape from his uncomfortably gendered life.

Prem's earliest memories are of hunger and an alcoholic father, of beatings from hir mother and the injustice and fights around having to do the housework with hir sisters while hir brothers were exempt. Spending longer hours in school was a way to escape the drudgery of chores at home, and a growing participation in various sports ensued. Ze recalled, 'I had lots of certificates.... I was doing athletics—high jump, long jump, running, everything. I played in inter-school tournaments, always came first. Participated once at district level and won there too.' Ze was good enough that 'neighbours suggested... I would get a secure job in the police and so that was also what made me take this seriously'. This is perhaps the clearest statement from any of our respondents about excelling on the field as a passport to a better life, and is noteworthy for how it speaks to class just as other narratives might speak to gender.

Many respondents took up sport in a dedicated manner around puberty, which itself usually implied stricter dress norms being imposed on young 'girls' as well as restrictions on mobility outside school hours. Playing games allowed for some leeway, such as being able to wear less gendered clothes—shorts, trousers, tracksuits, rather than the hated 'feminine' school uniforms.

Those who found it difficult to come to terms with menstruation or with having breasts were able to build a positive relationship with the body through pleasure in its agility and speed. Other physical activities, such as dance and theatre, also allowed those engaging in them to use their bodies in ways that were self-affirming.

Of course, there is more than one way of transcending the recalcitrant body. Kamal, disabled since childhood, found and honed his own set of abilities and skills, playing chess and becoming a carrom champ. He also played cricket, football and 'shuttlecock' from the wheelchair in games organized by the disabled people's association he helped set up. He was always on the boys' teams, he says, and speaks of being unable to go for a game in the US as he didn't have a passport, being unwilling to get a document that identified him as a woman.

'A World of Our Own'

Playing a sport clearly enabled several respondents to meet other gender non-conforming PAGFB, which not only helped them feel less alone and more 'normal', but fostered early intimate connections as well. Arun described hir first sexual relationship as the 'cricket relationship'. Sumit said of hir football team in college, 'Many persons there are like me, they have girlfriends.' Aditi recalled:

> My group of friends... are all straight, hence, I never shared my personal life with them. But in cricket, I met many friends like me... we were like tomboys with real short hair.... In cricket I met others who were girlfriends with each other in the team.

And Monu called it 'a world of our own':

> There were seven of us who used to play football.... We were all alike, wore similar clothes.... In that football scene homosexuality is normal and heterosexuality is abnormal. The coaches also knew all about this and they would never interfere... as long as we played well. So that was one world and home was another story.

Taking part in a sport meant many things to many people. You were part of the cool, hip crowd. You were a hero, girls followed you around. You could dress as you pleased and wear your hair short. Playing a game or being an athlete, biker or cyclist gave you greater mobility and you could stay out later. Being on a team meant opportunities to travel to other parts of the country. And, of course, it meant finding a community and romance, sometimes even a career.

It is not only competitive sports or athletics, but also other collective spaces and activities outside the confines of the classroom that may be affirmative and enabling. Santosh wasn't keen on studies, but he enjoyed the National Cadet Corps trips that allowed him to give free rein to his gender:

> I was very happy in the camp—a boy surrounded by ladies! At night, the girls wore salwars and nighties, while I wore my male clothes…. I slept with different girls. In my mind, I was a boy and my partners saw me as a boy…. I'd say to the girls, 'I want to sleep with you.' I acted like a rowdy. I would climb trees to get them mangoes. The way I made eye contact was like a boy makes with a girl.

'Women's Sports'

While PAGFB who do not identify as 'woman' may find sports and other physical activities more accommodating of their gender, many who do identify as 'woman' also find affirmation here as well as a release from suffocating circumstances.

Falguni, an only child, recalled how she hated dolls, hated playing with other girls and was mean to them, but enjoyed playing every possible sport with boys, climbing trees and fixing household appliances. Although her father encouraged her wanting to be 'like a boy', buying her jeans and shirts, the extended family objected. She said, 'I love physical exertion. I enjoy trekking and cycling. I used to cycle [long distances]. I hate sitting-at-home activities.' Neel did athletics, played volleyball and kabaddi with the boys who were her childhood friends and won prizes in school as part of women's teams. 'My family supported me and allowed me to do sports. I had no experience of violence of any sort.'

Not all our 'woman' respondents were as lucky. We have seen in Chapter 4 how Kavi's family stopped her from playing cricket. Saumya had a similar story—made to do household chores while her brother wasn't, considered 'the dumbest child on earth by her mother'. She loved cricket but was unable to continue playing when the neighbourhood game shifted to a public maidan. 'As you grow older you start getting your periods, start being like a woman in your body, so you stop. I missed playing cricket and still do. I could have taken it as a profession if my parents encouraged me.'

Hemlata was forced to do a great deal of housework, unlike her brothers, and grew up fearing her father's beatings and feeling unloved by her mother. She was also beaten in school by male teachers and sexually abused by several visitors at home. She appears to have found some solace and a sense of pride in becoming a district-level kabaddi champion and winning prizes for rangoli. 'I also liked singing, but no one encouraged me,' she said, adding, 'My entire childhood was so filled with fear that I could not pursue my interests.' The feminine talent of rangoli was approved of by her mother, but playing kabaddi was not, while school picnics and excursions were forbidden.

Alpana's grandmother derided her for being a girl, and for being dark and fat, telling her, 'You're not a girl, God fell short of mud while making you.' Hurt and confused, Alpana nevertheless refused to be either the girlie girl her mother could enjoy dressing up or the cricket-playing son she knew her father—who coached at a cricket camp—would have preferred. 'I wanted to play football, not cricket. For me it was less of a game, more contact, play in mud, get drenched in water. [I] used to see the neighbourhood boys all muddy. Maybe that's why my dad didn't want me to play.'

All too often we find parents trying to impose their own interests on their children or preventing them from following their individual passions. Especially in the case of sport, in an ironic reversal of their usual advantages in other areas, 'woman'-identified respondents faced more obstacles than those who were more overtly gender non-conforming. For many, their engagement with sport ended with school or with college. While ciswomen found other playing spaces and opportunities hard to access, trans* persons may have stopped because of forced migration. The urgent need to earn a living, with competitive sports not paying enough, was also a factor.

The persistence of gender segregation in sports evokes mixed responses. Arun, who played cricket at the state level (in the teeth of family opposition that included beatings and house arrest), asserted, 'At one level the divide is problematic. People must see it as sport. Women's sport does not mean that women cannot play with men.' Ze referred to hir years as a player as life-changing, and said ze had to stop because there just wasn't any money in women's sport, not to speak of the lack of facilities and coaching. Yet, ze agreed that these all-women spaces allow for a good deal of gender transgression and diversity, and 'there are more lesbian, bisexual and transgender people' in these teams, especially in sports like cricket, football and in some places basketball, which allow all players to wear trousers or shorts. Hockey is less popular among queer PAGFB as everyone has to wear skirts.

Despite the odds against them, of the 12 people connected to sport, two did manage to find their dream vocations in related professions, one as a physical education teacher and the other as a physiotherapist. A third had plans to give up her current job and start a sports-related business. Others reflected on what might have been. Jamuna, who was captain of the girls' team that she fought to start in her school, said, 'Had I not gone abroad, I could have been playing cricket. It could have been a serious career.' Kanika, planning a future in academics, said, 'I have big interest in sports.... I used to participate in badminton tournaments. And win prizes. I have played cricket right since childhood with my brother. Sometimes I feel like I should be a sports journalist.' It's noteworthy that all those who found their calling in this field or felt they might easily have done so were living within the family fold when they spoke to us. Those who lacked even this basic support had little choice but to give up such dreams.

Other Creative Pursuits

In the cracks and spaces between school and home, and sometimes with their support, our respondents pursued many other interests and passions besides sport. Whether it was finding solace within the covers of a book or finding the writer within, in taking on different personae in theatre, picking up a camera to recreate their visions or raising their voices in song, many respondents managed to discover oases for themselves in a difficult world.

Literature

While still in college, Juhi's discovery of Urdu poetry jerked hir out of an uneasy membership in a right-wing group that hir father's political leanings and influence had led hir to join. 'It all ended, as in active participation in this kind of stuff, when I fell in love.... After that it was all about Ghalib, *shairi* [poetry] and ghazal.' Reading poetry together or writing poetry for a lover played a major role in all hir relationships. Besides its other attractions, romantic poetry with its inherent abstractions may also have been a useful means of soothing any troubled sense of transgression.

Jharna came from a home environment where her parents were always fighting. 'Enjoyment was less and torture was more' was how she summed up her growing years. In the midst of this she discovered the magic of words. She began writing poetry when she was 12 and never stopped. Through a succession of day jobs, she has continued to compose and read her poetry at *mushairas* (gatherings at which people recite their poetry) and to pen song lyrics professionally. She said, 'Poetry is my life—that is my skill.... When I was 24 the way I thought of my future is not where I am at 44—I meant to be a successful lyricist, not a struggling teacher.' Jharna's way with words also led her to other forms of writing, from academic guides for students to television serials.

Maushami used writing as a way of coping with abuse. 'I tried to kill myself [many] times because of the sexual abuse. I had no security. I started writing poems since I was 6.' She was an avid reader while in school and continues to write short stories and poetry.

Others too spoke about writing and reading as abiding passions and of how books had been a refuge during difficult times. Vimala, who faced extreme violence from her natal family, said she would read voraciously on everything from a young age: 'I would read one book and be immersed in it for a week. I am someone who lived in a dream world.... I would read poems and imagine and fantasize about the different... ways of loving.' Today she sees writing as her main skill and area of interest. She has written poetry, some of which has been set to music, as well as prose articles and interviews for magazines. When asked where she sees herself 10 years from now, she remarked, 'I will be sitting quietly somewhere and writing. It's a dream.'

Devi is also a published author. Ze co-authored a book while working for a feminist NGO, no small achievement for someone who grew up in poverty and learnt to read and write only at the age of 36. Ze spoke with some pride of the many women's movement songs ze has written—enough to fill another book, ze said.

For Sandhya, books became very important:

> I used to take out books from my father's trunk and read them. In one such search I found a volume on Swami Vivekanand.... Then I went and got influenced by all the gurus.... After this I started reading—all kinds of books. After the library started in our village, I was the only girl who went there and sat and read.... I loved the romantic novels and would stay awake nights to read them.

Later it was writing and receiving letters that made hir feel appreciated at a time when ze was grappling with questions around hir body, gender and sexuality. Ze kept up a long correspondence with a man who wrote letters for a radio programme ze liked; when eventually they met, ze was able to tell him about hirself and feel understood and accepted. Ze also wrote regularly to a woman friend ze was hopelessly in love with. 'Even today when I read those letters I can feel the anxiety in me.... I had kept copies of all of them because I thought that I was writing very nice letters.' Here was an exchange of words that was building towards heartbreak, but the writing was in itself an act of enjoyment.

Theatre and the Performing Arts

Six people spoke of an intensive involvement with drama, and some continue to be part of amateur or professional theatre groups. Neha, for example, enjoyed dramatics and singing in school. From there it was a small step to theatricals at home:

> I would send out invitations to everyone in the house. I would ask them to come to a certain room at a specific time and would put out chairs.... I loved putting on performances. These were mostly film dance numbers or I used to put up small plays like the 'Three Little Pigs'. I would rope in my sister and cousins.

She liked learning classical music and dance, but chafed at the discipline and disliked having to touch the feet of 'a guru who was never friendly and never smiled'. Neha still enjoys music, watching plays and dance performances, but prefers working backstage. 'I'm not as confident and fearless as I was in my younger days. And have lost interest in performance.'

One respondent came into theatre because of her mother, a theatre director. The very first play she took part in influenced her deeply:

> I had done a play with my mom on female infanticide and travelled all over... with it.... It had a profound impact on me.... Because [in] village after village people would openly tell us that they would kill the girl child because they did not have money to pay for her dowry.... I was 12 at that time and it was a bit crazy to hear everywhere that girls are useless.

Theatre continues to be an important part of her life and she has learnt much from it.

> Theatre as I know it, I have learnt mainly from my mum. Lots of physical work and the basis of it is to be very comfortable with your

body, and each part of your body acts and it is very, very physical....
So theatre training gives you a certain comfort with your body,
which then may have had some effect on my gender or how I hold
myself in public.

Another respondent also looks at her work in theatre through
the lens of body image and gender concerns—from default roles
imposed on her when young to a conscious engagement today.
She spoke of being 'taller and bigger' than her peers, which meant
she 'could play married women's roles' from the time she was
quite young. She grew up in a Kolkata neighbourhood where
they 'used to do a lot of theatre, and festivals were celebrated by
doing Tagore plays'. Performance on stage has continued to be a
passion for her, resurfacing later in life from both her personal
experiences and the work she was doing:

> Every time you go to the doctor, anything that is wrong with you is
> linked to your weight. So even if you have a cold it is because of your
> weight. So for me it is about how I use those things productively and
> that's how [the show I have been doing] came up. And I thought
> of performing it because I had told these stories many times and
> they had been funny. I realized the power of performance when
> people from the audience have come up and cried and said that
> it was representative of their lives and it was important for them
> to have heard someone else say it. When I do trainings on gender
> and sexuality, it is like performing, the only difference is that [in
> theatre] there is a stage.

Chandni too engaged with issues of gender while essaying
certain roles in school and college plays. In hir girls' school ze
always got to play the boys' parts. Then in hir coed college hir
favourite role happened:

> [It was] a Victorian play called *Charlie's Aunt*. He's a guy who wants
> to meet his girlfriend. It was the time of chaperones, but Charlie
> couldn't find a chaperone. So he gets one of his friends to dress as a
> woman, to dress and act as his aunt actually. I was the aunt.... I was
> a woman acting as a man pretending to be a woman. I look back on
> it with great fondness. I found it very easy to do. [Playing the role

of] a woman in that kind of play is to me very farcical… a mock estimation of what I think a woman to be.

Karthik never had a chance to be involved with student dramatics. His parents were daily wage labourers, and when his father had an accident, Karthik had to drop out of school to work full time. His opportunity came later—a series of relocations brought him to live and work with members of a community of hijras and take part in plays meant to raise awareness about their issues.

> I wanted to be a great singer…. Now that I am part of the drama troupe, during rehearsal I get the opportunity to pursue my hobbies of singing and break dance. I sing film songs whilst working, and when I do not sing, people will ask why I am quiet, what is the matter, why am I not singing?

Singing at work is a sure sign of satisfaction and the fake moustaches 'man'-identified Karthik dons for some roles must also be a source of pleasure.

Prem too got into theatre only after hir forced migration to a big city, when the members of hir LBT support group worked on a play together. Today ze wants to 'take theatre seriously. Our theatre should be known nationally. I am very passionate about it. I also want to make a documentary film about my own life so that many other people may not have to go through the same pain as me.'

While some respondents who were involved with theatre also spoke about dance, at least two people wanted passionately to be dancers. Sam was made to learn Bharatanatyam by his mother, but he wasn't interested, perhaps partly because the teacher used to beat him on the legs. In any case he preferred dancing to film songs, which allowed him to take on male roles. He also liked to choreograph his own numbers rather than submit to the steps created by others. His mother disapproved, but that did not deter Sam. 'When there was no one at home, I would dance with [the music on] full volume. My sister and I had the same room. After she got married it became my room and I used to dance every day for about one hour. Learnt from TV.' Having to leave home at an early age and earn a living, he was unable to access formal training, but dreams of taking lessons and starting his own dance group.

Dance is a passion for Rahul as well, and his dream vocation. He said with regret, 'I can't dance freely because of my body.... Right now I am wearing a binder. Earlier I couldn't dance at all. I was conscious of my upper body.' For now dance is in abeyance as he is concentrating on earning money for a very specific purpose:

> At an age when people are thinking of their career, I am thinking about my surgery.... This would not have been the case if I [had been] born male. Then at this point I could have concentrated on dance as my career. I can't waste any more time... the next important thing for me after my surgery is dance.

Music

Just like being made to learn classical dance, being taught to sing or play a musical instrument is a conventional aspect of how PAGFB are raised, and many respondents were put through their cultural paces accordingly. Some loved it, others resisted having to learn and for yet others it became a serious interest later in life. Here we attempt to read music differently, in terms of its significance in the lives of those who were breaking rather than adhering to social and cultural norms.

After Jai was compelled to drop out of school and take up a full-time job, he sang professionally with an orchestra several times a month, travelling to festivals and also singing with a folk song group. He banks equally on studying further and working with computers, and on his talent for singing. 'I love to sing and so would like to be recognized for that, maybe not like Yesudas or some such figure, but still known a little bit.'

For Vasu, having to drop out of school meant the loss of playing spaces, but singing continued to be a solace. 'All the time I keep singing,' he said, adding that he would really like the chance to deejay and to sing 'in front of everyone'. Yet, there is an inherent difficulty: 'The only thing I feel sad about is that my voice is not deep like a man's. I feel sad that others make fun of me.'

While Jai and Vasu had no musical training, another respondent's entire life was structured around hir classical music lessons from the time ze was 9. Ze trained for 16 years with hir guru till his death, then continued to learn from other teachers. A professional singer, ze is also a sexuality and gender rights activist. From someone who now sees music as hir life, it is interesting to hear that: 'I was more keen on dance, but my mother said that you cannot dance all your life but you can sing. So she sent me to sing.' Although hir guru said ze must wear a bindi and bangles, and never allowed hir to cut hir hair—something ze only did when ze was 25, after he passed away—over time he became the person who understood hir best.

Ze talked of hir desire to work on sexuality and gender through music—something ze has already begun doing as a playwright, a new-found occupation. Ze also elaborated on hir ideas about gender and voice. One of the things about the singing human voice that deeply interested hir was the indeterminate gender of the trans* voice, which ze would like to recognize and celebrate:

> When I heard Kesarbai, then I thought that her voice was a full circle. You could never say clearly that it was a man and you could not say it was a woman singing. So then I practised and practised and it just did not work out. Then it was Bhimsen Joshi.... What I like about my guru though was that he never stopped me from doing all this.... He also felt that you have to search for a voice of your own, and if you do not want a female voice, then do other practices but do not try to imitate.... I know how to play with the texture of the voice so I am constantly experimenting with it and trying out things. Now I have it in my head that I want to figure a transgender voice. So I do this whole thing of purposefully going squeaky, full bass, the whole range. The texture remains the same and it is actually playing with the volume within the voice.

This was one respondent who had not just made hir passion into hir dream vocation, but was constantly recreating its meaning and pushing its frontiers.

Photography and the Visual Arts

Sunny went to an 'open school' where ze formed a deep friendship with some other boys. 'I could wear what I liked and I had those five friends and I was doing photography, so I was totally happy.' A diploma in photography and video led hir to a career in television. 'I want to be a cameraman for wildlife photography,' ze said. Hir desired profession allows hir to do exactly what ze loves while being precisely who ze is.

Two other respondents are visual artists: one has been working for some years and is an established practitioner; the other is completing her studies in art and design. Both spoke of the relationship between their art and their politics.

Simran, the design student, is interested in exploring all sorts of visual forms and media, from street theatre to animation. She described a project that she did at her college, inspired by her cousin, a transwoman:

> I wrote this book... which had four stories—one was [my cousin's], another of a gay senior of mine, [then the story of] a transgender woman... who blogs.... and the fourth story is of a cross-dresser in Lahore, a Muslim man who likes to wear silk but is not allowed, and has a child.... The book had six coarse silk panels for each story. The idea of the book was to talk of the differences between transgenders, transsexuals, cross-dressers, hijras and others, who are all different, but people tend to lump them all together. So one part was identity and the other was that they were written in a manner that [says], 'We are also like you, you straight people.'

Meghana recalled from hir pre-teen years in school how recognition 'from my parents and society that I am good at drawing and painting was a positive thing. I won many competitions. It was the only affirmation.' Tracing hir trajectory as an artist, ze said that in hir first year of college 'something amazing happened... I was introduced to photography.' Soon ze was not only an avid photographer with hir own dark room, but keenly acquiring hir own 'education in culture'. Meanwhile, ze became part of a feminist collective, which began to shape hir worldview. Today, several years later, hir queer feminist activism and hir artistic practice come together in work that brings together photography and other visual media as well as performance, and is often preoccupied with issues of gender and sexuality. Ze spoke of what made hir begin to use hir self and hir own body in hir work:

> Because the work is visual, and visual arts... is about representation, both self-representation as well as representing others... it creates a problem in the Indian context because not many people want to be [made visible]... because of certain circumstances. So I started to use a lot of myself in the work and performing in different ways within the work because I do not have to get permission from myself.

One can only imagine how liberating that must be for someone who had to fight parental opposition at every stage and about every choice in hir life.

Conclusion

Being different from the norm is not an easy place to be in, especially when one is young. Not having a language to talk of the unease between what one wants to be and what one is expected to be can also be disconcerting. Given society's mega-project of making 'good citizens', 'good boys and girls', through the disciplining, intimate spaces of the home, school, community and neighbourhood, any variance from the norm is seen as rebellion and quelled immediately through strictures and punishments.

There are some spaces even within these systems that offer relief from the usual. By allowing articulation of different aspirations, they inadvertently provide the ground for playing out one's fantasies, becoming the small window through which a bit of the self can be explored. 'Women's sports' allow participants to wear clothes and haircuts that are not really 'women's'. They not only facilitate the kind of mobility, friendships and exposure that 'girls' would otherwise be deprived of, but also help create a more positive equation with the body than that enforced by society. Likewise, theatre and the performing arts enable the playing out of fantasies that may otherwise never have been explored, and the language of literature enables an expression that can compensate for the absence of conversations with others.

Some of our respondents managed to make these interests their professions; they were able to create adult lives for themselves where these passions were nurtured. Others found new interests that built on their non-normativity. But we find that for most PAGFB there is a closing in of any such spaces as soon as their education is over. Thus, many respondents, especially those who came from the margins of society, did not manage to find any such space. In any case it is easier for those with privilege of class, caste and location to break rules and live by their own norms. It is those on the margins that are forced to fit in and obey. It is no surprise, then, to find that their access to the non-normative professions and interests is also fairly curtailed.

Diversity of all kinds must be nurtured, and spaces for multiple explorations and expressions need to be created for everyone. Everyone needs to have access to spaces and opportunities even in their adult lives to pursue what triggers their creativity and inspires them. Those from the margins need this even more because it is the margin that challenges the mainstream, that pushes the envelope and makes the world more diverse, and questions the complacency of the normative.

7

Work and Livelihood

We spoke to queer PAGFB who are employed in a variety of occupations, ranging from researchers, teachers, daily-wage earners, artists, engineers, police officers and mediapersons to those employed by corporates and non-governmental organizations. Their journeys have not been easy; in fact, they have been fraught with difficulties. At the time of the study four respondents were unemployed, while three were studying.

Most PAGFB, irrespective of being queer, are not raised to think of economic independence as a central concern, especially in contrast with PAGMB, who are raised with not just the expectation but the duty of being financially independent, as well as being primary providers for the family. This differentiation adversely affects the career opportunities and trajectories of PAGFB. The socialization and commensurate exposure necessary for a public working life is denied to them.

All this affects those who are queer even more acutely as the lack of economic empowerment threatens their ability to live on their own terms. Livelihood issues for queer PAGFB may differ from those of other PAGFB, as workspaces reflect rigid societal norms and mores around gender and sexuality, with fixed rules around clothes and dress. When queer PAGFB move out of their familial heteronormative superstructures, their limited access to education and skill-building institutions creates almost insurmountable barriers to finding and retaining employment. This is exacerbated by the pressure to conform to the gender binary, and the complete lack of social capital and support networks. For a few of our respondents this has meant a day-to-day struggle for work, shelter and food, which not only further impacts employability, but also gravely affects their physical, mental and emotional health.

Although PAGFB are not, by and large, brought up to fend for themselves, class and caste circumstances compelled a few of our respondents to start working in order to supplement their family income. In this chapter we explore how these very types of marginalization of caste, class and circumstance combined with those of gender and sexuality wield a great impact on our respondents' lives, trapping them in a vicious circle of deprivation.

Starting Early

Many of our respondents started working at an early age, almost half before they became adults (see Table 7.1). Six people started work before they were 14 years old, the minimum working age as defined by Indian laws. One of the factors that contributed to this was the economic circumstances of their natal families. A few others felt an internal drive to start working early in order to be financially independent sooner rather than later. A third impetus for some respondents was their being forced to migrate and fend for themselves in order to be able to freely express their gender and/or sexuality.

A few respondents grew up in natal families that lived with economic hardship and no monetary security. Devi, who challenges the assignation 'woman', said that ze had to start working at age 6 or 7 to support hir family. 'I worked in a quarry, worked in the farms, worked to build roads and worked in building construction.' Ze recalled becoming strong by lifting

Table 7.1: Age of Starting Paid Work

Started work at age	Respondents
<14 years	6
14 to 18	16
>18	28

and transporting bricks on construction sites. As ze was unable to complete hir education and didn't get the opportunity to learn other skills, ze continued to work in occupations that required manual labour well into adulthood.

After dropping out of school, Vasu started accompanying his mother when she went to do domestic work. 'I was never paid anything.... I started going for housework only when my father died. I never did like it. I just went to help my mother.' He started working for wages when he was 12 and continued to work in the same household for the next three years. He went on to work in other jobs that required unskilled labour.

Coming from a poor urban family, Sumit, who identifies as 'transgender', started working when hir father suffered a heart attack. Ze took on the responsibility of hir father's work as a building contractor: 'All his half-complete buildings, I managed to complete them.... Before Baba died, only two of my sisters had got married. Me and my mother managed the weddings of the other five.' Ze was not able to complete hir 12th standard, but managed to open hir own provision and photocopy shop, which enables hir to support hirself and hir family. Ze also distributes newspapers and paints banners to supplement the household income.

Falguni, who identifies as 'androgynous woman', came from an urban, middle-class Brahmin family. Her father was depressed, had quit his job and had a fraught relationship with her mother. Falguni started working in her summer breaks at 15 or 16 as a salesperson at exhibitions of consumer durables. She worked and studied till she dropped out in her second year of college to pursue a full-time career. 'I couldn't cry or show fear as my father couldn't be a man, couldn't be supportive.'

While these respondents had to start working early due to familial circumstances, there were others who felt a need to be financially independent, regardless of the family's economic status. Juhi started working at 13 because 'I had this *bhayankar* [immense] discomfort about living in my parents' house. I wanted to be independent.... So there was this huge need to earn money.

Some of us as friends, gang-type, we got together.... to drop off milk and newspapers at people's houses.' Later on ze went on to do sundry jobs such as sales in exhibitions, taking orders to sell firecrackers and selling shaving kits to men. This type of work was very unconventional for a PAGFB from a conservative, middle-class, Brahmin family, but Juhi managed to sidestep the norms around hir gender as well as caste/class background by couching the work as something ze did in hir spare time.

Sara came from a traditional, middle-class, Muslim family that lived in a small town. The boys were always given more pocket money than her, so by the time she entered her teens, she had been driven to find ways of earning small sums of money. Apart from raising pigeons and selling them, she recalled, 'Once, during my summer holidays... I opened up my library. I would put *Twinkle, Phantom*, Urdu novels, English novels, comic books on rent. I really enjoyed making money. I also rented out video games, one game for four annas.' And with her love for *meetha* [sweet] paan, she started her own mobile paan *patti* [shop]—'I would say that you can get it in the market for one rupee and I'm giving it to you for two rupees. Why? 'Coz it's at your doorsteps, also customized. More *gulkand* [sweet preserve made of rose petals], etc. as per your preference. Everyone bought it and they really did enjoy it too.'

Remarkably, respondents like Juhi and Sara were able to undertake non-normative courses of action to access their own independent source of money. These pursuits, be it selling shaving kits, consumer electronics or starting a paan *patti*, were unique in multiple ways—breaking not just gender rules but those related to caste, class and religion. While there were enabling factors, they were both keenly motivated and impatient to attain fiscal independence and, thus, insulation from their families' rules.

Some of our respondents were compelled to join the workforce early as they had run away from home due to violence faced or conflicts around gender and sexuality. Anand, who ran away from home at 17, with only Rs 150 in his pocket, started tutoring 11th and 12th standard students so that he could afford a hostel while he went to college. Had he not had to run away from home, he would have had the monetary support for further studies.

Sam left home before he could complete school and so had difficulty in finding economically sustainable employment. A queer support group helped him get a job as an office assistant in an NGO. At the time of this interview Sam was still working in NGOs as career choices outside supportive NGOs are not readily available to him.

It's important to note that in both these stories, the individuals were able to find and keep jobs as they chanced upon people or groups who helped. For others who may find themselves in similar situations there is no structural support or any social safety net.

Circle of Deprivation

Whether our respondents started work early or late, they had to rely on themselves in order to survive. Finding jobs was challenging for various reasons: lack of education, language skills and/or safe workspaces. Even when respondents found jobs, it was an uphill task to retain them. On the whole finding sustainable employment was more complicated for people from marginalized backgrounds, and gender and sexuality issues added yet another layer of difficulty. The violence wrought by the structures of family, school and other societal institutions is compounded by economic and social displacement when an individual runs away from home. This displacement added another factor to what we have called 'the circle of deprivation'. This deprivation is not just of home and education—there is unfamiliarity with a new location, possibly the language(s) spoken there, as well as the loss of a family home.

Apart from the pressure of finding a roof over one's head, queer PAGFB are unable to tap into the support networks they may have accessed in their home town as well as the urban networks of people who have emigrated from their home communities. These migrant communities offer new arrivals help with housing, securing informal sources of credit and job referrals. These community ties and networks generate access to information and resources in a way that we term social capital. This social capital is available only to in-group members. There is a large variety of specific benefits that flow from the trust, information and cooperation associated with these networks, creating value for the people who are connected. These largely parochial networks are heteropatriarchal in nature. Thus, anyone who has left home without the explicit assent of natal family and community, be they queer PAGFB or a heterosexual cisperson defying caste boundaries, will not be able to bridge ties and join such a network. This means that such individuals get further enmeshed in a circle of deprivation.

Those who have no familial support or social capital find their source of livelihood in the informal sector, which makes their employment extremely vulnerable and fragile. Any instability related to housing, health or personal circumstances that results in even a day-long absence at work means the loss of that particular job. The absence of family, extended family or even community support means that the individual doesn't have support to deal with the compounded issues of lack of employment as well as other concerns related to basic survival.

Santosh, who worked as a driver, had to take long road trips as part of his job. These journeys got very tough to undertake as he was the full-time carer for his partner who had several mental health issues. Due to lack of support systems for him and his partner, as well as inflexibility on the part of his employer, he was eventually compelled to leave a job that he loved.

Gender-transgressive PAGFB face other barriers to career advancement within their workplaces. While some may not be able to wear the clothes or sport the hair length of their choice, others may encounter difficulties working in environments that are pervasively heteronormative. This means that finding and keeping employment or work is incredibly difficult and eventually leads to critical lack of control over their circumstances and their ability to live their lives in the manner they want.

Clearly, it is the most marginalized who are most likely to be trapped within this vicious circle. Most are unable to survive in newer spaces due to the lack of privileges of caste, class, education and other skills. Irrespective of their determinations, dreams and passions, keeping their head above water is an uphill task. People who are trapped in the circle of deprivation seem to face systematic structural violence. This is heightened by the fact that the concessions and safety nets which employers—as well as the state—should provide are often not in place.

Prescriptions around Appearance

Whether it is dressing on the job or gender expression in the pursuit of work, it seems to have a critical effect on an individual's ability to get or keep a job. Kavi, a sports teacher in an urban school, testified that her superiors and fellow teachers had problems with her appearance:

> I dislike wearing a sari. It takes a long time and exposes part of the skin and you have to wear a blouse.... In schools here teachers are forced to wear a sari but salwar is not allowed. I fought with the headmistress. She asked for a note from me saying that I wanted to wear a salwar. I said it is not in her authority to dictate my clothes.

This in spite of the fact that there is no official rule requiring teachers to wear saris. Another teacher, Hemlata, shared a similar experience:

> When I was recovering from burns and could not tolerate clothes around my neck, I requested whether I could use a Punjabi suit. The principal said that to give you permission to wear salwar kameez, we need to ask others so that they are mentally prepared. Why should I get permission for what I am to wear or eat or with whom to sleep? This is my personal question.... I had to get a medical certificate, which I did not think was necessary.

Despite getting a 'sanction' from a medical authority, she was also judged by fellow teachers to be a 'bad wife and mother' because she stayed for after-school activities.

These gender boundaries show up even more starkly with those who identify as 'man' and their gender expressions. Divakar, a respondent with intersex variations, told us of his struggle to get a job despite having the correct qualifications. The first time he applied there were very many vacancies, but his application was rejected 'because I had attached a recent photo which they said... did not match with the certificate. At that time everyone who studied with me got a job, even those who had got some 40 to 45 per cent marks.'

The next time he applied for a post he was publicly ridiculed. 'When they were taking the applications, they made fun of me in front of everyone, saying, "See, this is Divya, and look at the photo! And look at her!"' In the end Divakar was compelled to go to a hospital, and undergo prolonged tests and humiliating scrutiny from the staff there so that he could obtain a certificate stating that he was male, to include in job applications.

Take the story of Jai, who had to start work in a fish-packing plant as no one else in his family was then working. 'During this time, at home, I still had to wear a churidar, but in the fish factory one had to wear uniform and coat and cap, and fully pack oneself and I liked that.' Despite having to work night shifts, odd hours and give up the school he loved so much, Jai liked one aspect of his workplace: the chance to wear clothes of his choice. Once he ran away, all the possible job opportunities he came across in the city required him to wear a churidar. Luckily, a job opening cropped up in an NGO where he was able to be himself. While queer PAGFB have migrated to urban areas in an attempt to live their life freely, they are not always able to do so.

After completing his 12th standard, Rahul cut his hair short and charted a plan to get a job in order to pay for a sex reassignment surgery (SRS):

> Before even my board results were announced... I went to so many places for interviews.... I had short hair, wore pants and shirts. I wasn't very hep then. Anybody could recognize me as a girl. In the interviews my answers used to be right, but I think they took my appearance negatively.

In the end he got a job at a McDonalds outlet. However, he had a trying experience, with co-workers and management questioning his gender expression. 'I used to speak in [a] masculine way. They wondered why I spoke like that... and when I told them that I was a boy, they would try and convince me that I was not really a boy.'

Sometimes even playing by the rules and wearing the appropriate clothes can be problematic if your hairstyle and body language differ from the norm. Aditi, who works in the police force, used to enjoy wearing the official uniform of trousers and a shirt, but her joy was short-lived. 'People look down at you and call you names. "She is not interested in marriage so she must be a lesbian." When people know you are like this, then they keep torturing you to get married.' She said that social events at work see most women police wear saris and jewellery, whereas her shirt and trousers mean that she gets taunted and pressurized with questions about when she will get married. She once enjoyed her job, but now looks forwards to leaving and starting her own gym.

Even when one has their own business and doesn't have a boss or co-workers, navigating gender and sexuality in the workspace can be tricky. Alex, who describes hirself as 'between transgender and lesbian', testified:

> People called me sir, but for the last couple of years they are a bit confused.... When I go to the bank... they say sir/madam, they are a bit confused, and I just repeat that I am Ms. Before they say anything, I do a formal introduction to avert any confusion.

As is evident from these varied experiences, workspaces seem to mirror the larger heteronormative institutions and structures.

There are rare occasions when the workplace can be an enabler with regard to dress. Coming from a conservative Jain family, Saumya was compelled to wear salwar kameez to college despite wanting to wear jeans. When she went to work, she was able to prevail over her family as well as explore her dressing and gender expression further. '[I] had to dress formally at work, like trousers and shirts, skirts and blouses. All [the people] wear these, so it is no longer butch/femme clothing. Or a gay/ straight thing.'

'Male' Occupations

As evinced from some of the stories, not being able to dress, look or behave like a 'woman' can mean tension, conflict, stress and violence. How does this dynamic operate in occupations that are largely male spaces or termed 'men's' jobs? Saran, sharing her experience working as a cinematographer, said, 'This is a man's scene, not a girl's stuff. I think I am amongst the first five [women] to be behind the camera.' In a male-dominated field, Saran had to be constantly aware of how she communicates as a professional because 'sometimes it gets in their way, the fact that a girl can tell them smarter ways of doing things; hence, it bothers them. [So] I have to be extremely tactful, and—without hurting their ego—I need to tell them.' As a queer PAGFB, she felt that she could not behave like many of the other women in her field—the 'typical girl'. According to her, this archetype helps many women navigate her field.

Sara, a producer, echoed Saran's sentiments about working in the media world:

> Direction is a hard-core line, it's like a masculine profession. When you shoot, there are 25 to 40 men, light boys, spot boys; in between all that there's this one woman director. The woman can be of two types, either the typical girly type who flatters the DOP [director of photography] or the type who will take charge, be clear and say exactly what she wants. I have never had an issue, and people do ask for my directions.

She narrated one particular incident at a conservative TV channel where she used to work. 'Many people passed comments on me…. But I gave back comments like nobody's business—a room of 10 men used to fall silent. They used to call me sir to trouble me.' She also used her own strategies to deal with gender- and sexuality-related negativity in her workplace. She said, 'In terms of gender, however straight people are, they don't define themselves, so why should I define myself? I am what I am. Take it or leave it was my attitude.'

However, harassment around gender or sexuality was not limited to male-centric professions or workspaces. Sometimes the work culture of an organization is pervasively heteronormative and patriarchal. Chandni, who says of hir gender, 'I don't articulate it as something specifically', is an editor at a stock brokerage where hir boss is a man who thinks that women can't do much work. 'When he first joined he tried to flirt or tease, relating to you in a gendered way where gender looks like [it does in] a Hindi film.... Even today I don't know how to relate to my boss properly... macho and traditional. It's a scary combination.' Ze also spoke about the pressure and questions about why ze wasn't planning to get married, citing that there were no non-normative women in the office with the exception of one divorcee. 'Work has become a little macho and loud with back-slapping. The women there tend to play the part—giggling, demure and coy. There's no woman going against the tide. I don't deal with it, I just keep to myself.'

The idea that male professionals expect their peers to behave like 'women' in order to go about their daily business is something that affects all PAGFB. This is true even of the medical world, as Monu, a physiotherapist, testified. 'The only thing I feel is that if I was or could have been someone who dressed like a woman, then I could have got many more patients. The doctors pay more attention to girls, but not to someone like me.'

While PAGFB are generally compelled to behave like 'women', queer PAGFB who pass as 'men' in the workplace are forced to behave like other cismen working with them. Karthik has worked in construction all his life, starting with breaking stones in a quarry at 9. 'At work, I am aware that... they think I am a man. I try to make my voice deep and strong.' But people notice and comment when he doesn't change his clothes and bathe after shift like the cismen. The pressure to look and behave in socially recognized ways, of being 'women' or 'men' deeply colours workplace dynamics for queer PAGFB.

Sexual Harassment

Other than conflict related to gender, respondents spoke out about explicit sexual harassment while at work. One 'woman'-identified respondent spoke of having to travel to another city on a business trip with her male boss:

> He took me out for dinner and during drinks, he started talking about adultery.... I said, you are here, your wife too must be with another man, and that fucked his head. He got sloshed though he was trying to get me drunk. He left me alone and went straight to his room and slept off. This made me grow up professionally overnight.

While such harassment may take place with any PAGFB, queer or not, Jai's story was rather different. At the fish-packing plant where he worked, he had a relationship with a female colleague. Their co-workers not only policed the relationship but actively harassed both partners:

> They felt that something was not 'right' and then they started spying by pretending to sleep and observing us. They saw us being sexual and then told us that one of us had to leave, both could not work there anymore. Both of us decided to resign as one could not have worked there alone, it would have been difficult.

Jai and his partner were meted out such harassment because their apparently 'lesbian relationship' challenged norms around heterosexuality. But moral codes around normative sexuality are strictly enforced even in heterosexual contexts. Hemlata, a school teacher, was dismissed from her job because she had a relationship with a male colleague. 'My affair was published in the newspapers and a signature campaign was started against me. There were discussions—"How can a married woman fall in love with a married man?" I was taken to be a bad woman.' Due to her gender, her desire and sexuality seem to have been censured and policed more than her male colleague's.

Sunny mentioned a particular incident with hir boss.

> I always treated him like a guy interacting with another guy, so when he asked me to go out for a burger, I thought nothing of it. Then when he asked me if he could come up home after the burger, I still thought nothing of it. He started to act weird and tried to kiss me, he made a reach for my chest, but because I keep my ID card in my pocket, he got nothing but the ID card in his hand and I wriggled out of his grasp.

This was sexual harassment compounded by a violation of Sunny's gender identity. After that neither Sunny nor hir boss acknowledged the episode, but he targeted Sunny by giving hir the most difficult shifts.

In Sandy's case, the perpetrator of sexual harassment was hir female boss who used to flirt with hir and call hir to a hotel room. Eventually they had a relationship, but after hir boss broke up very abruptly with hir, Sandy faced a toxic environment at work. 'She treated me very badly. If I did good work I was put down and if I did bad work I was yelled at. For two years... I was going through this and did not even know what to tell people.'

Even when a queer PAGFB can pass as male, it doesn't ensure a workspace safe, as is evident in Santosh's story.

> I worked for a month as an assistant in a full gents' hotel. I got Rs 35 and three meals a day. Nobody guessed I was female—we all slept together. I'd wake up early and go to the bathroom, or go outside to the public bathroom. But I got scared by gay sex, which I saw and learnt about for the first time. The manager would have sex with several guys, call them one by one, and I was afraid: what if he comes to me?

The pressure of harassment and of being outed meant that Santosh quit his job and was compelled to leave the city to find employment elsewhere.

All these examples illustrate how in the workplace the nature of consent is inextricably tangled with power imbalances inherent in relations between co-workers, or equations between subordinates and their superiors. The avenues for redressal or support regarding any incidence of othering, taunting or harassment of a sexual nature seem to be very few and possibly tough to access for all PAGFB. When Murali worked at a bottling plant the owner was blackmailing and abusing the women. Ze left when the owner insisted on meeting hir alone.

When queer sexuality and non-normative gender enter the picture, the nature of sexual harassment changes based on a new set of prejudices coming into play. Whether one is explicitly targeted as a sexual object or due to their sexual liaisons or relationships—through creating hostile work environments or quid pro quo harassment when a superior's sexual behaviour is rejected—all of these are stories of sexual harassment.

Other Kinds of Violence

Such harassment at the workplace compounds the circle of deprivation. Losing employment due to discrimination and violence can mean forced multiple migrations, as in Santosh's case, or struggling to eke out a livelihood, as in Vasu's. When he started a part-time job, he described how the owner felt uncomfortable about his being a runaway. 'He was scared that if something went wrong, this kid has come from home and is staying here. And also, I am a woman dressed up as a man.' The owner was worried that if the police came asking for Vasu, then he would get into trouble and so he said, 'While you can work here, keep looking out for other jobs.' Vasu quit that job and was on the lookout for employment when we met him.

In other stories we heard of the workplace being a site of violence due to varied reasons that both PAGMB and PAGFB potentially face, such as class, violent customers or supervisors, or just a toxic work environment. For example, Sam's first job at 17 was sewing at a garment unit. He had only been there a week when his supervisor beat him up because he was doing something incorrectly. Sam hit him back and quit the job. Initially he didn't inform his mother, but when she found out, Sam got a beating from her too.

Sometimes, the violence is not as overt, as is apparent from one respondent's experiences at her workplace. She is from a nomadic tribe and felt that her employers were dismissive and disrespectful when it came to her caste, class and sexuality. She was annoyed when they used her then-husband's dominant-caste surname as hers in one of the project proposals. 'How could they just surmise? I did not want to use his name at the workplace. This also reflected the organization's position on caste.... I requested them to change it to [my own surname].' When she bought a flat, derogatory comments were made:

> I had taken leave for 10 days to paint my flat so that I could move in. But this was commented upon—'Why paint, because later you will have to whitewash.' From their talk I could gather that I deserve nothing better than whitewash.... This was a class comment.

NGOs as Workspaces

Sometimes the only workspace available for the multiply marginalized and disenfranchised is the space of the NGO. Many respondents reported working in NGOs that hired persons with varying gender identities and a lack of formal education. Murali, who identifies as 'FTM', left hir village because ze wasn't free to express hir gender there. After moving ze managed to get a job at an NGO for LGBT rights where ze was able to dress as a man. 'It was a safe space and comfortable life.' Notably, though ze speaks very little of the local language, ze had studied up to the 12th standard and was able to take on general administrative work. Sometimes NGOs such as this one are the only recourse for gender-transgressive PAGFB to find a toehold in the formal employment sector.

Prem, who had studied up to the 12th standard too, ran away to a metro with hir lover. Ze found a job in an agency that worked with domestic workers. Hir employers insisted that ze wear a sari to work, which made hir very uncomfortable, but ze had to fend for hirself and hir partner, and so was unable to assert hirself. Eventually an NGO offered hir a job. 'I wanted to… wear pant–shirt, smoke, etc. So the day I got a job, I went and cut my hair and went in pant–shirt.' Ze is currently unemployed, but the avenues available to hir are low-skilled jobs at NGOs with no potential for learning or self-advancement.

Similarly, Bhargavi, who was unable to complete hir 12th standard, ran away to an urban centre. Ze got a job as an assistant at a drop-in centre at an NGO. Hir job was to make tea, take photocopies and similar sundry tasks. Despite two promotions in two years, Bhargavi has not been able to add to hir skillset as there is no scope to take on skilled work and nor can ze afford to take time off work to study further.

But not all NGOs are supportive of non-normative gender and/or sexuality. Devi, who comes from a poor, rural family and wasn't able to access any formal education, eventually joined an NGO working on women's rights. As part of this work, ze organized meetings in *bastis* [urban settlements] to discuss the concerns of single women. The NGO clamped down on Devi when people started discussing lesbian relationships in their meetings. This led to Devi becoming disillusioned with hir work. Ze said, 'When the oppression became too much to bear, I just quit. The women's movement gave me new life. But a certain way of thinking caused me such deep hurt that it will stay with me forever.'

Another trans* respondent spoke of how even an LGBT NGO space was problematic and intolerant of certain non-normative sexualities and genders and of non-monogamy. 'There was no space for us who had different sexual preferences. If we questioned this, we feared losing our jobs. They questioned the multiple relationships among us… and I had to answer all their questions.' Respondents also spoke about having to fight for wages, to be referred to in their preferred gender pronoun and for opportunities for promotion.

Several NGOs, especially those working on human rights and gender and sexuality concerns have created space within their set-ups for a wider range of gender and sexuality expressions. Thus, queer PAGFB have expressed comfort in taking up such jobs as they are closer to their realities. However, it seems that these can be safe, affirmative places in a limited measure. At times, they also become spaces where certain kinds of marginalization or deviations can mean oppression, a loss of rights and, sometimes, livelihoods. At the same time, the kind of work that is on offer may not be sustainable or have a potential for growth in terms of a fulfilling career or a sustaining job—they tend to be dead-end and basic-level jobs. This type of employment is a very short-term measure, and a focus on not just giving people a job but creating skills that enhance livelihood opportunities and enhance employability is urgently needed.

Privileges that Even the Odds

For queer PAGFB who are multiply marginalized, displaced, estranged from family or have faced ruptures in their education, the routes to economic independence are limited. However, for those who had some privileges, the struggles were somewhat different.

Sara moved to the closest city for education and found work in the mass media field soon after dropping out of college.

> In my childhood, my mother had got many offers to come and teach English. [But] my father didn't allow my mother to work…. This really affected me. No one made a path for me… I had to break the barriers and move ahead.

Despite dropping out, Sara said she got her job because 'the media is a line where you can be an undergrad or an MA, it's open to [everyone]'. Ironically, she was able to get a job because her family had given her an English language education and she was able to work only because she wasn't living with her family anymore. Her passion for her work and, ultimately, her savings from years of working enabled and emboldened her to start studying again. She decided to undertake a part-time bachelor's degree. 'I'm sharpening my skills by studying…. My weapons are film and video…. I'm studying after 10 to 12 years. The plan is to graduate because if I want to go abroad, I have to study in the same line that I'm working in.' Planning a career and being able to pursue it is a privilege that many queer PAGFB from multiply marginalized backgrounds are unable to access.

Saumya's story was not very different. She comes from an urban, middle-class family that expected her to stay at home and do household tasks rather than study further or go to work. She fought opposition from her family when she started working at the age of 20. At some point she decided to pursue a long-distance MBA. This would not have been possible for her to unless she was economically independent as her parents believed that she was not good at either studies or work. Critical in this pursuit was support from her partner. Now, after completing her MBA, Saumya continues to do well in her career and lives with her parents whom she partially supports with her salary.

Sandy, who identifies as 'other' and comes from an upper-middle-class family, had a turbulent childhood as well as ruptures in her education and had to fend for hirself very early. Ze started with low-skilled jobs in sales and then found work in the English print media. However, when ze moved to another city to live with hir father, he soon threw hir out of the house. Even so, Sandy was able to find and keep a job at a prestigious media company. The trajectory for hir, then, is radically different from that of other queer PAGFB who went through locational and familial displacement. Privileges of caste and class swing the odds remarkably in one's favour despite marginalization based on gender and sexuality. For people with class/caste privilege, getting that first opportunity is the crucial step to expanding their horizons.

Dream Vocations

Going beyond the need to survive or even succeed in their careers, some of our respondents managed to find professions close to their hearts. A few who were denied the opportunity to pursue their interests managed to circumvent such roadblocks by finding a similar domain or a way to connect back to their passion. Kavi, who identifies as 'female', spoke of how her family stopped her from following a future in cricket as they felt she was a girl and needed to be protected. She decided to stick to sport academically and completed a master's in physical education. While she never got an opportunity to realize her dream to play cricket for her state, she now relishes her work as a physical education teacher in a school.

Another sports buff, Monu came from an urban middle-class family that didn't like 'girls' in the family to play. But ze went against the tide and eventually played professionally for hir state's football team for four years. Then ze suffered a ligament injury that ended hir career. Yet, as ze said, 'I have very good memories of my sporting life and feel that world is ours, there are others like me, so I would like to remain connected to it.' Ze trained to become a sports physiotherapist. Now Monu travels widely with cricket and football teams, participating from the sidelines and sometimes even on the field.

One of our respondents is a musician, a career ze is very passionate about and which is able to provide for hir needs. Ze also uses hir professional success to connect to another passion—exploring gender. Ze spoke about the texture of voices and actively looks for trans* voices. An acclaimed singer, ze is on the way to fulfilling hir dream of connecting hir music and hir activism. 'Composing and rock band music—that is my dream. Travelling, singing, generating money, routing it to different organizations.'

A fair number of our respondents found fulfilment in their careers around issues of gender and sexuality. They find this work meaningful as it connects to their lives, politics and lived realities. Geeta was following her heart when she started working with NGOs on concerns around feminism and gender. In the future she plans to do research on sexuality. Kamal found that activism was where his passion lay, particularly with organizing around people who are marginalized by disability as well as identity, such as queer or commercial sex workers:

> I want to give a voice to all those who have no opportunity to talk of their concerns. What is the reason for this problem? Sending one postcard, I could collect 7,000 people with disabilities, so why not now? We have to struggle for our own rights. I have to survive and also bring others together to struggle and survive.

Whether it is working on these issues through organizations or by way of personal activism, such work was often emotionally and personally affirmative for many. Ranjana, who ran away from her urban, middle-class family due to marriage pressures, said, 'I have passion for women's rights, so that will definitely continue, and sexuality rights is a part of it. I will be dead if I don't work on these issues.'

Maushami started working at an NGO that focused on sexuality at a time that she was going through an internal conflict about her own sexuality as well as struggling with self-destructive behaviours like cutting. Her workplace turned out to be supportive. 'No one judged me, questioned me. When I was in a relationship with a transgender man, no one questioned me about how come, as I had [had] a boyfriend earlier…. I started feeling much better.' For yet others the NGOs where they worked at were instrumental in providing them support, be it to resume and complete their education or to cope with domestic violence in their homes and communities.

One respondent is a visual artist of repute, who explores gender and sexuality in hir work. 'My role as an artist is not to present the right answer or right solutions always but also to create a problem or to create a question, perhaps a discomfort.' Ze also said:

> I always feel, when I see queer stuff from the Indian context, that there is a kind of self-affirmation that I cannot find [elsewhere]. Of course, you can relate to queer stuff made in other parts of the world, but I just feel like the situation, context, vocabulary, circumstances are so different locally.

Acceptance at Work

A few respondents also spoke of how their workspaces and/or certain colleagues were supportive of their non-normative gender and/or sexuality. When Ujwala, who has worked in the non-profit sector on various issues ranging from crafts to development as well as gender and sexuality, came out to a colleague at an NGO where she worked

> she just looked at me and went off. Next day, I got a beautiful letter from her saying, 'Sorry, it took me by surprise, and I am happy for you and proud of you.' The staff was told, everybody. If there was a homophobic joke, they were told, 'Sorry, this is homophobic.' And in fact there was a treasure hunt organized between my office and [my partner's] for my birthday, with the whole staff getting involved.

Amidst stories of disapprobation, control and harassment due to outings of sexuality and gender, Ujwala's story sets a very positive precedent for support for marginalized sexualities in the workplace.

Anand could not use his preferred pronoun or preferred bathroom at any of his workspaces. However, that changed at one particular job due to a supportive supervisor. Anand recounted that he had gone to work with a rakhi tied to his wrist:

> [My senior colleague] asked why the rakhi. I just looked at him. He said, 'You're a girl, aren't you?' I don't know from where I got the courage, I said, 'Not really.' He said, 'What?' Then he closed the door and said, 'Ok, now tell me.' I said, 'Do you know about transsexuals?' He said. 'Yes, are you one?' I said, 'Yes, I am.' He said, 'Cool, so then why do you let these guys call you [by your given name], what's your name?' I told him, 'Anand.' He said, 'That's how they should be addressing you.'... So he calls all the people in that centre and says, 'Who is this?' They say, '[old name].' He says, 'Wrong, this is Anand and he's a he, and I want him to be addressed in the correct way from now on.'

After exploring the different ways in which people have been harassed at work and shunted out of jobs because of non-normative sexuality and/or gender, Anand and Ujwala's experiences seem quite unique—finding allies in the workplace who strive to the best of their capability to make their lives easier. In the absence of non-discrimination policies, even one person in a position of power can make a difference. While this can go a long way in making people comfortable, it leaves them vulnerable to the vagaries of chance. An overarching system of support structures that respect, affirm and adequately cater to the needs and requirements of persons marginalized because of gender and/or sexuality is needed. These would range from using people's preferred pronouns and enabling access to preferred bathrooms to the recognition of the non-heteronormative family that someone may have.

Conclusion

At the time of the study 27 respondents were earning a monthly income of less than Rs 10,000. Of these, three were students, while another five were neither employed nor living with or being supported by their natal families. There were eight people earning up to Rs 5,000, which is below a minimum living wage. This figure of almost half of our respondents earning minimum or just about the minimum living wage is a stark indicator that their material conditions had not changed for the better, leaving many of them still struggling for basic survival.

As we have seen, while an initial education enabled employment opportunities commensurate with their level of education, circumstances such as forced migration, outings at workplaces and conflicts around gender and sexuality limited the employment and career prospects of many of our respondents. The circumstances of those forced to migrate and who, therefore, never finished school/college seems to have left them the most vulnerable to systemic violence. Poverty, violence due to transgressions of norms and rules, ruptured education, forced migration, lack of job security, discrimination, lack of social capital and support networks, physical and mental health issues all come together to form an almost insurmountable barrier: the circle of deprivation.

Some non-profits provide much-needed employment to disenfranchised queer PAGFB, but the scope of these jobs is limited and doesn't provide opportunities to realize one's potential. As our interviews show, this has meant a constant reliance on NGOs as well as an inability to survive outside them, creating an untenably long-term dependence.

Those respondents who have succeeded have done so because of an early opportunity and access to class and caste privileges. There is need for such opportunities to be provided to as many people as possible so that they acquire a skillset useful to survive in the mainstream job market. NGOs need to consider providing these opportunities through scholarship programmes to people interested in certain careers or vocations. However, this is not solely the responsibility of groups working on gender and sexuality or human rights. NGOs working on livelihood issues as well as those working with the youth should take cognizance of the needs of queer PAGFB. Helping queer PAGFB to find the skills and qualifications they require is the only way that they will find sustainable and meaningful employment or careers.

The non-profit and for-profit sectors, as well as publicly-owned entities should take it upon themselves to create queer-friendly policies and workspaces. This must include being more inclusive and respectful of difference, be it with regard to gender, appearance or sexuality. This must be visible not just in hiring practices, but also with workplace provisions and arrangements. We need labour laws and workspaces that espouse anti-discrimination norms, as well as safe access to restroom facilities of choice.

While our concerns in this book have been centred around gender and sexuality, it is important to recognize that any sort of autonomy, in this or any other aspect of life, partially hinges upon financial independence. Hence, all PAGFB should be encouraged to think of themselves as financially independent beings. In the long term there needs to be a paradigm shift in our attitudes towards PAGFB participation in the workforce. It needs to be recognized that most adult women work, and they should have the opportunity as well as choice to work for their own sense of autonomy and independence.

8

Public Spaces

In the mainstream view, 'women' seem to be associated more with the private sphere of home. Most PAGFB, whether queer or not, are restricted from accessing public spaces, especially while growing up, unlike PAGMB, who access these spaces with a sense of entitlement learned from childhood. While PAGMB have the licence to hang out or loiter in public spaces, PAGFB are expected to have a legitimate purpose that allows them to inhabit these spaces and then only at 'appropriate' times. One of the frequent justifications given for denying similar access to PAGFB is that such policing is for their own safety. In this way, rather than making the other users of public spaces as well as the state responsible for equal access and equal safety, the burden of staying safe in these spaces is shifted to PAGFB themselves.

Access to public spaces for PAGFB is further influenced by ability, gender, class and location. These factors dictate how you can behave, what you can look like and what you do or not do in a particular space. In essence public spaces themselves not only shape, but are designed by normative expectations around gender, caste, class and ability. Whether it is wheelchair-inaccessible public transport systems or pedestrian crossings that exclude the needs of disabled persons, it is often the multiply marginalized who face difficulties in accessing a large variety of public spaces, including bathrooms. Further, those who transgress gender norms and are marginalized by class and caste are often forced to migrate, leaving them most vulnerable to violence in public spaces. Importantly, even when queer PAGFB face violence in their lives, they usually have no recourse to support from state agencies such as the police. While many referred to the institutionalized bias against PAGFB, our respondents shared only a few stray personal accounts of overt police violence.

In our conversations respondents narrated their experiences of traversing various spaces, both urban and rural, being perceived either as 'women' or as transgressing the strictly enforced gender norms of society. They also spoke of their specific and often unsafe experience of spaces segregated along gender lines, apparently for the benefit of 'women' who are seen as 'needing protection'. In the process we also heard of many personal strategies developed in order to negotiate differently difficult spaces.

Location Matters

A significant number of respondents said how it was impossible to live the way they wanted in their hometown or village. Transgressions from the norm were quickly picked up and pointed out in closely knit semi-urban and/or rural areas. Some reported being called names or being discriminated against while growing up. One person attested, 'In Tamil they used to call me *pondi-chati*—it means you are born neither a male nor a female.' Knowing everyone in the village or neighbourhood means that people who do not live normative lives are acutely visible and vulnerable.

Jai, who identifies as 'man', recounted that there was someone in the next village who was PAGFB and lived as a man. Jai never managed to speak to this person, who was a daily wage labourer and by and large ostracized by everyone. However, there was one incident. 'He came up to my father and spoke a bit and after he left, my father said, "Such persons are wrong and should be tied and beaten and killed. She should be thrown in the fire." So I got scared.' Jai was afraid he too would be seen as 'one such person'.

Kirti can never break some codes where he lives:

Having lived in the village all my life and worn saris, it is hard to imagine what I would look like if not in a sari. And I would have short hair if I had a choice. I would have smoked and drunk more freely.... Once [my partner] and I tried to smoke inside the house, but people from outside wondered about the smell. So we stopped and haven't done it again.

While Kirti cannot break these rules due to fear of verbal or physical persecution, there were instances where people contravened such norms openly. When Divakar migrated to the city, its anonymity meant that he had no problems passing as male. This holds him in good stead when he returns to visit his natal family in the village where he was raised as a girl: 'In front of known people I try and walk with as much confidence as I can. I walk in my village with one shirt button open.' Now, after having reclaimed his space in this way, Divakar is not afraid to go anywhere, any time.

Others also experienced migration as liberating, as the influence of social and familial controls was diminished. Sara recalled, 'My father said do what you want to do in [the big city], not in [this town].' She moved to the nearest big city when she was 15, and now says, 'I will never get the same sort of freedoms as I do living alone if I went back home.'

The privilege of an urban location, which for many was also a space away from home, enabled our respondents to take up space in male-dominated areas, cut their hair, wear shirts and trousers, as well as walk and talk differently. Quite a few mentioned that the very first thing they did after running away from home was to get their hair cut short. Such as Sam, who was living on the streets after leaving home. Today, he can confidently access barbers who cater to a male clientele. Another respondent said, 'The first time the barber... looked at me with doubts. He could not question me, as I was his customer. Now that I am a regular, they do not say anything.'

It is not just the people who are gender transgressive who experience freedom in anonymous urban environments; these sites allow gender-conforming people to break norms too. Laxmi, who migrated from her village to a large city, said, 'I have more freedom to move around. I have the freedom to dress in jeans.' The city has been vastly empowering for her and she faces no problems there, whereas even now, when she visits her village, she is subjected to comments and censure from not just neighbours, but also her own friends.

While relatively anonymous urban spaces allow some room for negotiation, not all spaces can be as easily accessed or used by PAGFB as they can be by cismen. Spaces that most respondents felt safe accessing were homes and other private spaces, as well as semi-public spaces like coffee shops and malls. However, class privilege and the ability to spend are significant enablers for access to the latter.

Freedom and access are not uniform across urban areas, of course, especially when we consider certain locations and even cities where gender codes are strictly defined. Neha remarked:

> In Madras, the notion of a Tamil woman, Tamil identity is very strong. In Bombay, you can see different types of people. A woman of a certain class walking down the road, bald or with short hair is not so easy. Once I move to another city, it's like I renegotiate with the city.

These thoughts are echoed by another respondent:

> If I were a boy, I would get more freedom and liberty to stay out till late. I feel comfortable to be out alone till about 11 pm. But after that I feel safe only if I have someone with me, otherwise it is not safe in Kolkata.

A few respondents spoke about the affirmation they felt in reclaiming or subverting male-centric spaces in urban areas. Jharna, who identifies as 'woman', stated, 'After leaving home… any inhibitions I may have had completely went…. I can eat alone, stand on the street and have paan or chai alone. If people stare, let them—I don't care.' Saran, who is sometimes mistaken for a boy, said:

> All of those daring days of mine… starting at 10 or 11 in the morning. We would be on the road all day, sometimes at the

> cigarette shop, sometimes at the back of the car, sometimes keep my
> bag and sit under the tree.

This sort of staking claim to 'male' spaces challenges prevailing notions of safe spaces for women.

Passing in Public

However, even when in an urban space or when one has other privileges, whether one passes as a 'man' or a 'woman', or neither, affects gender performance, negotiations and safety in a public space. Although Kanika likes to shift between masculine and feminine expression in public, ze said, 'I was returning from school and a lady was passing by and she remarked, "God knows whether she is a male or female." She said it consciously so that I could hear her, and I was in salwar. I was irritated big time.' PAGFB in public spaces who are read as 'butch' find that this cuts both ways—some women find them intriguing and approachable; others, especially those with male companions, are often hostile.

A public space can turn unsafe very quickly if someone is questioned about their gender. Respondents have been harassed, abused, threatened, even beaten up. Vasu, who identifies as 'male', said:

> I am not scared of being out, but only, no one should find out that
> I am a woman. If they guess through my body shape that I am a
> woman, then it is an issue. Sometimes when I wear a shirt, one can
> make out…. I am afraid of my body. What if when I am just walking
> along, someone comes and does something to me, assaults me?

Sam had this story of travelling in a bus:

> Some young boys had got in and they were teasing me, 'Is it a boy
> or a girl? What's underneath?' and also saying *gaalis* [abuses] about
> mother. I got very angry and screamed at them. Then they realized
> on hearing me that I was a girl. So then they said that they would
> take off my clothes to check. But no one in the bus supported me.

The driver and the conductor did not stop the bus. Then I jumped off the running bus when it slowed. Had I not jumped off, they would have pulled off my clothes.

Jai told us of an incident in the neighbourhood where he sold fried fish for a living:

Some people started beating us and then even passers-by joined in. They were shouting abuses and so on. I too shouted at them. This went on for about half an hour.... When the fight began some had said, 'We will rape you,' but later they said they did not know that I was a woman.

It's clear that people picked on and harassed both Sam and Jai, despite recognizing them as 'women'. The verbal harassment was obviously sexualized to shame the act of gender transgression itself.

Passing in a chosen gender unequivocally may provide gender transgressors a modicum of safety in certain contexts or situations. As Chandni said, 'Once my hair grew out and I became bustier, the questions stopped.' For some, using specific clothing helped with passing in the manner they preferred. Planning what to wear for public outings can thus be incredibly important. Since there is recognition for only two genders in the public sphere, people are forced to choose between them so as to avoid derogatory comments. Arun, who identifies as 'genderqueer', spoke of hir method:

I always wear this T-shirt inside a shirt.... From the beginning, I [have felt] like that one shirt is not enough. While playing cricket, it became my practice.... No, I cannot wear something sleeveless in public. But shorts I can wear if they are till the knees.

Other respondents spoke of using tight clothing to make their body outline visible so as to pass as women in certain spaces.

Similar experiences are echoed by people who chose to cut their hair—short hair helped them pass in their chosen gender.

But when Prem visited hir hometown, ze wore a salwar kameez and grew out hir hair to be read as a woman. Others too spoke about using hair length if they wanted to pass as women.

Another essential gendered cue is voice. Some respondents shared their strategies around voice in public spaces. Sandy purposely uses hir voice to effect in sticky situations. 'But I do use the loos in airports and my trick is to talk loudly on my phone and making sure my voice sounds female as I am entering a bathroom.' And Anand, who identifies as 'man', said, 'I let the friends I'm with do the ordering so I don't have to speak, as my voice is the one thing that can give me away.' Other gender-transgressive PAGFB narrated how their partners step in when necessary.

To fit convincingly into their chosen gender and be recognized as such by others, people usually have to exhibit normative behaviours clearly associated with the perceived gender. Anand, for instance, adopted certain behaviours to 'fit in' during his college days. '[I] used to roam around with guys, do gymming, cycling, late night drinkouts.... I was like a full goonda.' Rahul talked about fitting in at the call centre where he used to work. 'The whole team was an only boys' team. They were fine with me. They used to do boys' talk with me. About girls, drinking, etc.' Karthik, who identifies as 'man', said:

> From my gender performance, people think I am a man. They identify me thus by my walk, the way I dress or talk and work.... Sometimes, male friends bet on girls and I am expected to and also challenged to do the same.

Sometimes, the passing in a certain gender is so successful that respondents have even had it entered on official documents. Sunny, who identifies as '50 per cent male and 50 per cent female', said, 'All the papers had been ticked male just by looking at my face... PAN [permanent account number] card male, passport male, voting ID.' While it was very satisfying for hir to be perceived as male unambiguously enough to be issued an 'official' stamp, this was juxtaposed with the constant fear of being found out: 'My mother has been so harassed and so much money was being spent on changing it again and again, that I have stopped feeling happy; now I just make sure they tick female.'

Gender-Segregated Spaces

Nowhere is gender as inscribed into the binary as it is in the spaces that are segregated. Gender-segregated public spaces, hence, remain the most contested and difficult to negotiate, even in urban centres. Most notable amongst these are public toilets as we saw in the example earlier, but also reserved seats in buses, train compartments, security checks in malls, airports or anywhere else. These are spaces that are marked with conflict as the body is interrogated, for gender has to be proven.

Sandy, who identifies as 'other', said:

> I hate malls because you have to go through the body check at the entrance and that is always a tense moment. At the airport... I have a uniform and wear a tight T-shirt where the boob outline cannot be missed.... This last flight back to Delhi, the lady cop at Mumbai airport poked my breast with the body scanner and asked, 'Are you sure you are a woman?'

As Sandy's body and space was violated in an airport, so was 'woman'-identified Saran's in a mall:

> I was entering a mall and... and the next thing the guy is taking the machine and ready to frisk me. I said, 'What are you doing? Are you awake or sleeping?' He says, 'Your hair.' So I said, 'If I am bald does it mean I am old. If you grow your hair longer are you going to be a woman?'

Navigating gender-specific spaces requires forethought and calculation. Juhi, who identifies as 'androgynous', spoke of hir strategy when using local trains, 'I would actively make some effort to indicate that I'm a woman. Maybe wear a haversack where your breasts jut out so everyone knows that you're a woman. So, no one would get violent with you or just shove you out of the compartment or anything.'

This violence ranges all the way from hurtful remarks to physical abuse. Ironically, women-only spaces are supposed to be safe for PAGFB, but many experiences in this study testify to their being the most violent towards gender-transgressive people.

Aditi, who identifies as 'woman', was harassed by a fellow commuter in the ladies' compartment. She was travelling after having partially changed out of her police uniform. 'In the train, once when I was in half-civil, a lady saw me from the back and asked if I am a girl and started passing comments. I get angry when some people do it deliberately to poke fun.' Shaming the gender transgressor is a common occurrence.

Those PAGFB who openly transgress gender norms also may face a different kind of harassment from cismen. All 'women' anyway face sexual harassment from cismen in public spaces. However, when a PAGFB is also seen as gender transgressive, the violence from cismen takes a very different form. Vasu talked about using the men's entrance in buses:

> It's not comfortable having the men touch you, as they move around and go past you. But then I have not given it much attention, thinking to myself, of course, I am a man. But then if they touch me by mistake in front, then they would guess that I am a woman. If men begin to guess and think like that, it's a danger isn't it? That's my only fear. Otherwise I am not too bothered with men touching me.

Rahul, who passes as male, had this story to share: 'Once I was in bus… this man was sitting next to me, he was gay… and put his hand on my thigh. I moved it. He thought I was a boy. He ran away after that.'

Harassment and conflict over gender and sexuality in public transport has been dealt with by accentuating or permanently modifying appearance or attribute, ignoring or challenging attackers and, if they had it, using their class privilege to circumvent travelling by public transport altogether. When asked, a few respondents said that they would love to hire cabs or to be able to ride and own bikes or cars. Some, though, had specific vehicles in mind, like a BMW X5!

Public Toilets

There seems to be one public site that is unequivocally prickly and contentious. While the police and security forces are allowed a legitimacy to enforce certain 'rules' in public spaces like streets, parks and malls, toilets are where many citizens assume a moral right to question an individual about their gender as well as their right to be there. For many gender-challenging individuals anxiety and apprehension are precursors to a bathroom visit— where their gender must approximate the public perception of either 'man' or 'woman'. Toilets are perhaps one of the most vexed locations in the public area, where one's gender undergoes a minute scrutiny by people at large. For people who challenge their assigned gender, both 'male' and 'female' toilets can become violent places. Accessing bathrooms is problematic not only for people who transgress gender norms, but also for disabled people. Be it in terms of space requirements or other arrangements, non-normative bodies, whether trans* and/or disabled, are routinely invisibilized and marginalized.

We asked respondents about their experiences of using public toilets as well as their thoughts on an ideal toilet system. Some individuals do not use public toilets at all. Prem is scared of using them as two of hir trans* PAGFB friends were publicly beaten in the course of using a women's toilet. Similarly, Arun said, 'I do not use public toilets. I really don't, even in long distance buses…. One, it is dirty, but mainly, I do not want to create a crisis. I drink water, but I can hold.' The practice of 'holding' that Arun referred to seems to be common enough to have earned the moniker 'tranny bladder'—'holding' till one can access a safe toilet or possibly restricting one's intake of liquids.

The decision of which toilet to use can be a challenging one and can depend on the strategies available to the individual. Some respondents feel comfortable using the women's toilet when they are accompanied by an individual who can pass as 'woman'. In such circumstances finding a safe space to pee becomes a privilege. Even some of those who identify as 'woman', but do not manage to fully pass as such, have spoken of being challenged while using women's toilets. Priya, who identifies as 'woman', said, 'I might be mistaken for a boy sometimes, but I just turn around, look at the person, and they figure that I am a girl.' Other individuals use smiles, clothes or their voice to enable them to use women's toilets with more ease.

The problem is often exacerbated for those PAGFB who do not identify as 'woman'. To be able to use women's toilets, not only are they forced into trying to pass as 'women', they also have to face ridicule from others.

Using men's toilets was sometimes a viable option for a few respondents. However, this was also not an easy choice. If the toilet has only urinals, it is problematic. Karthik said, 'I always go to the gents' toilets. If there is only urinal, I will not go. I will control myself.' For those who had the privilege of being able to access restaurants and other such spaces, there were often unisex toilets where no questions are asked and a degree of cleanliness is maintained. For others it was a constant decision to be made. Sunny said, 'I sometimes hesitate, wondering which loo I will feel like going to today. I see how people react and make my choice accordingly.'

Alex, who identifies as 'between transgender and lesbian', said ze never had any difficulty in using men's toilets as long as ze could access one with closed doors:

> It was better than going to the ladies' toilet. I started wearing earrings and going to the women's loo for the last four or five years because changes started coming in my body and I began to feel the need to go to the women's loos.

With age, not only has hir toilet preference changed, ze also feels more confident to challenge the transphobia ze encounters:

> Sometimes they again look at me and I just give them smart answers. Now even at this age people still stare at me. I have had women screaming at me this is a women's toilet, I have to say and yell back can't you see that I am not a guy? It's such a waste of time I would like to ignore [them], but sometimes it's beyond one's endurance.

Since public toilets can be problematic for individuals across a range of gender identities, we asked our respondents for an ideal system. This was not easy due to the various concerns not only for trans* persons but also for 'women' in this patriarchal world. Some respondents believed that it would be best to include toilets for trans* persons along with toilets for men and women. However, there were concerns of being outed or being singled out as a transperson.

Jai said: 'We cannot have specific loos for FTMs as then everyone will know. At the same time, common bathrooms are also not a possibility as I do not want to share common space with men. So I have no answer.' While many of the male-identified respondents felt that unisex toilets were preferable, safety concerns for women were paramount for them. Rahul, who identifies as 'boy', said, 'Unisex toilets won't work. Women's safety is at stake with unisex toilets. I don't think we can forget this fact.' The other consideration was that of hygiene. Alex said, 'I am also quite worried about hygiene. I never sit on the pot. I stand or do the invisible chair. Men's loos are the worst… women's toilets are very clean in comparison.'

Priya added another layer to this discussion:

> A different system of toilets could be that of unisex toilets because I know friends… who have to face discrimination, can't use ladies' toilets…. But yes, sharing toilets with straight men is a concern…. I do not mind sharing toilets with queer men, but I don't feel safe with straight men. I think there should be two toilets, one for men and the other unisex.

The issue of public toilets is a tough one to tackle. Meghana, who identifies as 'androgynous', said, 'Frankly, I feel like it is too unreal. I would rather learn to deal [with it] better and have men learn to pee better, and ideally it would be best to have a set of public toilets [with] many toilets inside and anybody can use it.' At one level, as Juhi pointed out, the issue is about something without categories, but the solution is being sought in terms of categories: 'Such categorization serves only to emphasize gender while possibly marginalizing individuals who are already on the boundaries of gender.'

Queer Couples in the Public Eye

Since 'women' occupy such little public space in any case, they are anyway not really seen in public even with other 'women'. Even when they are seen, strict gender segregation in our society allows for intimate friendships between people of the same gender. Ranjana testified, 'It's not very evident…. It's not as if people can make out that we are partners. So there is not so much awareness about us.'

While Ranjana and her partner passed as women and were invisible as a couple in public spaces, others are not as comfortable. Kanika recounted hir discomfort: 'I used to get very uncomfortable with this girlfriend who would cosy up with me in public spaces and people would stare at us.' So ze would use any excuse to get out from such spaces.

Closeness between persons of the same gender comes under the scanner when there is visible gender transgression. Once again it is the combination of gender and sexuality, and it is the more gender-transgressive person who may be targeted, but the safety of both persons could be called into question. Nidhi recounted an incident in the park with hir girlfriend:

> From the public, in general, we have to bear a lot. They say dirty things, 'Is there a lack of boys that you girls are together?' or 'Come and sleep with me.' One afternoon we sat at the lake and one girl came and sat near us. She edged herself closer and closer to me.

> I was wondering what was happening. Then I saw her make a phone call. After that, suddenly we were surrounded by six to eight boys. They called [my partner] my *maal* [thing or object]. And they threatened her, saying, 'Your girlfriend won't be with you all the time. We will find you and rape you.'

In this instance, because one of the couple was gender transgressive, though clearly a 'woman' in the abuser's eyes, they were targeted. It is this visiblization of transgression, be it related to the way a person 'looks' or 'behaves', particularly when gender and sexuality combine, that can spark hostility and violence.

As in the case of Monu, who faced the wrath of a neighbourhood gang of boys when ze had a relationship with a girl in the same neighbourhood. They came to Monu's house with sticks to beat hir up. 'It had hurt their egos that these are girls, they have affairs with girls, and here we are boys, we are seeing all this, sucking our thumbs and not able to do anything.'

When one of the partners was able to pass in public as a person of the 'opposite' gender, sometimes it was safer for the queer couple. Vimala who is married to a 'man'-identified PAGFB, said, 'When both of us go out now, for many years, we have not had any reaction because he is understood to be a man and I a woman.' Murali, who lives with hir partner in a rented house, was seen as her brother and not as her husband, 'as she is older than me and bigger in size. I tell them she is my sister. Recently, the shopkeeper near our house asked me about her and I said she is my sister. We do not look like husband and wife.' To continue to be accepted and avoid intrusive questions about why there are no children, Murali and hir partner keep up the sibling story.

Brushes with the Police

While queer PAGFB often find refuge in urban centres where gender norms seem to be relatively relaxed, it is not the same for PAGMB. Codes around dress and behaviour for PAGMB are far stricter, so any gender transgressions leave them very vulnerable to harassment and violence from the public and police alike. Also, PAGMB who culturally have more access to public spaces, often have sexual encounters with other PAGMB in these spaces and, hence, are subject to even more violence, especially from the police. This is not true for PAGFB as they do not access public spaces as much; the norms around their gender expression are not as strict; and they do not usually have sexual liaisons or openly cruise for partners in public spaces. As a result the violence they face from the police in the public arena is very different from that faced by PAGMB and may be less common.

Queer PAGFB face police violence mainly when they run away from their homes as a couple because their families seek direct intervention from the state in such situations. When Kamal and his partner ran away, she left her family a note telling them about their relationship. Using this note as proof, Kamal's partner's family lodged a case of kidnapping against him. So the institution of the police, duty-bound to protect the rights of all citizens, found a variety of ways in which to pursue and threaten Kamal with arrest at the behest of his partner's family, even though they were both adults.

One respondent was compelled to run away from her natal family who practically put her under house arrest after a friend outed her relationship with another PAGFB. The two ran away, along with another woman friend. After a failed three-way suicide pact, in which the friend died, the respondent and her partner were imprisoned and interrogated by the police:

> At the age of 21 years, I was arrested and taken to the police station.... The police used foul language and ridiculed me. They asked vulgar questions and showed their power by raising their voices and shouting at me. I did not experience any sexual abuse there, but my partner did.

With PAGFB who are visibly gender transgressive, there have been instances where the police have read them as men. Sandy told us of one such incident: 'I got slapped by a policeman once, in a crowd outside the American embassy and I do not think he realized that I was not a man.'

Significantly, in spite of the fact that many of our respondents faced a lot of violence, they never managed to get police help even when they tried. Neha spoke of a time when she called on the police for assistance when she was lost on a trip. 'The police were very amused.... It was obvious that all the men were drunk and they were making fun of me.'

Vasu tried using the provisions for 'women', but to no avail:

Once, when there was a fight in the house and I was beaten, I went to the police. I was bleeding badly and so I went and complained that my oldest brother beat me. I had gone and submitted a complaint to the Women's Cell.... He wasn't even made to come to the police station. I felt so worthless in front of all of them.

Conclusion

Be it as individuals or with partners or friends who challenge gender norms, the capacity to occupy certain spaces and publicly live as per one's preferred gender is accessible only to a few who have privileges in society. As in every other situation, those marginalized in multiple ways are the worst impacted.

Many of our respondents who moved to cities to escape social norms in their hometowns or be free from the strictures imposed by their families found the anonymity of urban spaces to be empowering, but to a limited extent. Due to the very 'masculine' character of public spaces, most PAGFB do not access them as easily and 'rightfully' as PAGMB. And when they do, all PAGFB face a certain kind of misogynistic hostility and violence. Thus, public spaces remained problematic for our respondents even in the largest of cities, and they faced harassment and violence in buses, toilets, malls and other places.

While gender-segregated spaces have been mandated as safety and convenience measures to ensure equal access for 'women', sometimes even these spaces can be markedly unsafe for gender-transgressive PAGFB. This is because the arrangement stems from a binary approach to gender. For those who do not pass as strictly 'man' or 'woman' such spaces, paradoxically, become sites of harassment. In fact gender-segregated spaces can and have been unsafe for PAGMB as well.

To be able to make a difference to all PAGFB and to those who wish to live lives different from the normative, it is imperative that public spaces are not grounded in the gender binary. They need to be rooted in diversity as well as in gender specificity that is not exclusionary but guided by sensitivity towards all genders, especially in public amenities like transport, toilets, neighbourhoods, streets and parks.

Barriers to public spaces for gender-transgressive people, as for women, disabled persons, working-class people and others variously marginalized have a domino effect as they affect access to obtaining education, employment and healthcare services. The law and order forces entrusted to ensure safe and equal access for all citizens need to safeguard people's rights rather than police their behaviour. It is important that such changes be made both spatially and culturally, as equal and safe access to public space is a basic human right, and is yet another terrain where reductive binaries and heteropatriarchy must be challenged.

9

Intimate Relationships

Given the pervasive homophobia and transphobia, it is astonishing that most queer individuals are able to seek, let alone find, intimate partners. We find the same intensity of romantic connections as everywhere, with the common dream of a future together, cemented by marriage. And yet, along with it we also have many other features that recur persistently and disturbingly in far too many of our respondents' relationship trajectories: the violence of forced marriages; the scars of sexual abuse; not being able to talk about your lover as a lover; not being able to share either your passion or your grief with those around you; suicide or attempted suicide.

For most queer PAGFB, intimate relationships tend to be burdened by an unusual weight of insecurity and mutual dependence, lived, as they are, invisibly, often after leaving natal families and relocating, without social sanction or adequate support structures. They are the one place where a person's gender and sexuality get most deeply affirmed, while the world around is at best unaware of and at worst violent towards these crucial aspects of the self. And because they affirm so much that others deny, they can also become sites of intense trauma when things go wrong.

While the less familiar narratives of their sexual and romantic relationships abound in the same tropes that we encounter freely elsewhere—passion and pleasure, jealousy and heartbreak, highs and lows—there are significant variations on all these themes. An intimate relationship between two women, or a woman and an FTM, or an FTM and a genderqueer person (to cite just a few possibilities) is also a love story that ends up breaking many of the rules, no matter how conventionally it may (seem to) begin.

In this chapter we look at how such relationships played out in the lives of our respondents, at the pressures they faced and the coping mechanisms they found, the joys they recalled and the sorrows they survived, their negotiations around gender, and the varied range of their experiences and articulations of intimacy.

Early Romances

Most respondents did seem to find—or be found by—romantic partners in every likely place and under every unlikely circumstance. The classroom, the workplace, the house next door—all these were common backdrops to their early and later romances, dalliances as well as long-term bonds. Relationships in most of these spaces happened very early despite the lack of openness or acceptance. Respondents lived their intimacies in secret, or faced ridicule and punishment.

The subjects of early crushes were almost always older people—seniors in school or teachers in college, neighbours or distant stars from the world of movies, sport or music. Many public figures are used to a certain amount of adulation, but how does a woman of the world react when it is a friend's 'daughter' rather than son who shows a more-than-ordinary interest? Fortunately for Sunny, the older woman ze fancied was neither outraged nor horrified. Instead, she accepted the 14-year-old's request for 'friendship' and helped Sunny figure hirself out over the next few years:

> I used to call her at night and chat a lot.... I used to cycle to her house and sit outside.... I would leave flowers at her doorstep.... I told her about my trauma at school because I had to wear the girls' school uniform. But then [she] told me something very important... 'You are actually a boy but the school authorities do not have any brains so you are just playing a role there. You are wearing a skirt because they have made you play that role.'... This made me feel

> okay. I wear my skirt and I am playing a role, but when I come home it's the real me.

It was this woman, 20 years older than Sunny and a good friend of hir mother's, who laughingly made a pact to marry Sunny if she was still single when ze turned 18, gave hir an article to read about sex-change surgery and eventually persuaded hir to get in touch with a queer support group.

Others were not as fortunate. One respondent was 8 when ze and hir closest friend, a slightly older girl who worked in the former's home, fell in love with each other:

> When we got into a relationship, no one knew. We would have sex and no one knew. We lived in our own world. We planned to get married…. She would wear a sari and I wanted to wear a skirt…. At some point we were both so inseparable that my grandmother teased me that I had no sense of caste because I ate with her. She was more worried about the eating because she had no idea of the other things that were happening!

The older girl, a bright student who intended to be a doctor, hanged herself after her father stopped her education, sexually abused her and tried to force her to marry her older sister's husband. Our respondent was 16 by then; it was more than 10 years before ze could even begin to process the trauma: 'I could not speak to anyone. Everyone knew that I had lost a close friend but… [they] had not seen any other two people like this.'

The fact that this story was about very young people only points to the paradox of how 'natural', in a sense, their intimacy was, while being utterly non-normative in ways that were clear even to them even then. Still, they were able to escape detection for years because a sexual relationship between them was unimaginable to others. While not all such intimacies between 'girls' manage to evade scrutiny or censure, it is interesting to speculate that had the older partner been a boy, the inseparable twosome might have been wrenched apart much sooner.

At the same time for our more gender-transgressive respondents looking different helped get a lot of attention from other PAGFB, especially in the sports arena. Aditi, who, like several others, met her partner on the playing fields, said:

> [Since my] college days, because I was a tomboy and I was famous in sports, girls were attracted to me.... But there was one girl... whom I liked and got attracted to.... I used to coach her [in] kabaddi. So we became friends and our relationship grew. We were together for seven to eight years. Now she told me last year that she wants to marry.... I know this boy because I used to meet him now and then with her, but I never thought that there was anything between them.

Aditi's recollections of being popular and being pursued by several girls because she was good at sports were echoed by other respondents, and so was her experience of a very specific type of betrayal: that of being left by a girlfriend or woman-identified lover for a 'boy' or a 'man'. The latter phenomenon looms large in the lives of queer PAGFB, especially (but not only) those who are gender non-conforming. For many, it goes back to early adolescence.

Kanika recalled hir interactions with a girl in hir school, an admired senior:

> She told me to come to her house and she wanted to show me something. I was deeply in love with her, so I went. It was dark [inside]... and she suddenly kissed me. I was shocked, but I liked it. This was my first kiss. I felt she was also feeling the same way I [felt]. But after that came the boyfriend.... Now I realize that she was experimenting with me.... I was giving her the attention and she liked it. And I got hurt.

Sunny had a clear analysis of just what was going on in hir first romance at the age of 14 with a girl in hir class:

> Things ended badly with [her], she got married. Her father was a real dog, he kept a strict watch on her—no TV, no going out, he would pick up and drop her from school. That is when I realized that [she] did not have any access to boys and that is why she was with me. I was her best male option.

When Sumit's partner left hir to marry a cisman, it echoed a pattern from hir college days:

> Many girls used to come closer to me then. I used to think that they [were] coming to me because they [were] attracted to me. Now I think I was wrong. They were not able to get closer to men and so they were coming to me.... The girls were coming to try out physical relationships, I just kept falling in love.

Of course, it wasn't all one-way, with mainly heterosexual young women pursuing boyish-looking queer PAGFB (not all of whom, then or later, identified as men). With the arrival of puberty, everyone is busy chasing someone or more than one. A good number of our respondents recalled their multiple flirtations and early sexual relationships. Sam, Jai and Santosh, all of whom identify as 'man', pursued—and slept with—plenty of girls. Among those we have categorized as 'others', Prem had a relationship with a classmate in school, while Sunny had very intense crushes at the age of 11 and then again at 14. And among the 'woman'-identified respondents, Tuli had relationships with other PAGFB while still very young, while Neha and Jamuna had PAGMB partners in their early teens.

The list is not exhaustive, only indicative of how desire, like water, always seeks and often finds its way. It is what comes later that makes all the difference.

Getting Married

While some of the people we met *were* consciously trying to invent new ways of living, a majority of our respondents—whether by default or by conscious emulation—tended to follow the available heteronormative scripts for intimate relationships. Inevitably, these scripts had to be rewritten or abandoned, but they were often tried. A major plot point in these scripts is, of course, marriage.

As many as 10 of our respondents performed some kind of symbolic act or ceremony with their PAGFB partners as a way of mutually affirming their relationship. For some it was simply an act of love; for others a desperate bid to try and bind what was coming apart; for yet others an attempt to stave off forced marriage to cismen. But it was always meant as a talisman that would protect the relationship in some way, keep the lovers from being separated, beat the odds that were weighted against them.

It was very rarely that they managed to succeed. Kamal grew up in a middle-class farming family. When he and his partner ran away to get married and the latter's father filed a case of kidnapping against him, the whole business escalated and the couple found themselves at the centre of a media circus, being questioned by a horde of mainly hostile TV journalists. All through the ensuing crisis, Kamal's sister and brother-in-law were supportive, and soon his parents came around as well. Even as religious bodies continued to pass the buck, trying to rule on whether this runaway marriage—performed by a *pujari* (Hindu priest) with all the proper rituals at one of the holiest of holy temples in the region—could be considered valid, Kamal described how his parents upheld the union through other customs:

> In our ST culture, [a married couple has] to do a puja to Shivam. My parents took us both to... the temple and did the puja.... [My partner] is fully integrated into this community. [She] had to perform a puja to be accepted.

For almost everyone else, their marriages were a far cry from the socially sanctioned and celebrated unions between ciswomen and cismen. Performed in secret, usually without witnesses, they neither enabled the couple to live together openly nor could they serve as a guarantee against one or both partners being forced into marriages with cismen. Six of the 10 respondents who married their PAGFB partners were no longer with those people at the time of the interviews. Some had seen their partners forced into marriages with cismen that they were powerless to prevent.

Sumit and hir partner had a 12-year relationship and it was at her behest that they went to a temple and secretly got married.

Though Sumit's sisters did not know this, they affectionately referred to hir partner as hir wife. Yet, for all the good-humoured teasing, nobody really saw it for the intimate sexual and romantic relationship it was. Sumit's non-normative gender was completely accepted by both hir own family and hir partner's; everybody treated hir as the boy ze considered hirself to be, but hir sexuality was conveniently glossed over—a painful paradox that many respondents describe. This obliviousness made it perfectly possible for hir partner's parents not only to arrange their daughter's marriage elsewhere, but also, in all innocence, to invite Sumit. Ze did not go. This is hir account of how hir lover broke the news to hir, and the aftermath:

> So one day then she said, 'Come to my college to meet me.' For a few days, I [had been] noticing a change in her. I felt that she always was under pressure from many people in her extended family... So when I went to [her] college, she just said, 'I will be better off without you. My life will be better, so you leave me.' When she said this, I agreed and left. [Since] that day... in the last two and a half years, neither of us has called or met.... [I] have heard that she catches the bus [across the street] from my house, but I have not seen her.... I did not want to talk.... I could have talked to people in [the support group] also, but I chose to keep quiet.... Maybe I would have liked someone to at least find out why she left in the way that she did.

Here, we have an almost classic example of an intimate relationship that is lived in silence and ends in silence. Others broke up after they came to support groups, apparently for the usual sorts of reasons: differences among themselves or partners getting involved with someone else. Yet, the 'usual reasons' may not be comparable with what happens in socially sanctioned partnerships because the pressures are very different for those who are suddenly cut off from families and other traditional support systems, dislocated geographically, economically at a disadvantage and plunged into the hothouse environments of small new communities with evolving lifestyles and values that could be destabilizing at first. However liberating, for instance, queer and feminist critiques of marriage and of monogamy might be for some, or in the long run, they may well create personal or relational crises for many who till then have never even met other people like themselves.

Jai had already been part of a traumatic suicide pact with a girlfriend, who died while he survived. Later, when Jai fell in love again and eloped with his new girlfriend, it is not surprising that he should have wanted to 'marry' her again and again, 'some four or five times within three months, and since the parents did not know, they thought we were good friends going to the temple.... We would go to the temple and take off the *thali* [necklace that is a marker of marriage worn by women of some communities] and tie it again. Love is mental!' This love and this marriage crumbled very soon after the runaways arrived in a new place:

> I found out that [my partner] was having a relationship with [someone else]. I confronted her and she said that it was her choice and she could do what she wanted and had not written and given to me that she would be with me for life. This was shocking for me then as I felt that we had gone through so much and I thought one could have only one relationship.... We had a crisis meeting... and [my partner] clearly said that she... did not really love me but had used me to get out of the family.

Ironically, it was after one such crisis of infidelity that Prem felt that marriage would be a magic solution:

> One day in the shelter I got a call from [a community member] who was screaming at me that you have come here and spoilt my life.... I did not understand what this was all about.... [My partner] said that she and [the caller's partner] were having a relationship.... Then we all sat and spoke about it and sorted it between us. Next week I decided that we needed to get married.

That is a familiar part of the familiar script—love equals marriage equals monogamy. Neel distinguished between going through a symbolic ceremony and actually being married by making the marriage and monogamy connection clearly:

> I am not in that kind of a marriage—that is, heterosexual marriage. We are not married, but we decided to live together and did a *pottu* [kumkum bindi], [we] both put [it] for each other. She is a great believer. The decision to marry was hers.... Marriage is a positive thing for me. I had not wanted any other relationship, because in [the support group, people have] multiple relationships.... And I am afraid of all this.

For some of our respondents, marriage was premised entirely on its social approval and legal recognition. Roma, a 'woman', said, 'I have not even considered being married to a woman because marriage to women is not legal. It would be nice though.' Sandy foregrounded practical considerations when ze explained:

> My girlfriend even suggested that we go to some other country and get married there. She wants this because of legal protection.... Both our fathers are very vengeful men and God forbid if something happens to one of us in our young age, then they are unfortunately among our legal heirs. The law recognizes our fathers, mothers, sisters as legal heirs, but not our partners.

Some saw marriage as possible and desirable only after they had bodies that matched their gender, but Rahul spoke for many FTMs and transmen when he said, 'She should understand my life and think of it as a normal thing. There should be no comparisons. It is difficult to find such a woman. If I find such a person, I would definitely like to marry her.' Rahul saw his relationship as a heterosexual relationship and expected his partner to be a straight woman.

Being Together

Even when queer people are trying to redefine their relationships, the blueprints of how sexual intimacies are lived are very heteronormative. In the face of such dominant role models, a valid question that raises its head is: how do two people, both assigned gender female at birth, identifying with varied gender identities, apply notions of femininity and masculinity to their relationship? How do they negotiate prescribed gender roles and chosen gender identities within their intimate spaces?

Not many of our respondents had had many long-term relationships. There were a few, however, who had been together long enough with present or previous partners to be able to reflect on negotiating gender roles and other aspects of a shared life, whether lived together under the same roof or not. Anand fondly recalled of one of his relationships: 'Around the house, minor plumbing jobs would come to me and cooking was her thing, making the bed was her thing—I used to help, of course. All these things were unsaid. Buying stuff from the market was my thing.' He was happy doing housework, except for the cooking, as he had a strong aversion to this gendered task. He said that while he would wish his partner to give up her job if one of them had to in order to bring up a child, he would accept her choosing not to have a child. He also said he wouldn't expect his partner to look after his natal family members if they were ill. And yet, he insisted he wanted to be a 'stereotypical male'. Thus, for him, an open-minded, non-interfering, caring husband fit the mould of 'stereotypical'.

Neel had a similar, apparently contradictory, notion. She considered herself head of the household and was the one who earned, while her partner did most of the housework. Yet, she said there was no division of labour and that they shared the work as much as possible. Both took decisions jointly about spending money.

For Tuli, who identifies as 'woman', gender played out in an unexpected way in the space of her intimate relationships. She spoke about how in each of these she was almost forced to enact the role of a husband or boyfriend. While she may have been a somewhat reluctant 'husband', she also seemed to have liked aspects of the role. 'I started giving half my earnings to my girlfriend and half to my mother. Even after my girlfriend started working, I was the one who always had to pay.... She'd give me the money before we went out.' Tuli also had a relationship with a transgender woman, who saw Tuli as her husband although while Tuli herself did not think of their attachment as a romantic/ sexual relationship. But when the woman adopted a child and she asked Tuli to be the co-parent, Tuli officially adopted the boy. So she began to spend part of her time with this family of hers—a 'wife' and a child for whom she is a 'father figure'.

Ranjana and her partner had been together for 14 years at the time of the interview, after having had to run away to another city right after they graduated:

> We don't have a fixed idea of masculine, feminine, we really don't. It's other people's perception which sees her as masculine and me as feminine. But if you look at housework, she is a perfect woman. She keeps the house clean and tidy, cooking food.... But there is no clear thing of 'this work is yours and that work is mine'.....
> I also travel a lot. Also she loves me so much that she doesn't let me work. So patriarchal it sounds, na? So many men say, na, that my wife loves me so much that she doesn't let me work.... Sometimes I worry, so much of love, emotional dependency. I feel scared for her.... Head of the household—we both are, we both take decisions. It's really shared. It's not easy to be democratic. We have to convince each other. You can't say who dominates, sometimes she does, sometimes I do. I do trust our wisdom.

Other respondents echoed this sense of shared 'wisdom'. It might indicate their settling with greater ease into gendered roles or renegotiating them as they go along. It might reflect how their relationships enabled self-acceptance as well as mutual understanding.

Vimala had been in a long-term relationship with her PAGFB partner who identifies so completely as a man that he will not consider the term 'transgender' for himself. She spoke of their mutual understanding that allowed her to affirm his gender, while giving both enough leeway to set aside certain conventions:

> When I do household work, it is not neat and things don't become clean. So it's he who does the cleaning, cooking. I work outside. And if I am tired, my partner does all the work. And when I am well, he asks me to make him a cup of tea. So these things are done with mutual concern and consideration.

While Vimala and her partner had arrived at a zone of mutual consideration, comfort and security, others like Sandhya and hir partner were still grappling with the daily business of living together, struggling to redefine their selves and each other in the light of still new notions about gender and feminism. Ze sensed a host of contradictions in how hir 'woman'-identified partner saw hir:

> At one level she considers me to be her husband. But [she once]… said that we are living together as friends because we do not agree with this notion of a husband…. [Yet] she says, 'You go out and earn money… my dream is to look after the house, cooking, cleaning. Looking after our child, going out with you.'

Geeta, looking back on a relationship, reflected that while she and her partner divided housework according to what each one liked, there still were things that might constitute gendered roles:

> While I lived with [my partner], I think our roles were pretty gendered. I didn't like it, but I didn't push enough. I felt that I had much more of the mental clutter between the two of us. I think it's a gendered thing about who has the mental clutter in the relationship…. Nurturing was also gendered…. I think there was much more caring and nurturing that was being done by me. I think I went into a virtual mother mode. But this is also about gender and sexuality. I would never do all of this with a man. There is a lesbian urge to merge…. Drawing boundaries becomes difficult.

Manjula echoed this when ze said, 'I think the problem is that we do not know how to negotiate our independent lives while living together. This is the problem with all lesbian couples.'

The 'problem' was also acknowledged in Ujwala's description of how she and her live-in partner of 10 years had worked around it:

> We do a lot of hanging out together, but we also hang out separately and there is a set of friends that she may never hang out with. They can come over, we will have a great time, but if I am going out to meet them, she doesn't have to come, or when she is going out with her friends, I don't feel that I have to go out with her. So we keep our friends apart.... But now we are all growing old together and some of my friends are now her friends, separate of me. We have struggled with these negotiations of not being joined at the hip.

Not only were our respondents negotiating gendering of roles and playing around with them in a way that usually there was no stereotypical definition of one kind or the other, they also seemed to be redefining being together.

Monogamy and Non-Monogamy

Between the stereotypical 'joined at the hip' relationships of lesbians and the monogamous 'one partner for life' archetype of marriage, it is interesting to see how much our respondents spoke about monogamy and non-monogamy—their negotiations around it, their considered responses and their lived experiences. For some respondents monogamy in their intimate relationships was non-negotiable; for others it was an issue of mutual consent and an area of constant negotiation; for others still these were shifting spaces. Some people had a political take, others an emotional and experiential stake, and several had both.

In fact, this seems to be an active discussion in queer political spaces, especially those that are feminist. Not having any existing role models to follow, with there being no active demand for marriage, monogamy as an idea seems to hang more loosely here than it does in normative heterosexual married relationships. In a microcosm, non-monogamous relationships are almost seen as the 'queer' way to be, the more radical choice. And maybe this is what Ujwala was reacting to when she said, 'My understandings are changing and I am okay saying I am confused. For example, if you are monogamous, then I don't have an issue with that. I will not buy into the argument that non-monogamy is important to be queer.'

That was her considered view, refusing to privilege one way of relating over another. On the personal front she described a 'very, very heady' period of 'being in multiple relationships with all and sundry men, and being in that novel position about whether this one or that one today, and they all claiming to be in love with me'. Now, having been with a woman partner for 10 years, she admitted, 'I think more now about one-night stands. But then, is it worth the while now that I am in a relationship?'

Ranjana agreed with Ujwala in that non-monogamy could be too much to take on, and although definitely attracted to others, she respected her partner's wishes in the matter:

> I do know that I am bisexual. I have had crushes on men even after getting into a relationship with her. But to her, it's just me. Sometimes I feel proud and sometimes I want to tear my hair…. Non-monogamy has not been a consideration for her, for me it has been. But I understand that it is a tough one. Relationships are so complex. As it is there is so much on your plate, how much can we deal with?

Manjula, also guided by hir trans* PAGFB partner's wishes, found hirself in a conundrum:

> Initially, [my partner] was [all] for monogamy and I was very non-monogamous. I changed a lot for him because he wanted monogamy. Suddenly, one fine day, I realized that he is non-monogamous and I had changed and I am not able to change back…. At this point of time, I want some consistent belonging to one person, not get lost.

This sense of not belonging affects many queer people, estranged as they often are from their families and forced to keep a low profile in other spaces. In such circumstances many look to their intimate partners to be anchors amidst all the instability.

A few of our respondents who were in relationships that had lasted for years and been mutually affirming spoke of monogamy as a given, such as Jharna: 'In literature, there's a phrase, *eknishth prem* [a committed love], and it's a phrase I like very much and believe that's how love should be.' Then, there are those like Priya, who said, despite the recent break-up of an abusive monogamous relationship, 'I think multiple relationships are stupidity.'

Thus, for some, monogamy was their only choice, but for most of the aforementioned respondents and for others (as we shall see), it was a much thought out and considered choice, and definitely not a given. Many spoke of not wanting that one grand exclusive relationship. For them non-monogamy had always been, or had become, the preferred option. Neha, who wanted to have 'lots of' relationships, when asked if it is important to have love and intimacy to have sex, said, 'Not at all.' Sam envisaged a relationship with a partner who 'can stay with her husband and with me also'. Alpana said, 'I would describe myself as polyamorous. I don't believe in a lifetime commitment—I've been there, I've seen it, but I'm more comfortable with multiple relationships. I don't find it unethical.' Meghana spoke of how 'either you or your partner can go through phases where they are not feeling like having sex…. I need to have some other options so the burden to satisfy desire need not rest solely with one individual.'

Non-monogamy might mean sex without emotional attachment for some respondents; for others it might include what Chandni listed as 'one-night stands, friends with benefits, scenes, long-term friends with benefits'; for others still non-monogamy too might be premised on what Hemlata called '*apnapan*' (feeling of closeness), without which she cannot imagine being in any sexual relationship.

Many people also shared their experiments with non-monogamy. These were usually with (eventual if not initial) awareness and consent from all partners, but, of course, there are also covert relationships. One respondent said he had always been in multiple relationships earlier, but could access that sort of space only very rarely now; it was not something he could even discuss with his live-in partner of many years. He emphasized that he wanted to be with her always, but when she misunderstood him or fought with him, he sought others for comfort.

Others like Kirti managed to have more than one relationship more easily even though he lived in a rural area, isolated from a so-called queer community. Kirti had been in an intense long-term relationship with one woman, a neighbour, for two decades when he began an affair with another woman who had just gone through a divorce and returned to her parents' home in the village. Kirti's first partner was deeply hurt and refused to talk to him for a whole year, during which the second partner moved in with him. 'A person gets bored eating the same food every day, it is nice to taste something different sometimes,' said Kirti, but went on to speak of his emotional distress when his first partner began to ignore him. Eventually they made up. While the jealousies and difficulties continued, Kirti not only managed to keep both relationships going, he mentioned a more recent third one:

> I went to her place once for some occasion. The men and women sit separately. She served me tea and sat down next to me, stuck to me…. I told her that I liked her… and she told me right away that she felt the same way too…. I was grateful to God that she also turned out to be a lesbian…. Now I have these three partners…. [My second partner] knows about my third partner. She doesn't care…. But [my first partner] is dangerous. I don't let her come to know all these things.

Kirti continued to live as he wanted, although it created trouble for his various loves. Simran, who calls herself bisexual, on the other hand, took a clear stand when her pact was not honoured. When she went abroad for a few months, she had a steady boyfriend, but recognizing that both of them might want to be with other people, they set certain limits:

> Our deal was that I would not sleep with any other man, I could sleep with women. And for him, we had said that he could sleep with

some women but not have anything emotional, and the moment I came back, everything else would end.... But when I came back, this did not happen and at the same time I was being lied to. I said I draw my line here... and I dumped him.

Jamuna said that the logic of falling in love with someone and being in a relationship with them does not translate necessarily to sleeping only with them. 'If I want to sleep with someone else, why wouldn't I? Because she doesn't own me and all that.' But then, she went on to nuance her position and describe just what sort of non-monogamy worked for her:

I have never been in two regular sexual relationships simultaneously. One sexual relationship and a lot of flings or one-night stands is okay. Or fuck buddies is okay. But the concern of a regular sexual thing is that it may become [another] relationship and I don't think I want that since I am also a very romantic fool type person and I love focusing on the person in a big way. So multiple sexual relationships—one regular and one or more fling-y [is fine]. Almost all of my partners have also been in a similar set-up.

For Kavi the 'one or more fling-y' attempt did not work out:

I made friends with a girl. I told her that I was a lesbian. I flirted with her. I didn't intend to be in a relationship with her. I used to share this information about flirting with [my partner]. On a rainy day [this other woman] asked me to accompany her, we got completely drenched.... I smooched her intensely.... It was four months of friendship and three months of a relationship with love. When I left this relationship, I felt hurt and pain. [My partner] said that she couldn't trust me any more.... We are homonormative unfortunately.

Clearly, despite the heteronormative or homonormative notions that ruled many people's ideas of love and intimacy, a fairly large number of our respondents had practised or wished to practise non-monogamy while being in a primary relationship with one person. Saumya recalled how, in her 20s, she 'felt like experimenting'. She got involved with a woman colleague, which took a toll on her existing relationship:

> I was sexually with other women as well. Even after we had broken up, I was still waiting for her. In my head I never wanted to be with somebody else. Emotionally, I never gave myself to anyone else. But she had moved on. Eventually I too decided to move on and got involved with another person. So I am in a confusing space right now.

Given these difficulties, it was not surprising to hear Geeta say, 'I want something boring and stable. I have had too much of experimentation. I just want an uncomplicated old age.'

Arun talked of the complex negotiations that happen over a period of time in a relationship. Ze had been in another relationship for a year and a half and said:

> I have been trying to manage both the relationships, but now I feel that I cannot. With [my long-term partner] I feel there have been a lot of problems over the last three years.... I asked her to seek counselling so that she could deal with her emotions since I did not think that I could deal with [them].... But it became... the reason you are not taking it any more [because] you are in another relationship.... This does not mean that I have stopped trying to take it all because of the other relationship, it is that I had been trying all these days and I cannot.

Although all the tropes of a romantic relationship are imagined and fantasized about, none of them seem to work in these 'unconventional' relationships. Marriage is used to get social recognition and demand fidelity, but that does not work in the absence of a support network and community that provides such recognition. Roles go topsy-turvy because identities are not linearly defined— masculine and feminine are turned around in multiple ways. A sense of 'belonging' to one's romantic partner is what some pursue; others adventurously follow their hearts without a care.

We find that nowhere do gender and sexuality come together so completely as in the equation with an intimate partner.

Especially for gender non-conforming PAGFB, this very private space allows for a fuller expression and exploration of one's gender than, say, public spaces do. Depending on the extent to which such expression is encouraged or thwarted by a partner, depending also on how far people are able to negotiate gendered roles and expectations, whether in the sexual sphere or around household tasks while living together, these relationships can provide the greatest affirmation or inflict the deepest hurt.

Based on the interviews, we kept coming back to the question of what is it that these relationships really give people? What does breaking out of moulds really mean? These were spaces where some were able to explore new ways of being; where new languages were being created; where some were also lucky to have, even in fairly adverse circumstances, the possibilities of finding their own comforts with their genders.

Gender Affirmation

Some respondents traced how their sense of self, of what they were or were not comfortable with in a relationship, as well as the way they related to partners had evolved through a series of intimacies over time.

Monu had been in very butch–femme type of relationships while growing up, and had also faced a lot of flak for hir gender from her extended family and neighbours. Then ze met hir current partner, who was extremely supportive. She took on people who made snide comments about Monu, whether it was a nosy neighbour or strangers in public places. Monu said, 'She has made things very smooth for me.' Hir partner was so affirmative of Monu's gender that ze was even able to help out at the beauty parlour she runs, something ze said ze could not ever have imagined doing. Monu credited her with many changes for the better in hir life, ranging from hir own greater ease with hir body and gender to the way they settle fights without violence.

Like Monu's partner, Vimala's negotiation of her partner's gender within their relationship was affirmative, albeit not untroubled. She spoke of her own feminism, and her relationship with her PAGFB partner who identifies as a 'man', in a nuanced manner:

> Apart from considering himself a man, my partner used to be someone who abides by conventional societal man–woman relations.... He believed in marriage and wanted to marry his partner, and see ourselves as husband and wife.... My politics has changed since then, and so I am now prepared to call him a partner, not a husband. But that is my matter and not of the person I am with.... He is still within that system.... But it is as though I am keeping things to myself, in a way cheating myself and telling the world that I married a man.... That is the struggle with which I am living and am trying to explain to you.... In other spaces I will not explain, I will just say that he is my husband and... male.

Vimala did a careful and aware negotiation of her cisgendered privilege:

> There are many things he may not get, as he is biologically not a man, so this is a space for me to attain for him those things he desires.... But since I am the only one with whom he has a relationship, I have to compromise a bit. Although I don't see it as a compromise.

This recognition of cisgendered privilege in intimacies is essential because even though a relationship appears to be like the 'usual man–woman' one, the vulnerability that the gender-transgressing partner feels changes the mutual gender dynamics considerably. Heteronormative power equations get turned around, turning ideas of masculinity and femininity on their head.

'Other'-identified Sandy spoke of a former partner's instinctive understanding of hir gender. They shared not just a house, but also their politics and activism, so that there was a lot more leeway—Sandy even felt safe being 'feminine'—than in another relationship that was far more gendered and in which ze eventually found hirself reproached for being un-feminist in ways that felt unfair and violent. Ze brought to hir current relationship a memory of that conflict and a reluctance to have to explain hirself, whether it was about not wanting to wear a certain type of bra or not appreciating 'feminizing' endearments:

> I... have been fighting my gender battle all these years and do not want to do this at home. I do not want to educate someone, I want them to learn and find out. But she wants me to teach her and I do not want to do that.... The onus cannot be on me.

Yet hir present relationship gave Sandy the opportunity to admire how hir partner, who chooses not to call herself political is, as an 'openly gay woman', lived a life where she and other queer friends supported each other materially and emotionally, and where every choice was, ultimately, political.

Juhi's narrative of hir intimate relationships also traced a growth curve, both in terms of arriving at a greater comfort with hirself and dealing with interpersonal issues. At 16, she did, and was expected to do, all that a boyfriend does for a girlfriend— buying movie tickets or carrying her stuff for her or driving her around—without any articulation of the gendered dynamics. This relationship eventually broke up. Ze said in retrospect that the girlfriend was 'very straight, so it wouldn't have gone anywhere'. Hir second relationship, with a fellow postgraduate student, had the intensity of something both partners defined as 'love, pure love.... "Lesbian" was not used at all. It wasn't even "women who love women". It was more "soulmate" types.' Unlike hir first relationship where, for Juhi, sex did not include undressing, and there was a certain amount of awkwardness on both sides, this one was uninhibited. 'Since love was happening, the mundane issue of bodies and how you feel about your body, you transcend them.'

Hir partner, divorced when they met, eventually remarried and moved away. This felt like a 'huge rejection' and Juhi's next relationship happened soon after: 'It was a serious rebound... a married woman with an 8-month-old child'. The relationship was marked by a sense of extreme stigma, with the husband insinuating that Juhi was responsible for his wife's going 'off her head'. Things were exacerbated by the woman's guilt about keeping the child away from his father. It all felt extremely oppressive and closeted. In this relationship that lasted eight years, two things stood out in retrospect. First, that despite many vexations, it allowed for a lot of mutual growth; second, that both people believed strongly in the importance of communication. Juhi spoke of hir much greater 'comfort with my own gender, gender expression'. Hir partner encouraged Juhi to explore hir love of cooking, be more experimental with clothes by wearing more prints and colours, and reassured an unconfident Juhi that ze would be good at caring for a place of hir own.

Being able to talk things through, being able to process your own feelings and understand your partner's opens the possibility of space for negotiation and may make it easier to come to terms with aspects of the relationship—or of the partner's behaviour—that are troubling. Often, however, the power differentials between the partners made the conversations, discussions and negotiations that much more difficult.

Shifting Power Dynamics

Two things are abundantly clear. First, a conventional feminist reading of assigning less power to the 'woman' and more to the 'man' may not make much sense when the gender equation is more complex than that between a cisman and ciswoman. Second, there are no one-size-fits-all answers to any of the preceding questions because all interpersonal dynamics are also influenced by factors such as age, location, caste, class, ability, mental health issues, support or violence from family members and others, and—not least—the fact that individuals change and evolve within relationships, or from one relationship to another.

Age

While not many spoke of partners who were significantly younger or older than themselves, there were some intimate relationships in which age differences played a major role. Sometimes an older partner might use their age to assert authority; a much younger lover might experience anxiety about an all-too-likely future without the other; or both partners might have to deal with disapproval from familiars and misreading by strangers. In other words, many of the same issues that might crop up in less queer contexts, and yet with the twist of age added to all the other transgressions, of other norms.

Our respondents spoke of early crushes, sometimes on older people. Not all of them turned into relationships, of course, but Jharna's did. She was attracted from a very early age to her teacher, who was 30 years older. They went on meeting for 11 years:

> I used to write poetry.... It was the romance of my life, yaar!... We used to enjoy being with each other, though there was a big gap in our ages, in our cultures. She was a Jain, and believe it or not, I didn't even have a physical relationship with her, I couldn't even think of it, I was a child of 12. But one day she told me that she didn't like onions and from that day I stopped eating onions... it was my favourite.

It was only after Jharna left home to escape being forced into marriage that they became physically intimate, and at the time of the interview, their relationship was over two decades old. However, her partner remained closeted and Jharna still wavered between understanding this and calling her a 'very rigid person' and a coward. There was also a deeper complaint in the midst of Jharna's devotion on the lack of support when she left home:

> I had no guidance.... [My partner] could have guided me... but she was always too busy looking after herself.... I'm not complaining, but just telling you—sometimes commitment is not equal; an older person can also use the other person.

Jharna's worries about her partner's health were compounded by anxiety about her own future: 'I'm with the teacher till her last breath, but my life is still ahead of me, I have to live my life.'

Other Social Differences

Manjula talked of how ze and hir genderqueer partner, who was 11 years younger than hir, had to work through differences of age as well as class. 'I also had to negotiate with my parents not about his gender, but about his being poor and uneducated. Once my mother said that he is not even an SSLC [Secondary School Leaving Certificate] pass and you are a degree holder, how can this work?' And ze spoke of the pain of losing friends when hir partner 'could not adjust' to them or they to hir. Some friends simply refused to recognize the relationship, which sounds like homophobia at work, but with others the class difference seemed to have been the main impediment.

Manjula was open about hir relationship with hir friends, but Alex felt it was an ex-partner's upper-class status that caused her to keep their relationship under wraps.

> I was really into her… She belongs to a very settled, big [dominant-caste] family…. My whole family and friends knew that she was my girlfriend, but from her side, not a single friend knew about me, so there was also a class issue.

On the other hand, class also enabled choice in multiple ways, not just for individuals, but for many couples in intimate relationships too, so that when they were marginalized by their gender or sexuality, their class privilege—or that of their partner's—became the factor that pulled them back from the brink. This was especially so for those who lack supportive families or who had not found—and reached—one of the handful of queer support groups.

Sandy's partner, who was almost a decade older than hir and also more settled financially, provided the stability that ze needed and the space to deal with a tumultuous childhood and early years of adulthood:

> Today, when I say that she also brought me up, it is not about supporting me while I finished my education and paying my fees. It

was also just [her] telling me to calm down.... She was so calm and it was exactly what I needed.

Thus, in a sense, it seems that social privileges that accrue to one partner can work both ways. At times it was used against the other partner and left them even more vulnerable. However, others, who used this in a more aware manner, became the much needed support to create a space for both.

Gender

It is perhaps wishful thinking to expect PAGFB who identify as men to necessarily understand or act out masculinity in less conventional ways than most cismen. And yet, the kind of power that many cismen take for granted is simply not available to queer PAGFB who identify as men or as other than women. Hence, it usually falls to intimate partners to provide the much-needed affirmation and understanding, which puts an immense burden on relationships. Given the lack of significant support structures, many queer PAGFB are additionally traumatized when partners question or disrespect or fail to affirm their gender.

Santosh continued to encounter this kind of violence from his partner of six years:

My friends are FTM, but when [my partner] refers to me as a girl in front of them, or even when we're alone, it's very difficult to hear and gives me a lot of tension.... Sometimes when [she] says these things to me, I think she wouldn't be saying this if I was a man; it's because I'm born this way that she's saying them to me. Once, we were coming home, and on the way [we] had a fight [and] she called me a girl. I tied a rope from the fan and wanted to hang myself, but others... saw me and got help.

Sometimes the other person may not even realize what they are doing. One respondent said rather tellingly:

I was in two relationships with transgender men and both were abusive. The sex factor attracted me to them.... The person was not

> [operated upon]. So, of course, there were breasts and vagina....
> The second transgender person I was seeing was patriarchal, but
> well, he had great boobs.

While she recognized their abuse as located in their masculinity,
she was not able to see that her articulation of being attracted to
their body parts, which might be discomforting to them, could
also be some kind of abuse of cisgendered power.

A woman seeking pleasure from her FTM partners' female
body parts during sex subtracts more than a little power from
the 'patriarchal' side of the equation. There is clearly more than
one axis of power here; more than one way to read what is
happening.

Bhargavi spoke of the problems that ze and hir former
partner, a trans* PAGFB, had because of hir friendships with
another trans* PAGFB:

> [My partner] put many conditions and ordered me around. I did
> not like his behaviour. He behaved like a man, no differently from
> my husband.... When I got home from work [he] used to check all
> my calls.... [He] locked me in the bathroom for a long time, saying I
> should not go shopping with [the other person].... I was very upset
> for being falsely accused, and in my anger told [the other person]
> that I loved him. [My partner] got violent on hearing this and hit
> his own head with an empty beer bottle.

Possessiveness was part of what caused Bhargavi and hir partner
to break up. The other big part was gendered behaviour. Having
been married to a cisman and having been in relationships with
two trans* PAGFB as well as with a woman, Bhargavi offered a
comparison:

> [One trans* partner] liked doing housework and we did it
> together.... Now, with [the woman partner] there are no rules.
> Whoever reaches home first does the work. Often we share the
> housework.... With my husband I took it for granted that it was my
> work. When [the other PAGFB partner] used to order me around,
> I did not like it.

It is interesting that Bhargavi had different expectations from hir 'male'-identified PAGFB partners than ze did from hir husband. Was there a refusal to see the former as male in quite the same way or was there an implicit feminist politics at work here, a redefining of masculinity—and of one's own role—when with a PAGFB partner, no matter what that partner's own gender may be? A sense, certainly, of wanting more flexibility for yourself when you are with a self-chosen partner.

'Man'-identified Sam was in a relationship with a transwoman. The manner in which both partners expressed their gender and the ways in which the gender roles kept shifting indicated not just a high degree of complexity, but also an unconventional power equation. He said at one point, 'She started behaving like a typical woman. She would wash my clothes, bring me coffee in the morning. When I broke my hand in an accident, she bathed me. She is the only one who has seen my whole body.' Yet, in public spaces, the roles got blurred, if not reversed:

> She used to take more power. She would try to protect me in the pubs and clubs.... She always controlled me in how I expressed myself through my clothes, no smoking on roads, no drinking in bars, only at home.... She was giving me safety, but treating me like a female.... In pubs she would wear deep-necked dresses because she also wanted to pick up customers.... The men there would call me 'madam', so I was scared. In [those spaces] I do not even open my mouth. Only [she] would talk because otherwise people [could] find out from my voice that I am a girl.

In his relationships with woman-identified PAGFB, Sam seemed to have been on surer ground, his gender identity more stable.

Certainly, there tended to be trouble when a partner set fixed gender roles. Meghana, who calls hirself 'androgynous', recalled the complications in an early relationship ze had with an FTM person:

> At that point of time all kinds of things were very hard for me to grasp, even how to have sex. How do you touch your partner who

is trans?... It took me time to realize the layers and levels at which he wanted to be trans. I was not happy with many things, but I felt I had no space to say that because he was always reading it as being transphobic as opposed to a question of preferences, which may be differing.... What I found then very problematic in this relationship was... that we may be read as a heterosexual couple by others. This was completely opposed to my radical politics. I had a huge stake in claiming the non-hetero space. It was not just limited to sexuality... what it typically meant was I would then have to be the female, or the femininity role player for the other person to assert their masculinity.... I feel that somewhere it was both sexist and unfair to me.

What begins to emerge from our 50 interviews (although not always or unambiguously) is that most PAGFB who identify as 'man' tend to fit more easily into the available scripts for 'maleness' within intimate relationships, while some who identify as 'woman' and some of the 'others' appear to have a more nuanced and complex questioning of gender construction. This is not surprising considering that when you are a trans* person and identify with one of the binary genders, adopting all the stereotypes associated with them comes easiest. For others who identify with the gender that they were assigned or those that are struggling to find different names and identities for themselves, the stereotypes are meant to be challenged.

External Pressures

Relationships are also under constant attack from the outside. The utter lack of validation by families and other social institutions of relationships between people of non-normative sexualities and genders is no easy thing to overcome. There is a popular and specious argument that the same might be said of all intimacies that defy caste and community norms or class boundaries. While it is undeniable that all such relationships are actively—and often violently—discouraged, a double caveat is due: one, popular cinema and literature have always valorized the protagonists of 'illicit' heterosexual romances, while rendering other types of desire invisible; two, queer relationships are no less inflected by—and must be seen in the context of—those other prohibitions (and marginalizations) as well.

In the earlier chapters about respondents' experiences of growing up, we spoke at length of the ways in which families intervene violently, resulting in broken relationships, suicide pacts, or running away and forced migration. This non-acceptance from those considered near and dear leads to a lot of pressure on the relationship itself. First, because it then becomes the replacement for all emotional ties and, second, because there is no support system in place to take care of individuals moving away or not being compatible with each other, or even figuring out ways of being together.

Our respondents' stories of intimacy were not just their own, of course. Karthik's narrative left us grieving for his partner when he recounted the house arrests, blackmail and torture/beatings she underwent, trying desperately and repeatedly to be with Karthik right until her parents married her off. We also grieved for 'man'-identified Jai's partner, who did not survive their double suicide pact. However affirmative a partner may be, the lack of other support renders many such queer relationships untenable. Our respondents were, in a sense, the lucky ones who managed to reach support groups and find a community.

In our respondents' narratives, we also heard how they try to protect their relationships and partners from their own family members. Monu told us how hir mother was dismissive of hir partner:

> My mother too used to say earlier, 'She is lower caste, why do you go to her house?' My brothers and sisters would also say, 'That neighbourhood is *chhota log* [people of a lower social strata], it is not nice.' I would not tell [my partner] this. It would hurt her. I would argue with them that, 'What does caste have to do with anything? My relationship is with a person. She is so modern, that is better than being upper caste.'

Fed up of hir mother's constant taunts and realizing that ze had to look after hirself, Monu bought a flat in which hir girlfriend stays, but kept this fact hidden from hir mother because ze was not sure of how she and the other family members would react. Monu was trying to secure hir future and at the same time protecting hir girlfriend from the constant attacks from hir family.

Geeta had a house of her own and lived in the same city as her mother. She said:

> I am out to her but she does not accept [me]. She does not come to my house. My life is pretty invisible to her.... When I came out to my mother, she said, don't tell anyone in the family because then my brothers won't let me see my nephew or niece. I thought that wasn't really likely, but I didn't tell anyone. My brother, when he had seen [my partner] in the house had said, 'She looks like a you-know-what.'

The impact of this kind of disrespect was such that even though she broke up with this partner, she did not tell her mother about it 'because she might feel happy'. In a sense, even though the relationship was over, Geeta seemed to be protecting her memories of it and her love from the unwarranted attacks from her family.

As mentioned earlier, some of our respondents were forced into marriages with cismen and these relationships added pressures in their own way. Bhargavi had been married off by hir mother, who disapproved of hir relationship with a 'girl' who had been Bhargavi's classmate. Their clandestine relationship became known to Bhargavi's husband and 'when I was separated from my husband for a year [he and my partner] had sexual relations'. Ze saw some 'filthy' messages on hir husband's phone, sent to hir partner, but when asked, both of them denied having anything to do with it. Only when they finally managed to run away together did hir partner tell hir that 'my husband had tortured my partner many times. If my partner had spoken of this earlier, my husband would not have let us meet.'

For this kind of control over both people, it is not necessary that the man is a husband. One respondent was in a surreptitious relationship with a married male cousin who became extremely possessive and resorted to blackmail when she went away to study and got involved with another man. The cousin told her parents about her lover, so they discontinued her studies and confined her to the house. The second boyfriend came to her aid later, when she was caught up in a triple suicide pact that went horribly wrong. It is a story that needs to be told for its own sake, mapping yet again the depths of despair to which so many queer PAGFB are driven and the familiar betrayals by friends and family. Our respondent was by then in a relationship with a woman, who was also involved with another woman. Feeling hopeless and having decided to kill themselves, the three ran away together and booked into a hotel where, in the midst of much emotional turmoil and vacillation, one of them hanged herself. Our respondent's ex-boyfriend initially helped the two survivors hide, but tried to force her to have sex with him even during this traumatic time, and then led the police to them.

In some other cases the men that our respondents or their partners were married to managed to live with the fact that their wives were in relationships with other women, a fact possibly easier to take than a relationship with another cisman. On being told about Kirti's woman partner, Kirti's husband was mainly concerned with saving the marriage:

> My husband… was aware of my friendship with [my partner], but he did not look down upon it. In fact he would say that if I had such a friendship with a man, then he would have beaten me and left me right away…. He even gave me the permission to bring [her] home to live with us… but requested that I should not leave him. [She] came to live with us, but she could not bear the sight of him.

Another respondent spoke of hir husband's acceptance due to other reasons. Mala, who identifies as 'woman from outside but not fully a woman', is a tribal from a poor family in a rural area and was married off at 15 into even greater poverty. All through hir married life ze was abused for being childless. Over the years the husband had become less and less sexually active. When he consented to a medical check-up, the doctor found that neither Mala nor he could have children. Meanwhile, Mala had begun a intense relationship with a woman who worked at the centre. Ze told hir husband about it. 'My husband would say that because he has a deficiency, that's why I needed [her]. He knew it and was indifferent…. He [had known] of such relationships before me. There is a video theatre in our area where they show such films.'

Interestingly, just as Mala was not considered wholly female by the villagers, neither was hir husband considered a man: 'Now the villagers have got to know about me and my husband and they term us as hijra—neither male nor female.' The husband's own sense of his gender seemed to have made him both less compelled to be the dominant male, even though they lived within a very conventional community, and more tolerant of his wife's other relationship. In a sense, both Kirti's and Mala's husbands also allowed their other relationships to continue because they did not see them as threats to their marriage; they were secondary, not important enough. And in Mala's case, while hir husband thought he himself was not man enough, he felt Mala's woman partner was even less of a 'man' than him.

Violence within Relationships

Aditi attempted suicide after her partner began seeing a cisman while they were still together. Was her desperation entirely caused by the presence of another person in an emotionally intense and previously monogamous equation or was it exacerbated by the sense that the relationship was unsustainable because she and her partner were both women? From the many instances that respondents shared of contemplated or attempted suicide (and other forms of self-inflicted violence) in the context of their intimate relationships, it is clear that much of the pain stemmed from a feeling of hopelessness.

Many respondents spoke of self-harm in moments of extreme stress. When Prem's partner decided to leave hir, ze slashed both hir shoulders with a blade. Sandhya shared such an emotionally intense relationship with a friend in the hostel that their looming separation became unbearable to hir:

> We shut the door and I said that I [would] die if I do not get to live with [her].... We both sat and cried with each other for some time. Then I had a blade in my dissection box and had heard of people cutting their hands and writing each other's names.... So I said, 'Shall I show my love for you?'... I never wanted to cut too much, but did not realize how sharp the razor was.... Suddenly there was a big cut on my hand, showing the flesh, and [there was] blood all over. She saw it and fainted right there.

In Kavi's case a similar episode with her girlfriend outed her to family, friends and doctors alike. She was 20 at the time; she and her girlfriend had been quarrelling, largely because their families were getting suspicious. One evening Kavi saw her in a field but ignored her:

> The next morning, her mother came to me and said that she had taken sleeping pills.... She had written my name on her thigh, with a blade.... Four or five doctors questioned me. I got very scared. They asked whether I had spent the night with her..... In the prescription, they wrote 'homosexual love' and counselled me. Our families were told.

Respondents also related many kinds of violence between partners, which arose from gendered behaviour and expectations or from other problems like sexual jealousy and possessiveness. Priya was independent and earning very well when she started living with a butch-identified partner and encountered physical and emotional violence. Although they had a cook and a maid, and Priya was working long hours, she was expected to play a wifely role:

> My ex-girlfriend considers herself butch, I was the girl, the wife in the relationship.... She would call my family names, monitor where

and with whom I was going out, stopped me from talking to a male friend. She at various points was physically abusive, and it kept on increasing. She wasn't very different from my father. Once she threatened to rape me. That day I pushed her hard. It was extremely abusive emotionally.

Falguni described how her first relationship went from being something that calmed her to something that had a very negative long-term impact on her:

> She displayed a lot of possessiveness and it is my fault that I used to encourage it.... She slapped me but I did nothing back, and I took her back. And then it started getting worse. It turned violent after she got engaged. My tantrums, her anger—we used to have bad fights. She wouldn't express herself and I used to push her to speak. She used to beat me up, I said stuff verbally.... I cut off from everybody because she would be suspicious. It became suffocating.... She would put me down, call me a dumb fuck... humiliate me in bed—till date I can't feel physically for women too much. Till today I'm suffering.

Several respondents admitted to feeling, and being, physically violent towards intimate partners. Murali, who identifies as 'FTM', said of hir relationship with a 'woman'-identified partner: 'Small things flare up.... I was talking to my ex-lover. [My partner] got angry that we [were] still in touch and we started fighting. I do get violent.... She beat me once. In these three years, I have beaten her thrice.'

Sara confessed to having been violent in one of her relationships:

> She was violent with her words and I was violent with my hands.... I had fully lost it at the time, I used to smoke up a lot.... I was fully irresponsible... and she was a fully responsible, mother-type figure. She used to tell me what to do and what not to do.... I couldn't handle it.... I really [got violent] in this relationship, was a very bad child.... In my third relationship, I faced violence, all my clothes, kurtas were torn up by her, though I never raised my hand to her.

Chandni said:

> There are times… when people have driven me into a corner where
> I have felt violent. But I have never acted on it. That I see as the end
> of the relationship, as I don't like the person I am becoming when
> I am with them.

Jamuna too spoke about the element of violence in romantic
love:

> [I am] very, very stringent with myself about not hurting…. And
> especially in romantic relationships, it is devastating…. Other
> relationships don't hurt like this and I can't put a finger on why
> these relationships do. Especially when we do believe that these
> relationships are not central to your life, your other spaces are
> paramount, your other relationships are equally important, and
> friendships may be much more permanent—we know all of that
> and yet… there always is an element of violence to romantic love…
> and we need to set ourselves that standard to minimize the pain we
> give ourselves and each other.

The grand narrative of passion was replete with tales of power
play and subjugation, emotional blackmail and suicide, jealousy
and rage. In this particular queer context, however, the violence
often seems exacerbated by the intolerance and invisibility that
surrounds most transgressive relationships; many of the fault
lines within can be traced back to the lack of support outside.
The notion that one's desire or behaviour is abnormal, guilt over
parents being saddened by one's life choices, an overdependence
on an intimate partner leading to heightened vulnerability
and stress—all these become pressure points. And as a result,
relationships crack.

Finding Support

Of course, break-ups were not always by mutual, if troubled,
consent, but all too often because of forcible separation, forced
marriages, other kinds of natal family violence and the general

lack of support structures outside the family. Respondents listed a variety of reactions and coping mechanisms. Jai went to a counsellor who was not very helpful but was someone to talk to initially apart from the cousin who had been his only confidante. Given the prejudices of many mental health professionals, this was a risky enterprise, as Jai discovered. Others, like Alex, also accessed counselling. One person 'went berserk' and had a series of one-night stands with cismen as well as women.

For a number of respondents, just as the relationship had to be a secret affair, the break-up too had to be suffered in silence. For people living out their loves and desires and sorrows so much on the margins of society, all the usual issues surrounding break-ups seemed to get intensified.

Those respondents who had found queer support groups were less alone, although often the ex-partner was also a member of the same group and this was difficult to deal with. There are few spaces outside of the circle of queer friends and support groups where queer PAGFB can be themselves. Many respondents were involved with fellow activists and colleagues, which again made it hard to make a 'clean break'. One respondent in particular talked about the trauma of having to keep encountering her ex-partner in a space she could not withdraw from as community was the only thing that was holding her together. Some people did manage to remain friends with ex-lovers: Ujwala spoke of a man and a woman with both of whom she was able to achieve this difficult equation.

Devi used, rather wonderfully, the metaphor of flowing water for love and for letting love go where it will:

> It's a beating heart after all. If it beats [elsewhere] for someone else then it is a crime to turn it. If a stream is going on its course, will you turn it by making a dam? A relationship has been thus long, should we not cherish it? Like water, a relationship might change its course, but does that mean that we will now spit in it? Where earlier there was water now is it nothing? For me it still is water, it is a flowing stream. It is still good and I respect it. I talk to her sometimes, ask her how she is. I did feel alone, I was hurt. But I tried to understand, did not tarnish the whole thing.… To change

the course is akin to making a dam, bad for oneself and everyone around too.

For all respondents whose parents did not stand by them, who went against parental wishes, there were a few whose family members stood by them and created that comfort zone needed to deal with the ups and downs of romantic relationships. Even when they did not quite understand, they made an attempt. Saumya says about her parents:

> They accepted my girlfriend. They liked her. She was part of family spaces and celebrations. They are still wondering because now we have broken up and I have not told them directly.... They cannot understand how I can keep changing partners. When I introduced my mother to my [current] partner, she was upset.... So she told my father, who was very cool—'These days these things happen.' So he, who is more conservative, appeared very cool, so my mother also accepted.

All through Prem's multiple escapades and entanglements with hir partner, hir mother stood by hir even at the worst of times. At present she looks after hir child while Prem continues to live in the city. Kavi's mother, who earlier tried her best to 'cure' Kavi of her homosexuality, today lives with her and her partner. Sunny was supported all along by hir mother, sister and some extended family as well. Ze and hir partner also live with hir mother.

When Sandy was young, ze went through a major depression related to hir relationships and job, and was in a nursing home for some time. Hir mother and stepfather helped hir deal with this, as did a close friend. 'One of the things that really helped me then, was my friendship.... [My friend] was there for me and [I] also had a family that was very supportive and loving.'

Those who do not have such support work towards creating their own 'community', trying to realize their own visions of home and family. Geeta described her home as an open house: 'It was a space for queer people. It was a kind of space that you associate with family—secure, taking it for granted. In fact, at one point, I had to go sleep at another friend's house as my own house was full of people.'

Prem spoke of hir complex interactions with the small queer community within which ze now lives:

> [A] sense of community comes because the fights are all short-lived. With this same group of people I also find that I can share a sense of friendship, intense friendships.... We can at least come and cry before someone or the other, or share a joy with someone else who is like you and knows you.... It also gives [us] a chance to find jobs, to discover one's own talents and allows for a kind of freedom that you do not get elsewhere.

'Community' is the keyword here. The support groups that people find or create, and queer friends within these groups were the closest many of our respondents came to rediscovering a sense of camaraderie and of belonging.

Kanika, who felt suicidal after hir break-up, said: 'Even now that feeling is there, so I don't give myself time alone and stay instead with friends from [the group].... I just call her and tell her I want to cry, and she is there for me.'

Tuli was even more emphatic:

> My parents, sister, niece—this is my blood family. I have to take care of them, I can never leave them for any reason or anyone. But if you ask me to say from my heart who is my family, other than [my] parents, it's every member of [the queer group]—this is the family I can talk to, where I am at ease, which understands me. It is a *janmabhoomi* [birth-place] of mine.

Kirti rarely got in touch with members of the groups he came in contact with years ago after a local newspaper sensationally outed him along with his partner, but just the knowledge of these faraway friends was enough to keep him going: 'I used to feel I was the only lesbian. But now I know that there are more like me.... Without all these people, I don't know what I would have done.'

Conclusion

In a society that recognizes only one trajectory of adult romantic and sexual intimacies—that is, leading to marriage, which is more about responsibilities towards parents, families and community, and not really about companionship—there is very little rational discussion around love. And all intimacies that emerge in this environment are caught in the same dialectic of roles and commitments even when marriage is not really an option. So even though for those in non-heterosexual alliances the possibilities are multiple in theory, their lived patterns tend to become ensnared in the usual.

Yet, while outwardly there is a similarity, there are many departures that urge a more nuanced reading. The non-acceptance of such alliances means isolation and silence. The more conservative society is in enforcing the norms of heteronormativity, the greater the pressure that these relationships and the people within them face. When there is a general opposition to intercaste and interreligious alliances, and more restrictions are imposed on people, both young and old, wanting to assert their autonomy, those choosing same-sex/gender partners are under greater pressure to hide their relationships. This forced silence, then, just adds to the fragility of such partnerships. It also means there are no external support systems, making the people, the relationship and the experimentation within it that much more vulnerable.

Further, there is an absence of discussions around various other aspects—around issues of monogamy, control and ownership of shared material goods or of each other, and negotiations of power within the relationship that accrue to people because of caste, class, age and so on. In situations where there is no prescribed institutional framework to follow, there is a greater awareness of these concerns as there are no set norms for dealing with them. In principle this should lead to a possibility of addressing them more squarely. However, the general lack of conversation hampers such negotiations as well. So the mere fact that a non-normative choice is never enough to make a radical difference in the way a relationship is lived.

Our respondents' lives also warn us that a simplistic reading with a very standard understanding of masculinity and femininity (as comprehended from heterosexual marriages between cispersons) would fail to look at gender-transgressive individuals and their relationships within the context of their particular vulnerabilities. This is a lesson that some of us who were part of urban autonomous women's groups started learning as we heard Dalit feminists speak of their relationships with Dalit men, and as we focused on the particularities of understanding Dalit masculinities. While aggression and violence as an expression of masculinity cannot be condoned, masculinities themselves have to be contextualized in the particular vulnerability of the person and the relationship. Thus, one has to understand that reverse gender power may operate in a relationship between one person who lives in their assigned gender and another who cannot. The emphasis has to be on the intersections of the marginalities, which lead to complex interlayering and not simple additions.

And finally, instead of obsessing as a society about who can have sexual relations with whom and what they do in that interaction, we might make much more responsible adult relationships if we seriously started speaking of how these could be conducted, and of how consent and respect have to be at their base. In hierarchical societies, intimacies are never going to be made between two equals. Learning to recognize the power that accrues to us from our social locations and negotiating it within our intimacies is an important lesson that perhaps needs to start within the hierarchical institution of the family itself.

10

The Self and the Body

Our feminisms have taught us how persons assigned gender female at birth have laws, strictures and boundaries inscribed on their bodies in multiple ways. And the history of this subcontinent has shown us time and again how lines of family, community, caste and nation are drawn and redrawn across these gendered bodies. Our personal histories of learning to live with ourselves without fear or hatred, and with some degree of dignity and respect are strewn with stories of coming to terms with this social–cultural palimpsest that is the 'female' body and, more crucially, with stories of reclaiming these bodies for meanings we want to inscribe on them, through them, or journeys towards being comfortable in them and in our selves.

In addition to all these inscriptions and resistances that have happened on multiple fronts is a queer dissonance with the body. This may exist for some of us who identify as queer and not for others. The body is as much a personal space as it is a social one. Individual negotiations and the extent to which they are needed are as particular to each person as everything else is.

The 'gendered body' of which we speak is, then, one that is assigned gender female at birth but does not necessarily choose to align itself with that assignment. As we have seen, respondents identified their genders in multiple ways and often with individual nuance. Even those who identified as 'woman' had their fair share of negotiations with gendered expectations of the body.

In this chapter we look more carefully at the relationship our respondents had with their bodies—the language they chose to talk about their bodies, how they imagined—and lived in—their bodies, how they recreated their bodies as they moved through their lives, how they dealt with the changes that came upon their physical selves over time, how they desired their bodies to be, and what they could and could not do about these desires. We also observe the interaction of these queer gendered selves and bodies with desire itself and people's interactions with intimate partners, revisioning their own and sometimes their partners' bodies. We note the markers of health and wellbeing, both physical and mental, that our respondents' lives, riddled with the complexities of being lived against the grain, reflected. And finally, we consider the interactions they had living in their queer gendered bodies with public health institutions.

The 'Female' Body

All our respondents were assigned gender female at birth. This was obviously done by looking at the external appearance of their bodies at the time. And through their lives, the body continued to play an important role in the making of their genders. At the same time societal norms and restrictions continued to build on the sexual difference in the prototypical 'male' and 'female' body, thus simultaneously gendering it. All our respondents, irrespective of gender identity, had much to say on this co-constructedness of body and gender.

As all respondents were PAGFB, the struggle against imposed social norms for what a 'female' body should look and be like was part of all their lives. Irrespective of the genders that they choose for themselves, everyone had stories to tell about their discomforts with the notion of what their bodies 'should' be like.

Most people who identified as 'woman' answered the question on whether their body matched their gender in the affirmative. Being cisgendered, though, did not necessarily mean complete comfort either with the 'female' body or with the social norms around gender, and did not directly point to any particular gender expression. Norms around beauty and body size were challenged, and respondents reclaimed their bodies in their own ways.

Twenty-nine-year-old Roma said that she was not comfortable with her body because she was too fat. Her discomfort can be traced back to when she was younger. She hated wearing feminine clothes because they 'make me feel that this is not me'. As a child, 'I was wearing trousers, shorts and pants, almost all the time, and shirts and T-shirts. Until, in late adolescence, I became fat and PCOS [polycystic ovarian syndrome] was diagnosed.' After this, she was not allowed to wear jeans by her mother and aunt because 'they said that I look like a hippo and my bulges show'.

Jharna, who is now 44, has over time come to terms with her woman-ness. Yet she expressed her annoyance:

> If there were a naked woman and a naked man standing in front of me, I must confess that I [would] feel jealous of the man. I feel nature has given him the better body. Why do we have all these curves and things—if I had any control over it, I wouldn't want this kind of body [like I have] for myself…. If I could choose, I would want a *mehnat-kash* [hard-working] body.

However, she added, 'I don't like the typical way women's bodies are shown in the media. And I feel that is a figure that is being imposed on us. I don't think it's fair to one's body.'

Hemlata did a similar reclaiming of the 'woman's' body: 'My body matches with my gender. I have challenged the restrictions and the myths created around my body.' Such assertions point towards the feminist journeys that many have undertaken in their lives in order to reclaim and have a sense of pride in their bodies.

These are critiques of the norms to which female bodies are supposed to subscribe—norms around body size, beauty, strength, colour of the skin and other such factors. Society too is able to adapt itself to some of these critiques. The problem really is when the body does not match even this reclaimed 'woman's body'. What if it is not just that a person's body does not conform to the kind of 'woman's body' that a particular society expects, but is singled out as a transgressing body? Ujwala summed up this experience very well:

> Just looking different is such a difficult thing that you have to live with. When you know that you are not going to pass. When you know that you are not going to be woman enough because you are not curvy enough or not pass as a man because you are not hairy enough. So it is a very difficult terrain when you are caught in between and have to answer questions on practically everything.

Scrutiny of Difference

It is not only what society expects of a person's body, it is also about what the person expects their own body to be. Our respondents' voices told us that the body does form one of the most important markers of difference between the varied gender identities, and also that the nature of unease trans* persons have is often qualitatively different from that which cisgendered persons experience.

The variations between 'man'-identified trans* PAGFB and those who we have categorized as 'others' are also clearest in their articulations around their relationships with their bodies. For those who identify as 'men' there seems to be tangible and at times irresolvable discord between gender identity and body.

'Man'-identified Jai spoke for many like him when he said, 'There is a basic discomfort with the body that I feel. Even when I wear pant–shirt, I do not feel comfortable because the shape of the body is seen, and thus, I like to wear jackets, even if it is hot. I wear clothes over clothes, lots of layers.' And like many other 'man'-identified respondents, he felt his body did not match his gender at all, and if possible, he would like all of the following: 'remove breasts and uterus, have facial hair and body hair, and have all the things that men have, including a penis'. And when asked how he sees himself 10 years later, his response was: 'First of all, I would like to do a complete SRS.'

Some respondents who did not call themselves 'man' but chose a gender identity that put them among the multiple 'others', managed to come to some sort of terms with the materiality of the body, its social construction and the imagined self. They spoke of their journeys towards building a relationship with their bodies. Arriving at such comfort was not always possible for all of them, but several factors helped. Some spoke of the complex interaction between their body and their gender over a period of time.

Juhi, who calls hirself 'androgynous', said:

> It actually took me a woman lover, with whom I bought myself [a bra] I liked, which made me comfortable, which made me happy.... Overall, I would say that I have developed comfort about my body largely through my relationships. Before that I had seen myself as asexual. It wasn't that I thought of myself actively as a boy, I was dressing up like boys and playing like boys.... But there was no active awareness that I'm butch, I'm dyke or that I'm masculine, I'm male, nothing like that. But there was discomfort about being fat, having breasts, things like that.

Arun, who identifies as being 'gender queer', also saw hir journey vis-à-vis hir gendered body happening over time. Ze found the body yet another space from which to question social norms:

> Yes, I am comfortable with my body and I feel it matches my gender. Earlier I did not feel like that. I knew that my [feeling of] attraction is this, so the first thought that came was, if I have to be with a woman, I have to become a man. But then I started thinking that then I am agreeing with society that I have to be either here or there. Whatever sex I am in, I should have the freedom to choose how I should be.

Yet, for some, achieving a degree of comfort with the body was made very difficult because it looked different and hence was the object of continuous scrutiny every day. Sandhya, a person with intersex variations, felt that it is the social scripts of what a woman's body and appearance must be like that cause hir conflict, to the extent that ze did not feel comfortable identifying as 'woman' even though ze would like to:

> I keep feeling that there is something lacking…. In a sense, I do not
> have a choice and so have to accept it, but not because I like it….
> My [arms] look very muscular and the veins are seen, I do not want
> to show them and so always wear full sleeves. I feel like I want to
> have a body like a woman's and also wear clothes like women do,
> but cannot do it and so feel uncomfortable. I cannot live the way I
> want, have to always think of others. But I try to respect myself and
> to come to terms with what is there.

Society's rules and expectations around the body are fixed
and all of us are so attuned to these that anything out of the way is
noticed, commented on, oftentimes ridiculed and attacked. The
body, then, is the space where efforts are made to find a balance
between multiple things—between a person's own notion of their
body so that they see it as reflecting their gender, of the way they
want their body to be seen by others, and the fact that it is a body
continuously read by others—all this mediated through societal
scripts that are written in accordance with region, nationality,
class, caste, ability and most primarily gender.

The PAGFB body in the social space is almost always seen
clothed, dressed, attired. The length of hair, the clothes a person
wears, the way they hold themselves, their overall build—all of
these make up the complex articulations of body and gender.

Expressing Gender through Attire

The balance between what one wants for oneself and what will
pass scrutiny does not come very easily. Much effort is spent
on appearing just right. For some, that feeling of rightness has
to do with wearing the clothes of their choice to achieve a look
that works. Of course, there is no one set 'look that works', but
some like Murali, who identifies as 'FTM' and grew up trying
to deal with long hair and 'women's' clothes, have arrived at a
fixed personal style. Every day, when Murali gets ready to go
out, ze prepares the otherwise giveaway upper half of hir 'female'
body: 'To hide the breasts, I wear a men's stretch banyan that
flattens them, then a cotton chemise which does not stretch and
is stitched exactly to fit, then a T-shirt and then, over it, my shirt.'

Another respondent, who passes as the 'man' he identifies as, recalled the violence of being forced to wear something that was socially required but just did not feel right. At home there was never any problem over his dressing in boys' clothes and his father was always particularly supportive, but one painful event stood out in his memory and made him weep every time he recounted it:

> One day I had to go for a function to my sister's house. They bought me a skirt, blouse and half-sari, and wanted me to wear it. I said, 'No, I do not know how to wear [this] and do not like to wear the half-sari.' They pressurized me to wear it. [My] father said I had to wear it, and beat me.... Finally, I wore the skirt and half-sari and went for the function. I did not talk to anyone or eat anything. When I got back home, I fought with my parents and left home and went to [another town].

Quite a few respondents also had stories to tell of restrictions with regard to hair. Santosh could cut his hair to shoulder length soon after his 10th standard when he got a job and then to its present short length once he left home. As mentioned earlier, the very first thing many people did after leaving home was to cut their hair short. Even in times of acute crisis, in the midst of running away, some individuals stopped to have their hair cut.

Divakar is a person with intersex variations who eventually embraced the identity of 'man' after years of trauma caused by the appearance of secondary masculine characteristics that did not allow him to pass as 'Divya' any more. Unable even to speak of the woman he once was except in the third person, he spoke about the codes he has used to distance himself from her:

> Till college, Divya used to wear saris, lehenga–blouse, churidar.... Every day she would wear different saris, all colourful and pretty. Now my shirts are not so colourful but soon, step by step, I will change this also.... Divya used different soaps and make-up items. She had a full box of make-up—lipstick, powder, clips—she spent all the money that other people gave her on this. Now I

> use nothing other than Lifebuoy soap. Not even aftershave lotions, no powder, nothing.

So painful has his transition been and the two selves so disjointed, that to cope, he had to burn everything Divya had owned. This meant the loss of colours to which he referred, something he has been slowly trying to bring back into his life. His circumstances compelled him to make a complete shift in how he presented his body to the world, but some people were able to have a more playful relationship with their bodies.

'Woman'-identified Geeta's class and urban privileges allowed her to choose her attire depending on how she wanted to present her gender and her other identities:

> I have become more aware of dressing fairly respectable when you are meeting… government officials. I haven't actively challenged it, the 'good activist' thing…. I don't think that… to meet a minster, I would go wearing trousers.

Outside of her workspace she did manage to play with her appearance. 'I love boots. In my straight days, I had dyke-y shoes. My gender feels different in boots. Like, the boots I am wearing today I call my transgender boots. Flowery and tough and big at the same time.'

Sara settled slowly into her current look, which is considered fairly transgressive. She constantly gets asked if she is a woman or a man, and has to fight to make her way both in men's and women's spaces. She said that the most important change for her has been her comfort with being the way she is now. When she visits her parents, she does not alter anything about her external appearance. 'Today, sometimes, my uncles will say, "Oh, we didn't recognize you, we thought it was a boy!" It feels damn good. Those sort of comments I can take in my stride very easily.'

Manjula said that hir gender is 'confused' and this determines hir gender expression and clothes:

Some days I feel like a hijra so then I overdo the femininity. If I feel like a woman, I may wear a sari—I am speaking in very stereotypical terms here. For example, today I feel nothing, there is no gender for me. Then I dress with whatever is before me, nothing in particular. Some dresses are signifiers. If [I feel] like a man, then I like to wear a waistcoat and sometimes even make a shade of a moustache, nothing very visible, but just a bit.

This mixing of genders was for many the only way in which they could express what felt true for their own sense of their gender. Chandni, who does not articulate hir gender, elaborated on this:

You see many hijras turned out completely in *gajra* [strings of flowers generally worn in hair] and decked up, and sometimes you see them in pant–shirt. I'm like that. Most of my life will be in pant–shirt, but sometimes I will get decked up... though I can't go to their extent. When I do that, I feel like a hijra and also I feel like someone will see through it, will see that I am not this. Say, a hijra would feel like 'I am not completely female and that people can see it'. I feel the same way.

Meghana traced the shifts in hir gender through how hir hair, clothes and appearance changed as ze grew up. Ze described hir hair as being 'a big thing in my gender': 'The minute my hair becomes a bit unwieldy in my eyes, I can be in perpetual crisis and have a perpetual identity or gender or body crisis. For days I will not be happy.... I feel that nobody will find me handsome, perhaps because that's how I feel inside.'

Clothes, the length and cut of the hair, body language, overall attitude—these are the ways through which people try to express their gender and communicate it to the world. For some, there is an internal match with what society expects; some find themselves totally at cross-purposes with those expectations; and for some, the confusion is part of their expression. As Meghana put it, 'To pass, it is not always what you wear, but it's your attitude.'

The Visible Body

Beyond the layers added through clothes and haircuts and attitude lies the physicality of the body itself. Every part of the body is inscribed with gender markers—the more apparent of these being the ones most checked out by other people. When attire does not lead to an easy reading, scrutiny moves to the most visible features, such as facial and other visible body hair, or the flatness or the fullness of the bustline. These features are, in any case, important for a person's own understanding of their body and gender, but become crucial because of this continuous scrutiny.

Going by conventional notions of the 'female body', none of our PAGFB respondents was supposed to have noticeable body hair, especially on the face. Yet, bodies are all part of continuums of various kinds, and variations exist even at particular points along these continuums, resisting such efforts at classification. Thus, some respondents did have body hair, some did not. Their responses to body hair—whether they liked having it, what they did about it and so on—made for an array of different gender stories.

Most of the cisgender respondents spoke most readily of pubic and underarm hair, mentioning facial hair or hair on their limbs or chest only rarely—either if they themselves had it or if they were speaking as activists or feminists. Neha said that she was personally comfortable with her body hair, but has had to face taunts about it. 'I did go through a tough time with so much hair on my body. Mostly women do not have hair and comments were passed. Once in a fit of anger I took father's razor and shaved my face.' Others said that they did not mind having body hair because they were 'making a political statement around it' (Sara) or 'I am a gender activist, so well, I really have no discomfort with body hair' (Ranjana).

The 'man'-identified respondents began with speaking primarily of facial hair. For almost all of them the dominant feeling was that they wanted it not only to be able to pass as men, but also to feel right about their own selves. All of them had tried different methods of growing more facial or body hair, but to no avail.

Anand said, 'I'm hairless—wish I had lots more…. I shaved my legs to grow hair for wearing shorts, and even the little hair I had has never come back!' Vasu used a blade to 'scrape my upper lip and cheeks for hair to grow. Then I have taken kajal and drawn a moustache over my lips.' Kamal went to a medical shop and asked for medicines that would help him grow a beard and a moustache. 'They called me mental and said what I need is counselling not medicine. I was willing to pay any amount of money.' Karthik went to a proper doctor, but found they were at cross-purposes with each other: 'Two years ago I gave a doctor Rs 800 for a medicine to increase body hair, but the doctor gave me medicine to stop body hair. He gives this medicine to hijras to stop hair growth and he gave me the same.'

Interestingly and ironically, almost all our 'man'-identified respondents had even less than the usual amount of body hair seen on 'female' bodies. They spoke wistfully of seeing themselves with more facial and body hair, and hoped that starting on hormones would help them achieve this dream at some point.

The replies of the 'others' were more varied. Some just liked body hair, while some really wanted it. Some were sad that they did not have any, while others were glad they did not. Some had tried acquiring more hair, others had stayed with what they had and yet others regularly removed their body hair, mostly for reasons of hygiene.

Most respondents spoke of pubic hair only on being asked specifically about it. The question of like or dislike in this case seemed to come from individual preference and there was no stark variation in the responses. This was not surprising since pubic hair is not usually visible and it seems that immediate concerns around the body are mainly around the perceivable markers.

For the two respondents with intersex variations, hair was clearly a significant marker. Sandhya was glad that ze did not have hair on hir body as that enabled hir to pass as a 'woman'. 'If I had that, things would be very difficult. Then I would have to change my gender, there would be no option.' Hir fear was valid and corroborated by Divakar's story. Along with facial hair, Divakar started experiencing changes when in college. He said, 'Slowly I started seeing that my voice was also changing and my breasts... started shrinking.' The road map for the future disappeared in a haze of dismay; denial was impossible with facial hair that needed to be shaved every day and children asking, 'Why do you look like a woman, but speak like a man?'

The heaviness or otherwise of the voice as soon as someone speaks is one such aspect that each one of us uses to start assigning a gender label to the speaker. A voice to match their gender identity is something people crave and when this does not happen, there are ways in which they strategize and manoeuvre for their own sakes and for the world. The negotiation is difficult, both for those who do not have a conventionally soft, gentle, 'feminine' kind of voice but identify as 'woman', and for those who want to hear a robust, deep voice emerge when they speak. Some deal with this by changing the pitch of their voices in public spaces, others by keeping quiet.

'I Don't Want These Things'

Even when people are too far for others to check for fuzz on their faces or when their voices are not heard, there is the torso that impacts the language of gender—both its expression and its readability. Breasts seem to be the chief marker that people look at, especially when other social markers of dress and hair length confuse them. And even when the act of transgression is recognized as such—when the observer knows or guesses the birth-assigned gender—staring at a particular body part, especially at breasts, is a familiar way of humiliating the transgressor. As 'woman'-identified Tuli, who usually dresses in trousers and shirts, and has short hair, said, 'They look at my chest and not my face.... I've been asked to take off my jacket and I said, "Why? Want to see my breasts? Can I feel yours and check if they're real? I can't tell if you're a woman either."'

Though many respondents had discomfort with the size of their breasts or were unhappy like Tuli was with the way in which their breasts marked them in a particular manner, several other cisgender respondents were happy with their breasts. Their main complaints were around size and the way society sexualizes women's breasts. But most 'women' and 'others' had arrived at some sort of ease over a period of time and some even said that they liked their breasts.

Jharna mentioned the comfort she has developed over the years. She said that initially she did not like it that her body was becoming like a woman's and resented having to wear a bra:

> In society, men strut around while women go about with their heads bowed. So I started dressing like a man and wanted to distance myself from my woman-ness. But then, when I read Osho, I learnt to accept and to love my woman-ness.... I decided I want empowerment as I am.

Kanika and Mala identify their gender as other than 'man' or 'woman' but both said that they love their breasts. Mala said, 'I really like my breasts. [I have liked them from] the beginning. Even if someone asks for it, I will not give it.... I feel very proud of them. I like good breasts.' Others like Monu have moved from utter discomfort to some sort of balance:

> Earlier I always wanted my body to be covered. I was insecure about showing my breasts and vagina, feeling that the person opposite will know that I am a girl, so I used to wear a *genji* [vest] all the time. Now my mind has changed.

Some people did not ever come to terms with certain aspects of their bodies, which reflected the depth of the discord they felt. This was very evident in the narratives of some of our trans* respondents, especially those who identified as 'man'. Their breasts were on their bodies but not really part of them; close yet separate. As one 'man'-identified respondent explained, 'We call breasts *bachcha* [children] because they are stuck to one's chest. I don't really use the term, but it's community parlance.'

Respondents spoke either of never looking at themselves while bathing or having no mirrors around. Jai said, 'Inside, I am a man, but the outside body is not like a man and so even if I see my breasts while taking a bath or something, then I do not like it. No, I never look at myself in the mirror naked.'

Kirti, who had children after he was forced into marriage to a cisman, said vehemently:

> I don't want my breasts. But I can't cut them and throw them away. I have disliked my breasts [since] the time they started growing…. While breastfeeding my breasts supported me. They helped me look after my children. But that is all. I never learnt to like them or respect them.

Many spoke of how hard they tried to make sure that these unwanted things on the body were not visible. Binding or layering to make the outline invisible was common camouflage. Some had tried to bind their breasts after watching the film *Boys Don't Cry*, while others had evolved their own methods of binding. A couple of respondents spoke of binders that could be bought on the internet but were not yet available in India. Invariably, such severe binding and layering is not easy and not only constricts the chest, but affects blood circulation, leading to severe bruising for some, skin rashes and pain for others, and difficulty in breathing (or running) and in some cases also in eating.

Anand, who has been binding his breasts for many years, said he cannot eat when he's out because he feels choked with the tight binding. 'As soon as I go home I remove the binding and, therefore, there are no mirrors in the house.' Vasu, who identifies as a 'man', narrated how 'earlier, when at home, I tied [them] up tightly. Or wore a tight *banian*, of a child's size, and it would even cut my arms, making the skin red as it would be so tight. The arm would even blacken.'

Such pain and trauma borne when rendering breasts invisible is essential for people's own relationship with their bodies and how they want to see themselves. The physical pain is outweighed by the pain of seeing oneself unlayered, unbound, alien.

Many 'man'-identified respondents were keen to access a range of medical and surgical interventions that would enable them to pass in their chosen gender in society as well as to achieve a degree of comfort with their own bodies. How far one might go to achieve this 'right' body varied from person to person, and on occasion for the same person over time. Some like Sumit said they were lucky to have small breasts that are not really noticeable and so they do not need to undergo surgery. Others like Rahul felt that top surgery was essential for them to be able to gain self-confidence and to be able to live their lives fully.[1] It was not surprising that top surgery was a priority for several respondents.

'But They Are There, So Be It'

It is this dual need—of passing society's gender norms with ease and of comfort with one's own body and self-image—that underlies the clear difference between respondents' attitudes to those aspects of the body that are most visible and those that are not. Thus, menstruation, which also marks the 'sexual difference' between bodies labelled 'male' and 'female' but is not visible to other people, drew relatively mixed responses. While many respondents were unhappy with this biological aspect of their bodies, this was so across gender identities.

Yet, there was a perceptible difference in the nature of the discomfort—for those identifying as 'men', it was something that created discord with their gender identities, whereas for other respondents it was something that marked them as 'women' in ways that they did not like. Many people spoke of the irritation they felt when they first menstruated. Kavi, who had always been a sportsperson and who loved to play with the boys in her neighbourhood, said, 'When my periods came, I felt very depressed despite my mother counselling me. I knew my freedom would change. I felt something had happened to me—I felt, what's this, it doesn't happen to boys.'

Very few were aware of periods before they began menstruating. Some had to deal with the rituals around the first period, others had to cope with the restrictions imposed on them during periods and almost all of them tried to resist the changed ways in which they were expected to behave afterwards. Thus, it was not something that most people welcomed. For those like Santosh or Karthik, who identified as boys at the time, periods were and still remain a very difficult time. It came as a shock, almost like a betrayal by their bodies.

Santosh had not known about menstruation. When he got his first period, he thought he had cut something inside. He told his mother, who explained:

> I felt I should not [menstruate], but I got it because I am a woman. I had hatred towards it. I used to go to temples and pray to the God to stop this and make me a man.... I would not sit or follow the rules which we had [about menstruation]. I used to go out and roam around.

For some time, Karthik even managed to hide the fact that he had begun his periods. Coming to terms with them was something he found almost impossible:

> When I was 16, I came back to the village. People kept asking if I had begun menstruating and why I did not wear the half-sari. I lied and said no, even though I had started my periods, as then people would think of me as a girl. I denied it and kept it hidden.... It was painful for me as I did not want to let them see me as a woman. I do not want this, then why am I getting it?

This despairing question was asked by many. Others came to terms with it over time as something they had no control over, though they were far from feeling good about it. Some dealt with the irregularities and pain, and others with the general discomfort.

Alex, now in hir late 30s, who identifies as 'between transgender and lesbian', described how ze felt about hir periods: 'I almost forget that I am a woman. When the period comes it reminds me, "Hello, you are a woman." This is an unnecessary job.' However, ze never thought of surgery: 'By the time I came to know about all these things, it was too late. Now there are just four-five years left and I will just wait it out. I don't want to play around with my body.'

Among our 50 respondents, Vimala was in a minority of one when she said, 'I love my periods. Maybe I am one of those rare creatures who say this. It is the happiest time in the month for me.' A few others were indifferent to it or had no problems with it. Most respondents, however, across gender identities did not see why they had to suffer this invisible, silent marker of 'women's bodies', whose onset truly marks their gender socially and also creates physical and social discomfort. As Sara, who identifies as a 'woman', said, 'I get my periods regularly. I think any woman would be happy if she didn't get them. But they are there, so be it.' Or as Saumya, also 'woman'-identified, said, 'Anyone would like to get rid of them.' And while Neha said she would not do anything to get rid of her periods, 'I wish menstruation wasn't there to begin with.'

All of which indicates that even 'women' are often unhappy with what are seen as markers of their bodies. Obviously, those who did not see themselves as 'woman' faced even more problems living with such marker-ridden bodies. Yet, dissonance between how one imagines one's body and what actually exists does not necessarily mean wanting medical interventions or surgery. And even when intervention is sought, it tends to be a well-considered decision, based on concerns of possible long-term ill-effects and other health issues, money and the individual's need to achieve a consonant sense of self. There is no single template. If at all there is something that is commonplace, it is the fact that there are very few hospitals and medical practitioners who are able to provide the required information or services.

Medical Interventions

It is evident enough that many respondents had different kinds of discomforts with their bodies, quite a few of which were related to their gender identities. Almost all those who identified as 'man' wanted medical interventions, as did some of the 'others'. For a few respondents like Saumya, it was a fleeting idea in the context of a relationship:

> Years back I told my first girlfriend that I would change my sex just to keep the relationship. I said this to her to just have her stay with me and because she was married, etc. I do not know whether I would've done anything.

But for most, the changes they desired were crucial for their sense of self and it is these that we talk of here. And even for those who wanted 'all that men have', their own circumstances as well as the inherent technical impossibility of such complete transition made individual expectations fairly nuanced and real.

Murali expressed hir compromise with the situation: 'I have come to know that complete SRS is very expensive. So I will work on getting facial hair, removal of breasts and uterus.' And Anand spoke of his well-thought-out plans:

> I want to get top surgery, it has to be done, then start hormones.... Not to do bottom surgery afterwards is another complication altogether. If I like someone and she likes me, now she sees this guy she is attracted to and then what do I tell her? That I'm a girl? Now at least it's easier, and it's easier for the other person.

Some did continue to dream about getting everything possible done. But several were aware that not only is reconstructive bottom surgery quite expensive, but also that it might not be very reliable.[2] Several people also had fears about the negative impact of all these interventions—loss of strength, being unable to keep doing the work they were doing and not being able to continue living in the same place without attracting too much attention to themselves.

The compromises did seem half-hearted. Santosh, Karthik and Kirti all identify as 'man' and this is what they had to say:

> **Santosh**: If my breasts were ever made public I would kill myself. So I would like to get rid of them.

Karthik: Yes, I want to go through an SRS. No, I have not undergone any surgery as yet because I have no money. My wish is to be a proper man before I die.

Kirti: There are men and women and 50–50. For myself, I know God has given me the body of a woman, but I would have liked that of a man.

While not everyone who felt dissonance with their body wanted intervention and change, there were some who wanted different kinds of interventions. Bhargavi had a nuanced articulation of what ze would like:

I feel I should have a body without breasts, but I want a vagina. Half... of my body is comfortable for me and half... uncomfortable for society. Breasts are visible and can identify me as a woman. If I have a vagina, I have no problem, but for society it is a problem. If I had a penis, it would be a problem for me, but for society it would not.

Equally emphatically, Sandy, who speaks of hirself as 'other', said:

I do not want to keep my breasts and have often said that I want to remove them.... But they do not bother me to the extent that I would do so if there was a health risk. I can live with them. But I have no desire to change my vagina. It is also very important for me in terms of sexual pleasure and I have never desired to have a penis.

In spite of so many people wanting so many different kinds of interventions, at the time of the interviews only one of our respondents, Rahul, was undergoing hormonal treatment and preparing for surgery. He expressed the difference it has made to him:

Earlier I used to feel that the words are mine but it's someone else's voice. I was self-conscious about talking. Now I feel confident. It's my voice and my words.... The doctor had said there could be side effects. But nothing has shown up. I don't know if it's just suiting me or whether I am too happy.... Work has to be done to look how you actually want. I have heard that trans* persons still

> don't feel satisfied even after taking hormones, they gain weight,
> etc. That made my will power even stronger to not feel this way, to
> work towards what I really want. I dance, exercise, I walk wherever
> I can. You have to not look at side effects but at the benefits.

For many of our respondents medical interventions, including surgeries, were key to attaining the body that matched their identity and thus their sense of self. But there are several barriers in terms of both the availability of these procedures and access to them. To begin with, there is a massive lack of adequate, reliable information about these interventions in the public domain. Not only has there been almost no substantive research, most doctors are ill-informed about whatever little knowledge does exist. Moreover, the cost of such interventions is prohibitive enough to place them well beyond the reach of the people who require them the most. Only the few who were able to access detailed information, not just about the procedures but also their after effects, and had the financial means, were able to make informed choices more easily.

The 'Experts'

The women's health movements have worked hard at exposing the anti-women character of modern medicine and its practitioners. Their seeing the male body as the norm and viewing women only as reproducers, not really listening to their experiences and concerns, has been well documented. Our PAGFB respondents add another layer to this understanding—their tales of hospitals and doctors revealed practitioners' blindness to issues of sexuality and gender, their close-minded approach to patients' lived experiences and the heteronormative framework within which they operate.

To begin with, there was the common assumption that marriage would resolve all health issues, especially those related to the menstrual cycle. As Alpana told us, 'I always had this erratic date problem with my periods and twice or thrice I went to doctors who all said, "You get married and have a kid and you'll be fine," which was never an answer.' Or even for general health conditions, as Ranjana said, marriage is seen as the solution to all maladies. 'I... used to fall sick a lot earlier. When I was in the first year of college, I was taken to a doctor and he said, "Get her married, she'll be fine." That angered me a lot. I actually had a calcium deficiency.'

Along with this article of faith is the widespread belief that all PAGFB must, by a certain age, be married to cismen and should produce children as soon as possible. Manjula spoke of hir frustration with a gynaecologist who was very worried that ze would not be able to conceive because of PCOS:

> They assumed I was married and they were discussing amongst themselves that I would not be able to have a child and that they should talk to the husband. I said, 'I am not married and you can talk to me directly.' Then they changed and said, 'Oh no, you can get married, no problem, you will conceive.' And I said, 'No I am not getting married, but in any case the uterus is inside me, you need to talk to me, not to my husband.'

Another casual assumption is that those who are not married are not sexually active. This results in an anxiety about going to doctors, expressed by many people. Jamuna put it very well:

> When you visit gynaecs, they never ask you if you are sexually active. They only ask if you are married and then they assume that you don't have sex. And then they probably don't do a whole lot of tests because of that.... So now I have started telling them that I am not married but I am sexually active. The next level is whether to tell that I am not having only heterosexual sex but also different kinds of sex, which should change the way you should look at my body.

Of late there are a few doctors in some of the metros who are open to asking if the person is sexually active, but that does not really resolve the problem either. Chandni said of hir dilemmas:

> What is sex and what it means to a gynaecologist, I have no clue.... I wonder when people say 'sex', are they talking about orgasm, penetration? It isn't clear. I try to gauge what the doctor is looking

for, I try to provide a specific answer to the question. But it's tough to figure out what to say, or figure out what information to keep in or leave out.

Sexual lives are difficult enough to talk about; it becomes even more complicated to explain when your partner is a trans* person. Vimala told us of a ciswoman friend who was 'married' to a 'man'-identified PAGFB. The friend had some swelling in her groin and went to her doctor. Vimala accompanied her but was not allowed into the examination room till she forcibly entered when she heard her friend screaming. The doctors had asked her friend if she was married, and she had answered in the affirmative. On hearing this, and learning that she 'still' did not have children, instead of attending to her immediate problem, the doctors were trying to put something inside her to find out why she was not getting pregnant.

This incident points to multiple erasures. First, Vimala was translating for her friend, but the doctors did not want her there because they trusted their own knowledge more than people's own experiences of their bodies. Second, they thought that there could be no more severe health issue for a married woman than the fact that she had not conceived in spite of being married for three months. Obviously, then, 'marriage' to them meant, by default, marriage of a ciswoman to a cisman, which is in itself a narrow view. But even if they were to be excused on that score because that is the only form of marriage that is legally recognized, there is certainly no excuse for doctors imagining that all sexual relationships are heteronormative ones.

If non-normative sexuality and sexual choices are things that doctors have not talked about, then what really baffles them and the whole medical establishment are people living— and passing—in genders other than those assigned to them at birth. This gave rise to many tragi-comic situations for our respondents, but it is difficult to laugh at incidents that reek of such ignorance around the social realities of our bodies among those who are supposed to be experts in all matters related to the physical body.

Sunny narrated what ze thinks of as hir best experience of the medical system. When ze had to go for an ultrasound,

> the person who came to scan me thought I was male and put me down as male.... Then he put the ultrasound machine over me and began scanning. Halfway, he stopped and began to look really concerned. I began to get worried: what did I have? Cancer? AIDS? He just said that this may happen to one person in crores. He would not talk to me but he called for my mother. He told her, 'Do you know, your son has ovaries?'.... I was so pleased to be called her son, but I also was shocked at the ignorance of the medical guys, they are all dopes who are so dumb they cannot make out the difference between a man and a woman.

Murali spoke of the time that ze went to a doctor's OPD with another trans* person. Murali's file went in, but ze was not called for ages:

> [The] doctor could see me through the glass door... kept calling everyone but did not call my name. Everyone finished and left.... I then went directly and asked the doctor why I was not being called. She said, 'Your file has not yet come to us.' I showed the doctor my receipt. The file and receipt showed a female name.... The doctor was confused as she saw us as two men sitting outside.

It is not just that doctors do not get it. The trouble, really, is that they go on to advise, moralize and comment on what people are wearing or how they look. As Arun said, 'I am ill and have come for help and it is your duty to look at that problem and not talk... about my clothes, etc.... It is not your duty to give lectures on morality.'

For trans* and queer people all this means avoiding the medical establishment. It is also the fear of being forced into a situation when your birth-assigned gender is reinforced. Many people who identified as 'man' said that when they went to a doctor they gave their assigned gender, because the doctors should know and be able to treat their problems accordingly. Some, like Anand, however, differed. He said, 'I see doctors as a guy—so I pack as well as bind when I go to a doctor.'

Hospitalization, though, is another matter altogether, because then there are not only doctors, but also all the other staff and other patients to deal with, as well as the gender-segregated wards for patients. Kamal recalled being put in the male ward while his partner worriedly kept looking for him in the female ward. She kicked up a racket and he was finally brought to the women's ward. 'They kept asking her if I was really a boy or girl. Using the ladies' toilet was also a problem. Other patients created a problem. The doctors would not say anything, but the nurses made a noise about it.'

All such experiences made every visit to the doctor a dreaded affair. It is this very health system that those wanting changes in their bodies have to approach. It is such doctors who then become the experts who opine on whether they can have the interventions that they need. It is doctors trained in these narrow ways who are the source of information for what will work best for an individual choosing a medical intervention. And when the individual's body is itself non-normative, the medical reaction is even more adverse.

Divakar's body had blindsided him in his 20s and made accessing any livelihood options difficult. So he finally went to a public teaching hospital to try to get a certificate saying his gender was male:

> The doctors just stripped me... one after the other, did not tell me anything and just went away with the reports. They kept saying that they would give me the certificate, but they seemed to be just watching me with curiosity and showing me to everyone, including the students around.... After five days, I said that I do not have money and so I cannot come again. They gave me some money, but said that if I wanted the certificate then I had to come to the hospital for 15 days.... They were also giving me some injections and tablets. I have no idea what they were.

Divakar felt extremely violated in the way his body was made a spectacle of. What is striking in his narration is the fact that no one at the hospital had the knowledge to comprehend what he was going through and they did not think it important to explain what little they knew to him. He was able to come to terms with his situation only much later, with the help of a supportive NGO working on issues of gender and sexuality.

Living with a different body is not easy. The fear of being caught in a situation where you might not be able to tell someone about it is a constant source of anxiety for all those with bodies that differ from their gender presentation. Sandhya, another respondent with intersex variations, spoke of hir fears about falling ill, '[I] have not fallen ill at all so far. But I do… worry about being taken to the hospital if I am suddenly ill and brought, say, by the police when I am unconscious.'

Mental Health Concerns

The only professionals that people seem to feel a little more comfortable reaching out to and who also seem to be providing better services are the mental health practitioners—counsellors, therapists and psychiatrists. A little under half of our respondents had been to a mental health professional at some point, either voluntarily or referred by community organizations and support groups, or forcibly taken by family. However, given the heteronormative structures all around, bad experiences with mental health professionals too were only to be expected.

Jai decided to see a counsellor when he got into his first relationship because he thought what he was doing was an illness. The counsellor not only asked him to come back with his girlfriend, he also assured Jai that he would 'make both of them okay'. '[But] my girlfriend said, "I will not come as he cannot make any life for us and also that I did not ask him before loving and I do not want to see him now."' However, Jai went back to the same counsellor when he survived the joint suicide pact in which his girlfriend died. Deeply disturbed, he was looking for help, but was reprimanded instead: 'He scolded me and said, "Such things are not acceptable here, this is not America."' Jai soon stopped going.

While Jai had sought help on his own, Priya was taken to a counsellor by her parents after they came to know of her sexual orientation. She said, 'The second counsellor made my father sit in during the sessions, how unethical is that? She even said that my being lesbian was because of the atmosphere at home and me seeing unhappy marriages. In a way, it helped me because my parents took the blame.' These visits were soon discontinued.

Vimala's family also forced her to see more than one psychiatrist and she was put through aversion therapy amongst other things:

> When I imagine my current partner, he gives me a slight shock, and when I imagine the male friend, he withdraws it. That was his treatment. I would deliberately imagine the reverse and would have fun out of this whole process. And so it has not affected me. Then he would show nude pictures of men.

Others like Falguni sought help because they had problems in their relationships. But she was not happy with her counsellor either, who did not seem professional enough: 'The problem was that she already had some preconceived notions about me. I felt she "knew" me already…. Because when she spoke, she said things which I had not told her. So she had heard from elsewhere.' Falguni did not go back to her.

There were good experiences with mental health practitioners as well and they were a pleasant surprise. Quite a few of our respondents had managed to find through friends, community, organizations and sheer chance some really good counsellors. Anand and Meghana were both effusive when they spoke of their experiences. Anand was happy that not only did his counsellor help him deal with his depression related to a bad experience at work, she also accepted his gender identity without batting an eyelid. Similarly, Meghana said:

> I was very sceptical about finding somebody in India who would be queer friendly, who would be feminist, who would have secular principles, basically not be gender-phobic or homophobic

in any sense. I think I was very lucky and found an amazing psychoanalyst…. She has no judgement whatsoever about anything that I tell her. Because you have to realize I have a bit of [a] crazy lifestyle.

Many other respondents also were fairly content with their mental health professionals. It was not as if the experience was similarly or uniformly good, but at least people did find someone who was aware of issues around both non-normative sexuality and gender. As some of our respondents realized that their desires and choices were not welcome in the world at large, when they found that there was no space to speak of the broken heart and when their lives seemed just too difficult to carry on with, it was these professionals who helped them come to terms with their loneliness. Some even managed to seek help from psychiatrists to get that all-important permission to start some amount of medical intervention to change their bodies in accordance with their genders, and in particular with their own notions of their bodies.

Among the list of trained medical practitioners, mental health professionals, then, stand out as somewhat more aware about issues of gender and sexuality. Possibly the fact that both homosexuality and gender identity issues have been treated as disorders and discussed amongst the community of psychiatrists and counsellors, has led to a greater awareness amongst them. There are still practitioners like the ones that Jai and Falguni met, but at the same time there were many good ones too.

The other possible reason for this is that there has been much more awareness amongst queer groups and communities to find supportive professionals as they are also constantly needed. Considering the kind of lives our respondents lived, they reported a lot of depression, loneliness and at times confusion caused by the discord between what they felt and what was expected of them. The structures and institutions around them were obviously not supportive, and were exclusionary as well as violently imposing norms on their lives. All of this resulted in disturbed behaviour, including self-harm and attempted suicides.

Twenty of our 50 respondents had attempted suicide at least once, some as many as three or four times. At least seven others had seriously contemplated suicide, and some described the extreme depression that they went through at some point in their lives. One person spoke of recurring mental health issues that left her very traumatized and led her to attempt suicides several times.

Alpana said that she had had serious self-esteem issues even when she had been a child because of the way her grandmother treated her. When she grew up and got into an abusive relationship with a cisman, it drove her into depression:

> My insecurity went really high. I stopped eating because he always used to tease me that I was fat and not good looking, so I thought if I grew thin and grew my hair long, I'd get him. I couldn't sleep—had to take sleeping pills.

Our respondents' lives give us more information on not only the kind of problems that people face because of living their gender and sexuality differently, but also to the already multiple levels at which mental health issues do not get addressed in any systemic way by the health system. Respondents spoke of such issues that were unrelated to gender and sexuality, both in their own lives and in the lives of people around them. At least five people told us of the mental illnesses of people close to them. In one case it was a partner, but in the other situations it was a parent.

As young children they perceived the unwell parent's behaviour as neglect towards themselves, causing long-term trauma, which many were dealing with till date. Maushami, who carries the scar of neglect, said, 'My mother suffers from depression. She has never been taken to see a doctor. It's evident she is schizophrenic. There is much tension in the house because of this…. I am not blaming her but I think she spoilt my childhood.'

Neha had an equally tough time understanding her mother's behaviour, who had a chronic mental disorder. Even though Neha was abused by her father, when her parents fought, she believed that her mother was 'an aggressive, untrustworthy woman'. She added, 'My grandparents were aware of my mother's behaviour and took care of her…. No one bothered to inform me in any way or help me understand the situation.'

Even for those few of our respondents—and these were just a handful—who did not face direct trauma as children, did not come from violent families or were not abused by the people close to them physically, emotionally and psychologically for being non-conforming, the fact that they lived in a predominantly heteronormative society itself made the possibility of making positive choices in life extremely difficult. As one of our respondents who is a mental health professional said, alluding to their personal experience as well to that of many others:

> Living in a heterosexual, non-accepting heterosexist milieu, you need to be able to negate that in order to be able to establish yourself. To create you need to negate that, whereas the key is in synthesis…. Whether you acknowledge [those experiences] or not, you live with a certain amount of disability or resilience based on them. You can't wish away something, you can't forget, it's not a slate that you can wipe clean.

For the large majority of our respondents, apart from this general heterosexist environment, there were multiple other types of marginalization like caste, disability, and so on, as well as other kinds of violence and neglect to deal with, all of which made coping difficult. They found their own ways to be able to lead a life with some semblance of equanimity. The most commonly used strategy was that of withdrawing, staying quiet, crying, sleeping and dealing with things on their own because they did not know who to go to till they found those few friends or a community where there were people like them or an organization that could refer them to a trusted professional. Some spoke of addictions like smoking, drinking and doping.

A few people who had access to these activities spoke of creative things like reading, exercising, music, walks, pottery, gardening and yoga. A few others were drawn to religion. Most of our respondents, however, did not really respond as much to organized formal religion. Very few spoke of their guilt because of religion; instead, they chose teachings and interpretations that legitimized their realities. Interestingly, it was the serenity of the church or the temple that made them feel at peace, irrespective of whether it belonged to the faith they were born into. Chosen spiritual gurus like Osho, Ramakrishna and the Brahmakumaris, or merely a belief in the divine, also helped.

The Desiring Body

It was the belief in one's feeling and choices that essentially seemed to help many of our respondents to deal with everything that the normative world forced them to endure. And that is where once again the body and the material self comes in. The body, which is otherwise a source of discomfort and unease, is also the means to exploring sexuality, of sexual selves. An exploration that most of our queer PAGFB respondents seemed to see and speak of as fun, which turns this same complicated body into a site of pleasure. While doing this, there were constant negotiations with the normative, peno-vaginal definition of sex. Sometimes it inhibited people's expressions, but often the impossibility of this kind of sex with the people they desired, for most of our respondents, led to multiple ways of revisioning what sex meant, and especially of their expected roles in sexual encounters.

We heard many positive statements on masturbation. Saran said:

> I realize most people masturbate. And I have come to the conclusion that it is a very healthy outlet. Sometimes you are stuck with your work, nothing is happening, you're frustrated, not liking the way your relationship is going. You don't talk very well to your partner. When you masturbate and come back, you ease out immediately.

Juhi said:

> In the context of two people, how you feel while in sexual activity and after is coloured by many things. Whereas, when you're on your own, after an intense physically pleasurable experience, what are the thoughts you have about yourself, about your life are very, very, qualitatively different. It's not only that masturbation is very nice and beautiful, but also very important.

Several respondents spoke of finding pleasure in pleasing their partners. Anand and Sara defined themselves as pleasers. Kavi said, 'In terms of working towards pleasure, I work towards the pleasure of us both.' Vimala's concern for her 'man'-identified PAGFB partner was apparent when she admitted:

> I would have a lot of doubt and anxiety about how someone who does not undress can give the other pleasure and enjoy himself too. How does he get pleasure?… But he has said that when I enjoy [it], that is when he gets his pleasure. And he wouldn't do this if he didn't get sexual satisfaction.

There is no notion of sacrificing one's own pleasure; several voices expressed the idea of a mutuality in which one's own pleasure is also underlined. As Jharna put it, 'I would say every sensual touch is important for me and I work for it. And I take care that the person I'm with should also get maximum pleasure. When I'm in bed with someone, there is nothing that is bad.' Alpana said 'I'm very exploring in bed': 'Recently I have [had a] preference for bondage and other fetishes—[have been] into it for the last few months and really enjoying it, but even there I have no preference in terms of dominant or submissive.' And Kanika said:

> I love bondage, I love handcuffs and ropes, but it must be safe sex and consensual. And I love both, to dominate or being dominated. I love any bodily acts that are safe and mutual. I also love oral sex and I love experimenting with new things.

Besides variations in who and what different people were attracted to, many respondents recognized how the experience of sex changed for them with different people or from situation to situation. The openness with which all of this seems to be embraced not only challenges many aspects of the normative, but it also indicates the multiplicity and, in that sense, the queering of desire. Maushami, who had been in relationships with women and with trans* persons, said, 'With women you can be passive or active, or anything that you want to.... In other kinds of relationships I want the other person to take initiative. I love to get pleasure first.'

Meghana spoke about certain moments of intimacy that make hir feel genderless:

> It does not matter any more what your gender is, what your age is, what your colour is, skin is, how your body is. You are meeting at another place or level. And I really appreciate feeling genderless and feeling that for once I am not defined or I don't have to define.

Some, who said they were bisexual, had their own take. Simran said, '[With women] I have a natural tendency to move towards a mirror [image].... With men it is very different, though. There I need the absolute opposite.... I want anti-chemistry really.' Geeta, on the other hand, found the language of bisexuality itself limiting because:

> It reinstates the binary. Once at a conference I found an MTF [male-to-female really attractive. This attraction was because of the gender transgression. And then I figured the attraction was a broader thing, towards people who gender-transgress and not necessary in one direction. Bisexuality is binary, so if I am attracted towards gender transgression, then who am I?

Chandni narrated hir experience with a cisman thus:

> After some time he would tell me, 'You know, I'm not a lesbian, I have things you can put to use.' And, I would say, 'I don't want that,

I want your fingers.' So I realized later that I liked queer sex.... And not much role-playing—that's okay, but not in a fixed way.

It is also in these intimacies that lack of gender affirmations and negation of gender identities leave a hugely negative impact on a person. Some 'man'-identified respondents, fearing rejections of this nature, chose not to enter into relationships at all. But those who did manage to negotiate gender within their relationships, found the canvas and scope of roles much more complex, and even playful, in the sexual space.

Monu said:

One friend had asked me this question, 'Suppose her hand goes to your vagina. Then you will think that it is not a vagina, it is a penis. And if she thinks also of it as a penis, then what is the problem?' I also thought that when I am having relations, I do not see these as vagina or breasts.... Then I went and asked [my partner], 'What do you think when you touch me there?' And she also said the same, that, 'I do not think of it as vagina. I see it as penis.' Then I said, 'Then it is all right if sometimes you touch, but penetration I cannot have.' And she never does it too.

Kirti spoke of the unique method that he and his partners employ:

[My partner] used to say that I am her husband. After six months I made her my husband.... We used to mark it on the calendar and take turns. When I was husband I would penetrate. I would make love to her like a husband would to his wife. When she was husband she would do it like that... we always maintained this pattern. With [my other partner] for the last three years now I am the husband. But we both penetrate. With her the term 'husband' does not have much meaning.... There is a lot of equality between us so what is the point of husband–wife?

Kanika, who identifies as 'woman but fluid', described how sexual play operated for hir:

When I feel feminine I love being penetrated. There were times when I was penetrated by my partner and we fantasized that she

[had] a penis and we both loved it, it was the same when I became her man. But sometimes we had sex fantasizing both of us as girls or as men. Because we both switch a lot.

Conclusion

As bodily difference is a crucial aspect in all gendered power dynamics, the body is critical to any discourse around gender. Enquiries and studies, especially from the perspectives of those marginalized because of their difference—for example, women and disabled persons—have foregrounded the fact that there is no 'normal' or 'natural'; that what is termed 'natural' is in itself socially constructed; and that the language of the 'normal' is just a ruse to criminalize everything that is not in tune with the dominant discourse and practice. In fact, these engagements have shown how this discourse actually constructs systems of access, ability and capability.

The subject of feminism, however, has been the woman perceived as distinct from the man based on the assumption of fixed difference of the body. Trans* lives remove this direct alignment of gender with the body. Engaging with trans* PAGFB realities leads us to say that the gendered body that has been assigned gender female at birth is not necessarily a woman's body but is subjected to the same restrictions and rules to which women's bodies are subjected. This, itself, brings in new dimensions to our understanding of the gendered body.

The identities of queer and trans* PAGFB are in a way connected to the body in ways that those of other PAGFB may not be. An active choice of sexuality in the case of queer people and the dissonance that trans* persons may feel with their bodies make it possible to state once again that while the body does not determine us—neither our gender nor our sexuality—but is a vital aspect of our being. While it is foolhardy to say that the body is not important, it is necessary to continuously point to the inadequacy of defining people merely by their bodies, especially in set, restricted, constructed ways, however scientific these may claim to be. Our bodies, then, are as constructed as our genders are natural.

This possibility of skewing the alignment between gender and the body adds a nuance to our feminisms. It allows for a more creative and playful relationship with the body. It frees gender identity and expression from bodily restraints, allowing them to be lived through the imagined body as well. Each one of us, irrespective of gender, should be able to find legitimacy through the idea that we do not just inhabit our physical body, we also live in the imagination of it.

Along with such lessons for our individual lives come urgent reminders to revisit the knowledge and understanding of the 'experts'—those who help maintain and sustain the 'natural' and the 'normal'. In their eagerness to classify and categorize, they are collapsing the multiple ways of being that humans may and do discover. It is urgent that we recognize this diversity and move away from reductionist discourse around the body so that we understand that there are no clear-cut 'male' or 'female' bodies, and hence there is no need to keep constructing them in particular ways for reasons of social acceptance. At the same time there is urgent need to build expertise to help people craft their gender and construct their bodies in consonance with these imaginations in ways that are mindful of their wellbeing.

Notes

1. Top surgery is the commonly used term for bilateral mastectomy, that is, removal of breasts and/or reconstruction of the chest region.
2. Bottom surgery generally refers to complete hysterectomy (removal of uterus) and/or genital reconstruction.

11

Gender: Some Conclusions and the Path Ahead

Throughout my younger life, I have been coaxing out what I call 'inherent' gender, looking in the mirror and making changes till one is happy finally with what one sees [till] one is seeing an image that is pleasing to oneself. The tension is between creating the image that the world demands and the image that one wants. In that sense I view myself as having had to reconstruct the original. I am not sure what the age was when I got entirely comfortable.... Twenty is a good age as a reference point when the reconstructed image was complete, the process of removing the conditioning, the rules, etc., and finding what one likes. And even when one finds what one likes, it is a journey to allow oneself to like what one sees in that image. You are pleased by it but you are oppressed by the idea of it being wrong. And to then make that transition towards celebrating, and for me that celebration begins when you are happy with what you see [and] glad that the world is seeing it. (Sandy, 34 years)

In the prevailing binary system gender is not just biologically determined based on the perceived sex at birth, it is also a hierarchical construct, with both categories being mutually impermeable. This construct pervades every institution, structure and interaction. It is enforced by norms, maintained by an intricate system of rewards and punishments, and reproduced continuously by social and cultural practices. Binary gender is thus normalized into the very fabric of human existence and seems inevitable and unbreakable.

A rigorous and enormous body of work by feminists from all around the world have dissected and critiqued this system and laid bare its constructedness, its inherent oppression and inequality, and the effects it has had on women in different locations and spheres of life. Queer and trans* theorists have added to this literature, questioning the very assumption that there are only two genders. Different questions raised over time, from specific and distinct locations, have added to the richness of these debates.

We locate ourselves both in the women's movements as well as the queer movements here in India, though our debates with and departures from the mainstream currents of both are significant and our work is naturally influenced by these critiques. Through this study, our readings and political engagements, we find ourselves in resonance with the emerging queer and transfeminist national and international discourses.

The lives of our 50 respondents point to the nuance and diversity with which gender is lived. They reveal how gender is a complex interplay of many factors, where the extremely personal inner world interacts in multiple ways with the external one of society and culture. Their narratives, along with the political struggles and articulations of queer and trans* movements resoundingly tell us that not only can the binary structure be broken, by lives being lived differently in the here and now, but also that there can be different systems of gender. Our study helps envision bits of a new gender system that is multiple, egalitarian and porous, and adds to the ongoing conversations around the world.

Decoding the Binary

The prevailing system of gender assumes a completely dimorphic world, divided into men and women, as well as an absolute continuity between sex and gender. The binary works in two ways: one, it demarcates bodies into two sexes, male and female, based on a stereotypical understanding of genitals; and two, it ensures that the genders of all persons, based on a complex process of socialization (the subject of enormous bodies of feminist and other work), adhere completely to the sex that they have been assigned at birth based on their genitals. Of course, this system does not use the language of assignment, but rather that of 'born male' or 'born female', thus naturalizing and normalizing this dimorphism into every possible thought and activity of human existence.

By connecting the process of socialization to the sex assigned at birth, so that people become men and women by learning masculinity and femininity, this system is biologically determinist in two ways. In the first it connects the learned traits and trappings of femininity and masculinity to specific genitally distinct bodies, thus making each body predestined to living life in a particular manner. In the other it ensures that no movement happens between the two genders. Further, this system does not assign equal status to the two genders, but values men, masculinity and maleness higher than women, femininity and femaleness in every way. This difference too is coded into the binary.

In such a segregated, patriarchal, heteronormative society, roles are well defined—and narrowly interpreted—and are strictly adhered to, without being challenged or questioned too deeply. This construct has been so compulsory for so long that it even masquerades as 'natural'. There is hardly any room to manoeuvre or to create alternatives. These gender norms are enforced through a well-calibrated scheme of rewards and punishments. Those who conform are rewarded by societal and legal sanction, citizenship rights and familial support. At the same time, those who challenge or transgress find the norms enforced in extremely violent ways. This is true of both the public as well as the more invisible private spaces.

Families, aided and abetted by schools, keep trying to overrule young people's own desires in order to bring them up as 'good' daughters (or sons) and 'good' girls (or boys) in keeping with rigid conventions. Natal families emerge more often as a site of major conflict and opposition than of support and concern. Monitoring of gender expression, moral policing of sexuality and forced heterosexual marriages are some of the standard ways in which the norms of the gender binary are imposed. In such a scenario intimate relationships of people's own choosing could provide a safe harbour, but the normative system denies such unions both social recognition and legal rights—in other words, it punishes them.

Public spaces are built and designed using the gender binary as a principle. Segregation based on the idea that there are two mutually exclusive and coherent genders is used in restrooms, public transport, hospitals, checks at malls and airports, and so on. Ostensibly put in place for safety and security of all users, this system means that people are subject to scrutiny by figures of official authority as well as by any user of that public space. People who are seen as transgressing established gender norms face a gamut of punishments, ranging from denial of access to verbal harassment and/or physical assault. The situation of collective and individual policing of public spaces thus created relies on subjective estimations of a person's gender that are based on how they look and act. Ironically, the burden of safety rests on the individual and their ability to pass rather than the system that is designed for their supposed safety.

In such circumstances, living one's gender is often a delicate balancing act. On the one hand is the need for safety that brings with it the pressure to conform, and on the other the equally pressing need to be oneself, whatever that entails, whether it has to do with appearance or behaviour. No matter what strategies a person uses in order to fulfil both needs, vulnerability levels remain high, as does the incidence of violence, abuse, stigma and discrimination.

> For some of us, the meanings culture drapes upon our bodies are extremely painful and depressing. Worse still, a gender system tends to enforce monolithic meanings. Big breasts must mean one thing, hairy backs another, wrinkles yet another still, providing us little or no room to construct ourselves and create alternatives.
>
> Simply having our bodies exposed to social judgement can be painful and disturbing to some people....
>
> *What does it cost to tell the truth?*

> I guess if your sense of self matches closely with the cultural grid of what you should mean, and you find those meanings pleasing, then the 'truth' doesn't come too expensive. For the rest of us, though, it can cost a great deal. (Wilkins 2006: 551, emphasis original)

While it is clear that trans* persons face brutal violence due to the gender binary, they are not the only ones. Such violence has to be understood in conjunction with the violence that 'women' face within the same heteronormative patriarchal system. Recognizing cis privilege and understanding how it operates is crucial and needs to be more and more part of the ongoing discussions in queer and feminist spaces, but it would be incorrect to say that trans* persons are the only ones fighting gender battles. Every time the gender expression of a person does not match their perceived identity, the person is subjected to intense scrutiny, which is often violent. Hence, ciswomen, and cismen too, who defy the norms of masculinity and femininity have to fight long, hard gender battles with little or no support.

People who are marginalized by factors such as class, caste, religion or ability also face these battles incessantly given that the systems of oppression do not operate singly but in tandem with each other. All of these axes of difference complicate how the gender binary operates. Every society has its scripts for the ways in which people of a certain gender, age, body appearance and so on are allowed to express themselves. Yet, also built into these societal norms is the amount of transgression that is allowed, to whom and in what situations. For instance, the class we belong to determines the spaces we may access and the ways in which we are allowed to behave in them. Thus, PAGFB with more societal privileges are able to express their gender in ways that may not conventionally be very 'woman'-like, such as attire. In fact, a limited bending of some norms may, in certain circumstances, be approved and even encouraged.

The Two-Gender Fallacy

In living their genders people question the binary in many different ways and their thoughts on gender are articulated from these varied positions. There is no uniformity to these articulations or these identities. So when we speak of dismantling the old, rigid gender system and envisioning new ways of being, it becomes essential to recognize that binary, normative gender is challenged in a multiplicity of ways. As Kessler and McKenna (2006: 178–80) say:

> Unless and until gender, in all of its manifestations including the physical, is seen as a social construction, action that will radically change our incorrigible propositions cannot occur. People must be confronted with the reality of other possibilities, as well as the possibility of other realities.

The narratives of our respondents reveal to us how important it can be for people to live their lives according to their own sense of their gender, despite the difficulties involved. All of them, to a greater or lesser extent, transgressed the norms of the gender binary, indicating some of the ways in which these norms are challenged. All these narratives added a crucial layer to our changing understanding of gender itself.

Not only did 28 of the 50 respondents choose a gender identity different from the one assigned to them at birth, as many as 18 chose to name themselves in ways that lay outside the binary. Thus, one of our very first findings underlined for us the vast gap between people's assigned gender and what they choose to call themselves. In a sense their voices emphasize the need for self-attribution of gender. As Kessler and McKenna (1978) have argued, this reflects that such a self-attributed gender identity can be relatively independent of the gender attributed by others.

Such a process of naming and of arriving at a language that helps people speak of their lives so as to resist the terms dictated by the binary makes it clear that gender identities make sense only when these are self-chosen and self-assigned. To be assigned such a personal identity at birth by someone else, long before one has had the chance to discover or understand anything about oneself, is therefore patently absurd.

Just as there are multiple gender identities, there appear to be a multitude of ways by which different people arrive at the gender location or name that seems most appropriate and comfortable for them. Some may traverse long routes that bring them to that destination, while others may know very early in life precisely where they wish to be. Some people keep fine-tuning their gender expression till they achieve what feels like consonance rather than dissonance with their gender identity; others may not have the enabling factors of class, or of other supportive circumstances or affirmative relationships, and may feel the gap between self-image and reality more keenly. Some may be comfortable enough (or be allowed) to express their inner gender only in certain spaces and not in others.

Which is not to say that once you find the place that seems right for you, you necessarily live there or wish to live there for all time to come. Individuals might keep trying different genders till they find the one that 'fits' or they may adapt and alter existing genders to suit their personal requirements. Or you might stay with the name you have chosen, but keep modifying its meaning and its possibilities. People's lived realities indicate how gender identity may be fairly flexible for some individuals and relatively fixed for others. It is also evident that even when people do not feel such discord with their birth-assigned gender that they need to name themselves differently, they do almost invariably feel the need to question the normativity and the fixity of their gender assignment and of all that comes with it. In other words, it is an ongoing process of crafting one's own gender.

One of the critical insights we gained was that gender identity is both innate and constructed. We have learnt by talking to persons with varied gender identities and expressions that the question, 'Why are you "x" gender?', seems to have no answer other than, 'Because that is how I feel.' There is as much subjectivity in such naming of one's gender as there is a constructedness that has to do with making it intelligible to others in this persistently gendered world. Thus, the felt gender is refracted through the individual's social reality and expressed in ways that are allowed and possible within their location.

It is not surprising, then, for example, that a PAGFB who identifies as 'man' will adopt those traits of masculinity that are prevalent around him. If dominant ways of being 'masculine' are not under scrutiny in his society by and large, then these will not readily be reflected in his way of being a man. In all probability the prevalent traits might be even more obvious, in the sense that a transman might seem more 'masculine' to us because that is what he is projecting as a gender cue in order to gain acceptance for his gender identity. This performance of gender in public should not be read simplistically as attempts to access 'male privilege and power'. This study clearly shows that the very definitions of masculinity and femininity are highly nuanced, and broken in multiple ways, by people while living their felt genders.

One area where this happens most often is that of intimacy. Since societal roles and norms of gender are so clearly defined, it is easy even for those in non-normative relationships to slip into available stereotypes. But in families (natal or chosen) and relationships where there is greater acceptance, where traditional gender norms are questioned and challenged, where the possibility of conversations and understanding exist, and where genders are unquestioningly accepted in the ways in which they are felt, the meanings of 'masculine' and 'feminine' too are altered and tweaked. Since the binary system is premised on the mutually exclusive hierarchy of masculinity and femininity, this reconfiguration allows for multiple redefinitions, some obvious but many apparent only as and when the varied ways of being are recognized and accepted.

Gender, then, has to be seen as a process of discovery, a work-in-progress, inflected and influenced by class and caste and education, negotiated through interactions with strangers and within intimate relationships, working its way around obstacles and redefining boundaries. It is both a point of departure and sometimes of arrival, which is why it makes sense to speak of it as a journey.

The realities of these lives demand that violently enforced gender norms must give way to a more egalitarian and voluntary system of gender. The flexibility that we see in individual lives needs to become part of our societal collective consciousness. Whether the world is more or less gendered, gender categories must be made less rigid; strict gender prescriptions need to be relaxed. The consequent blurring of boundaries between existing categories will spell the end of the present structure that perpetuates itself by punishing those who transgress and rewarding those who conform or seem to conform.

This might seem like a radical transformation or as yet another revolution that might never come. But we need to remember that it is very much within our grasp because it is already true of lives being lived. When institutions and spaces are designed to facilitate individuals in moving across, straddling, claiming and redefining varied gender identities with greater ease and without fear of reprisals, the closed binary system with its increasingly implausible hierarchies and mutually impermeable fixed categories will have been transformed into an open, porous, non-hierarchical and multiple-gendered one.

Plasticity, Not Fluidity

We advocate movement and flexibility as opposed to stasis or rigidity. Does that, then, imply that we need to look at gender, or at an alternative system of gender, as being characterized by 'fluidity'? While people searching for a new language do use the term 'fluid' to indicate their dissatisfaction with the prevalent norms that allow for little or no movement, we carefully suggest 'plasticity' as a more accurate descriptor of how gender is constructed and of how it operates in an individual's life.

Gender can change for one person in their lifetime and the understanding of it that each person brings to their own identity can also change. This kind of change in genders and movement between different gender locations lends itself to be interpreted as a fluid system. We, however, would prefer to refer to this in terms of 'plasticity', with people occupying definite identities and locations, even though they might shift shape over time or move from one location to another.

'Plasticity', in this context, resonates with its use in the physical sciences. A physical chemistry book from 1922 called *Fluidity and Plasticity* states:

> We may now define plasticity as a property of solids in virtue of which they hold their shape permanently under the action of small shearing stresses but they are readily deformed, worked, or molded, under somewhat larger stresses. Plasticity is thus a complex property. (Bingham 1922: 216)

This definition distinguishes the solid state from the fluid (liquid or gaseous) state. Plasticity is a characteristic of a solid, whereas fluidity characterizes a gas (and viscosity a liquid). This means that solids can change shape, but they offer resistance to this process, and the more plastic a substance, the less the resistance to the same amount of force. A fluid, by definition, is something that has no shape and, hence, offers hardly any resistance to force.

In this context, in choosing to use 'plasticity' over 'fluidity', we see gender not as something amorphous and without definition; rather, we see it much in the manner as a solid, as holding a specific location and character (like holding a shape), but malleable enough to reshape. The required 'shearing stress' for any remoulding comes from the need for change felt innately by the individual, which itself is refracted by their location and the existing social structure.

We are using plasticity as a characteristic of gender. However, this also has some things in common with the everyday use of the word 'plastic'—any of a wide range of synthetic or semi-synthetic mouldable solids. Even if gender is understood in this sense, there are some convergences, as gender, in our understanding, is crafted out of an internally felt (organic) desire, which is influenced by external (synthetic) structures and metaphors prevalent in society, and expressed through the materiality of the body.

Our Bodies, Our Genders

A person's body is a space of continual and intense personal and socio-cultural dialogue, and often of dissent and difference. The body is as much a part of making oneself the gender that one chooses to be; yet, it is illogical to see this as a linear connection. It is foolhardy to say that the body is not important; yet, it is imperative to continuously point out the inadequacy of defining people merely by their bodies and that too in set, restricted, constructed ways, however scientific they may claim to be. And, finally, our bodies are as constructed as our genders are natural.

Not only gender, but sex too is inscribed on a person's body at birth and the socio-cultural prescriptions continue through life. At the same time, people themselves ascribe meanings to their bodies that sometimes work within the frameworks provided by their locations but often not. Each person also lives within the realm of their imagined body, whatever be their gender, whether assigned by society or chosen by oneself. In *Assuming a Body*, Gayle Salomon (2010: 77) says something similar:

> Social construction must not be construed oppositionally to a 'felt sense' of bodily being, for one can contend both that a body is socially constructed and that its felt sense is undeniable. What social construction offers is a way to understand *how* that felt sense arises, in all its historical and cultural variations, with all its urgency and immediacy, and to ask what it is, finally, that is delivered by that felt sense. (Emphasis original)

We must, thus, see the body as an integral part of a person's identity and understand any dissonance or dysphoria they might feel from their location within the matrix of their historical, material and imagined body.

Feminist critiques have laid bare the socio-cultural control and use of 'women's' bodies to construct every institution and structure of patriarchal society, be it class, caste, religion, nation, sexuality, ability, family, work, division of labour or any other. And given the lopsidedness of the gender hierarchy, all woman-gendered persons are fighting battles where their bodies are terrains of intense scrutiny and control, and, thus, also of severe trauma and violence. Trans* narratives and lives add a layer of difference to the nature of dissonance, dysphoria, violence and trauma of the gendered body. This difference also makes the imagined body and its inhabiting more complex.

Hence, it is important to see the need of gender-related body alterations that some trans* persons desire as crucial for their wellbeing and attainment of the self. This is precisely why it is vital to ask for and get the requisite medical services with minimal interference from either the state or the medico-legal professions.

However, the medico-legal professions are part of the same gender binary scheme that governs the rest of society and, therefore, while they control who can get what medical services, they also control how those people will qualify to get these interventions. Thus, the rules around 'passing and/or living in the opposite gender' for a required period of time, getting due certification from psychiatrists, and measuring the relative success or failure of each transition in terms of how 'successfully' or 'unsuccessfully' a person is able to live and function in the 'opposite' gender.

Maintaining the binary system in this manner reduces the space for seeking gender-related body alterations that might not fit the norms of 'becoming men and women' as prescribed by doctors. It also re-imposes the language of normativity on people wanting medical procedures and pushes them to fit into the system to be able to access what they want rather than enabling them to express their desires without always using the language of the binary. Dean Spade (2006: 329) speaks of this as a forced compromise:

The self-determination of trans people in crafting our gender expression is compromised by the rigidity of the diagnostic and treatment criteria. At the same time, this criteria and the version of transsexuality that it posits produce and reify a fiction of normal, healthy gender that works as a regulatory measure for the gender expression of all people. To adopt the medical understanding of transsexuality is to agree that SRS is the unfortunate treatment of an unfortunate condition, to accept that gender norm adherence is fortunate and healthy, and to undermine the threat to a dichotomous gender system which trans experience can pose.

As mentioned earlier, the limits of transgression are often built into the systems of control and reproduction since this helps sustain these massive systems while maintaining fictions of flexibility and accommodation. We believe that even in a society where more and more gender and body variations are accepted, people might still want medical changes. A truly transformative system would be one that relies on the person's self-defined desires for gender-related body changes without attempting to fit them into any predetermined category of gender.

Gender in Social Interaction

Gender has been so socially naturalized in the prevalent binary system that its expression is totally linked to its co-construction by others. Each of us attributes a gender to every person that we see and are perturbed when unable to do so. As a result, differently-identified people respond differently to perceptions of their genders in public and private spaces. There are no unifying similarities, but there are complex interactions between what a person wants to show, what is seen and the actual living that occurs in the interplay of these two factors. We have to recognize the role that societal attribution of gender has on a person's own perception and crafting of their gender. It is almost as if the expression of the identity is incomplete without the co-contribution by others in reading that expression. Gender is lived, performed and demonstrated in tandem with its continuous reading and attribution by others in each and every possible social interaction.

For those challenging the binary or the attributed gender, this process cannot and does not end with a single transgression. While there is an internal need that constantly challenges gender norms, along with it is the fear of having to fight the policing and violence people routinely encounter in trying to be themselves and breaking an increasingly dysfunctional binary. This is not easy at all in a normative world, where the divide itself enforces that transgressions too be in a certain way. So a 'man'-identified PAGFB might not just find personal satisfaction in dressing and appearing in an overtly masculine style, it might also make it much easier for him to be read in his chosen gender and to pass in different public spaces as well. It is more difficult, then, in the binary gender system for those who do not clearly present as 'men' or 'women' to pass or remain unnoticed.

Bergman (2006: 31) speaks of hir own experience of accessing something as necessary and non-confrontational as the bathroom:

> The bathroom is where gender performance meets public perception with a resounding *thwack*, one that sometimes hurts and sometimes reverberates down my butch life in unexpected ways. It's where I have to make a public declaration and I can never be sure which one might match what people are expecting from me, and the consequences for being wrong are always so unpleasant, because the wrongness is so basic.

From something as apparently innocuous as the bathroom to the role that a person plays in the workspace and in intimacies, the way one dresses and presents the socialized body, a balancing act is repeatedly performed—of trying to present one's non-normative gender using languages, scripts and readings that are moulded completely by the norms.

Varied transgressions, actually offer newer ways of living the binary as well. It is in all our collective interests to facilitate this opening up of the binary. This will also help transform many of the cisgender gender battles. To increase the possibilities of being, of living, of appearance, we all need to break the stereotypes by liberating our own blinkered visions of how we expect to see genders being expressed and lived. Presumption of knowledge in this case restricts the creation of new knowledge.

So perhaps it is time to ask and learn about the gender galaxy and the myriad meanings that people assign to various gender identities rather than remain stuck in the rigid, two-fold, familiar but restricted cultural collective contexts. All of us need to change how we think, work and behave, and start asking each person how they identify, rather than read, assume and attribute a gender to them. Gender, after all, needs to be consensual.

Gender, Sex, Sexuality: Systemic Shifts

One of the things that gets fundamentally transformed when we start thinking of gender in this manner is the system of sex and gender. Traditionally, sex and gender have been used interchangeably, and in ways that bind physical body characteristics to the social category of gender. It is believed that each person is born into a certain sex, either male or female, and this is wholly determined by the appearance of the external genitalia at the time of birth. This is why many queer and trans* discourses use terms such as 'female born' and 'male born'. However, we arrived at the descriptor 'persons assigned gender female at birth' to refer to our respondents.

Their lived realities indicated to us that they had little in common beyond the fact that they were all assigned the female gender at birth and, hence, this seemed to aptly describe them. While this gender assignment does describe a certain commonality of experience, it does not reflect the diversity of experiences due to various other locations of class, caste, religion, ability and sexuality that PAGFB simultaneously inhabit.

Rejecting the terminology of being 'born' a certain sex and choosing instead the assignment of a gender at birth entails the growing understanding that the categories of sex and gender are both distinct, though connected. In the traditional binary system discussed earlier, they are completely overlapping and almost bear a 'natural' connection. The early feminist interpretations of sex and gender separated them, helped change the meanings of femininity and masculinity, and expanded the notions of being 'women' and 'men'. This differentiation and separation, however, naturalized sex and socialized gender. The latter made it possible to be different kind of gendered beings, but the former made it difficult to transcend the 'biological reality' of being a certain sex.

Understanding gender in a manner that disconnects the material reality of the body from the ways of being and living one's gender poses a challenge to the 'naturalness' of the biological category of sex. Accepting that a person may want change in their body to match their sense of their gender implies that there can be nothing 'natural' about sex. Alongside this, the very fact that bodies can be changed and reconstructed in myriad ways challenges even the very notion of a prototypical 'male' or 'female' body.

Another challenge to these notions comes from people with intersex variations whose external genitals and/or bodies do not lend themselves to the neat categories of the binary. Each one of them, however, is assigned a gender at birth and brought up as a man or a woman. The medical establishment looks at the infant and makes this decision. The lives of people with intersex variations and the ways in which their multiple ways of being are force fitted into binary categories of sex indicate that sex is also constructed. The continuum of variations in life forms, which is often forced to fit into fixed categorizations by socially manipulated systems of making meaning, as is often done in biology, is done here by the medical system to once again present a constructed category as a natural one.

In their study on gender, Kessler and McKenna (1978) make an important point: that though we want to make genitals the basis for sex, it is only rarely that we are in a position to view each other's genitals. To this Miqqi Alicia Gilbert (2009: 96) adds:

> Sex is a biological and typically legal classification that, interestingly enough, does not play a major social function in a daily way.... [M]ost of the time we are actually dealing with sex category rather than sex; that is, since we don't actually know the genital situation of any given individual, we make assumptions and draw conclusions about sex based on gender display.

Thus, sex too is being attributed and read, in the reading and attribution of gender.

The assumed naturalness of the category makes it extremely difficult for those whose bodies do not match their perceived gender. Nowhere is it more stark than the field of competitive sport where men's and women's competitions are separate and, thus, there is a stronger scrutiny of the 'female' athletes. In the last few years there have been challenges in the public domain about whether people like Caster Semenya, Santhi Soundarrajan and Dutee Chand can compete in international sports. Countless others who live lives that are made 'not normal' because of these constructions of the 'naturalness of sex' live with constant interrogation and the ever-present fear of being outed.[1] Thus, it is imperative that any new gender system revisit, re-envision and reinvent the category of sex.

Finally it is because of the perceived notion of sex and gender that people experience sexism and misogyny. It is because of the strict categorization and not the nature of the body or desire that sexual and gendered violence and discrimination happen. Therefore it is almost impossible to talk of 'real women' and 'real men' (and absurd to talk only in terms of men and women).

Hence, we choose to say that actually persons are assigned a gender at birth which each one models according to their felt understanding of themselves, sometimes altering the meaning and retaining the name, at other times changing the name and creating new meanings, and sometimes even changing the names but living the same meanings.

This brings us to the third of the body-based naturalized categories that form the basis of this binary gender system—

sexuality. It further naturalizes two body types by ascribing to them the 'natural' desire for the 'opposite', thus normalizing heterosexuality and rendering all other desires impossible, punishable and targeted. Many struggles and battles against this normative model of desire have been waged by people who have been punished for expressing desire for those who are the 'same' and not the 'opposite', or for both the 'same and the opposite' or even when desire for the 'opposite' is expressed in unacceptable ways—outside the ambit of marriage or violating the accepted class, caste, or religious norms; desire for more than one at the same time; desire without the narrative of love and commitment; and many others.

Transforming the gender system from the binary to the multiple forces us to take another look at these radical articulations as well. While challenging imposed norms, are these still trapped in the language of the binary? For instance, what does same-sex desire really mean once we accept there are more than two sexes or genders? What meanings, then, do we attribute to heterosexual, homosexual and bisexual?

The rainbow of the LGBTHKQIA... allows all those marginalized by the binary system to challenge it together. The various identities, ways of being and politics, uneasily clubbed together under this umbrella, need to be mindful of the ways in which each of their articulations challenge or do not challenge the triad of gender, sex and sexuality. They are connected and yet distinct. And, hence, struggles against their normative assertions can partly be common but will also need to be separate.

If challenges are undertaken without a careful, critical understanding of each of these constructs, they could even work against each other. So the assertion of a lesbian identity of someone could force their partner into being 'woman' even if they did not identify as such. Asking for rights based on same-sex desire could push us back into the naturalizing of sex. And speaking of sexual behaviours as identities could come in the way of evolving a radical politics of sexuality.

A Transformative Politics of Gender

When the gender system changes from a binary, closed one to a consensual, open, multiple and plastic one, then it is not just the systems of sex, gender and sexuality that get shifted. Change, after all, is not just about making accommodations at the centre and contracting the margins, but also about questioning the ideas and powers that underlie the formation and the persistence of these structures.

As Michael Rembis (2010: 56) says in the context of disability and sexuality:

> Thinking more broadly about sexuality will no doubt prove beneficial, but we must also work to reshape the very notion of gender, sex, sexuality, eroticism, desire, and disability, and to subvert the power relations and class structures that undergird the maintenance of these ideological constructions. Fundamentally altering the way we see the world ultimately will be much more difficult than simply being more 'inclusive'.

Throughout this study and in this book, as we looked at the intersection of our respondents' lives with different social institutions like the family, school and college, workspaces, public spaces and even the intimate space of relationships with others and/or oneself, we came across possibilities of change in the short and long term.

Changes that would help more people be themselves, that would help greater inclusion, are needed immediately. However, if the existing system of gender, sex and sexuality is itself destabilized, then each of these institutions would be transformed over time. The division of labour and the demarcation of the public and the private can then be envisaged in yet another way beyond what early feminism did. More pertinently, it is rethinking the organization of care, of intimacy and kinship beyond blood that have the potential to revolutionize the ways in which we live our lives.

Radical change does not come about just by the presence of difference or its mere acceptance into the already established orders. Our study and our work show that the integration of a truly radical view of gender into society demands a deep connect to changes in all other oppressive systems, such as those of patriarchy, class, caste or ableism.

True transformation revolves around the reordering of society and social structures, but like all other critiques of the present socio-political-economic structures, no single shift can bring about radical change. A transformative politics is that which connects us to various people's struggles towards radical change in society—struggles that counter the growing cultural and economic right wing and the military–industrial complex, all of which are gaining more and more power.

To have no outlaws in the gender galaxy, the voices and lives of those outlawed by the present restrictive and closed system, have to critically inform the envisioning of this transformation. We hope this book and especially the voices within it, contribute towards this process.

Note

1. For a brief history of female athletes in modern competitive sport and the variations of 'sex' and 'gender' tests they have been subjected to, refer to Koh, Adair and Sonsken (2014). Also see Macur (2014) for Dutee Chand's challenge to the International Association of Athletics Federations guidelines that have resulted in her ban due to high testosterone levels.

Appendix

Some Terms Used

Queer: We use the term 'queer' in this book in a very specific sense. This refers to people who may or may not know or actively use the word for themselves, but who define their own sexuality and/or gender identity as not heterosexual and/or not cisgender. In this sense, all 50 respondents and all 11 researchers are queer PAGFB. 'Queer' is also used as an adjective for those individuals, collectives, campaigns and movements that self-identify as such, however they might define the term, while possibly also using other descriptors like LBT or LGBT or transgender.

PAGFB (person[s] assigned gender female at birth) and **PAGMB (person[s] assigned gender male at birth):** These terms, which were arrived at independently in our discussions in the context of this study (and which we are happy to find echoed by gender activists and gaining currency in queer discourse worldwide), reflect our understanding that none of us is born with a readymade gender; rather, it is assigned to us at birth based on the traditional conflation of sex, in particular of the external genitalia, with gender. This assigned gender may or may not match a person's own sense of their gender. All respondents in this study are PAGFB though not all of them belong to the 'female' gender or consider themselves women, just as all PAGMB may not be of the 'male' gender or call themselves men. Together, the two terms include all people, and every variation in gender and of body.

Trans*: This refers to all those whose own sense of their gender does not match the gender assigned to them at birth. Spelt with an asterisk, trans* is an umbrella term coined within gender studies (and borrowing from computer file nomenclature) in order to refer to all non-cisgender gender identities, including transsexual, transvestite, genderqueer, genderfluid, genderless, agender, non-gendered, third gender, two-spirit, bigender, MTF (male-to-female), FTM (female-to-male), transman, transwoman, other, man-identified PAGFB, woman-identified PAGMB and (m)any others.

Cisgender: This refers to someone whose own sense of her or his gender matches the gender assigned to her, or to him, at birth. Thus, a cisman is a PAGMB who identifies as man, and a ciswoman is a PAGFB who identifies as woman. To be cisgender, then, is to enjoy cisgender privilege, which a trans* person lacks in a world based on the gender binary.

Intersex variations: Human bodies have many variations and these could be at multiple levels. Thus, it is incorrect to talk of an absolute standard of 'normal' for the 'male' or 'female' body. We choose to say 'persons with intersex variations' as against intersex conditions to emphasize variations in bodies without pathologizing them. Intersex variations are congenital differences in reproductive parts and/or secondary sexual characteristics, and/or variations invisible to the eye, such as chromosomal and/ or hormonal differences. (For more information on issues and debates around intersex variations, refer to the OII Australia website, http:// oii.org.au.)

Pronouns Used

In the pronouns used in this report, we have tried to be faithful to the gender identities that people espoused for themselves. All those who identified as 'man' or 'woman' have been referred to by the appropriate gender pronouns: *he, him, his*; *she, her, hers.* For those who did not identify as either 'man' or 'woman', we have used the category 'others' and chosen the pronouns *ze, hir, hirs.*

Although everyone (with the exception of one respondent who was searching for a new way to speak of hirself) used either the male or female pronouns for themselves, we have used *ze, hir, hirs* to fill the gaps in a language which recognizes only the gender binary. These (provisional) pronouns are also a useful way of indicating the gender location of the respondent in question, rather than having to clarify the point in every instance. In places where gender is not being specified, we have used the generic plural *they, them, their, theirs.*

Bibliography

Against a Trans Narrative. 2008. Produced by K. Broom, directed by J. Rosskam (documentary). http://www.vdb.org/titles/against-trans-narrative (accessed 6 March 2015).

Asmi, N. and Bina. 1999. 'Fire, Sparks and Smouldering Ashes', *Scripts*, May.

Bergman, S. Bear. 2006. *Butch Is a Noun.* Vancouver: Arsenal Pulp Press.

Bettcher, T. and A. Garry (eds). 2009. 'Transgender Studies and Feminism: Theory, Politics, and Gendered Realities' (special issue), *Hypatia*, 24(3).

Bingham, E.P. 1922. *Fluidity and Plasticity.* New York: McGraw Hill.

Bornstein, K. 1995. *Gender Outlaw: On Men, Women, and the Rest of Us.* New York: Vintage Books.

Bornstein, K. and S.B. Bergman (eds). 2010. *Gender Outlaws: The Next Generation.* Berkeley: Seal Press.

Campaign for Lesbian Rights (CALERI). *Khamosh! Emergency Jaari Hai: Lesbian Emergence.* New Delhi: CALERI.

Creating Resources for Empowerment in Action (CREA). 2012. 'Count Me IN!: Research Report on Violence against Disabled, Lesbian, and Sex-Working Women in Bangladesh, India, and Nepal'. New Delhi: CREA.

Feinberg, L. 1996. *Transgender Warriors: Making History from Joan of Arc to Dennis Rodman.* Boston: Beacon Press.

Fernandez, B. (ed.). 2002. *Humjinsi : A Resource Book on Lesbian, Gay and Bisexual Rights in India.* Mumbai: India Centre for Human Rights and Law.

Fernandez, B. and N.B. Gomathy. 2003. 'The Nature of Violence Faced by Lesbian Women in India'. Mumbai: Research Centre on Violence against Women, Tata Institute Of Social Sciences.

Ghosh, S. and B.S. Bandyopadhyay (eds). 2010. *Of Horizons and Beyond: Glimpses of Lesbian, Bisexual Women and Transpersons' Lives.* Kolkata: Sappho for Equality.

Ghosh, S., S. Bandyopadhyay and R. Biswas. 2011. *Vio-Map: Documenting and Mapping Violence and Rights Violation Taking Place n the Lives of Sexually Marginalized Women to Chart out Effective Advocacy Strategies.* Kolkata: Sappho For Equality.

Gilbert, M.A. 2009. 'Defeating Bigenderism: Changing Gender Assumptions in the Twenty-First century', *Hypatia* 24(3): 93–112.

Haraway, D. 1988. 'Situated Knowledges: The Science Question in Feminism and the Privilege of Partial Perspective', *Feminist Studies*, 14(3): 575–99.

Harding, S. 1987. 'Is There a Feminist Method?' in S. Harding (ed.) *Feminism and Methodology: Social Science Issues*, pp.1–14. Bloomington: Indiana University Press.

Halberstam, J. 2005. *In a Queer Time and Place: Transgender Bodies, Subcultural Lives*. New York: New York University Press.

———. 2011. *Queer Art of Failure*. Durham: Duke University Press.

Harstock, N. 1998. *The Feminist Standpoint Revisited and Other Essays*. Boulder: West View Press.

Human Rights Commission of the City & County of San Francisco. 2005. 'A Human Rights Investigation into the Medical "Normalization" of Intersex People'. https://oii.org.au/wp-content/uploads/2009/sfhrc_intersex_report.pdf (accessed on 6 March 2014).

Karkazis, K. 2008. *Fixing Sex: Intersex, Medical Authority, and Lived Experience*. Durham: Duke University Press.

Kessler, S. and W. McKenna. 1978. *Gender: An Ethno-Methodological Approach*. Chicago: University of Chicago Press.

———. 2006. 'Toward a Theory of Gender', in S. Stryker and S. Whittle (eds), *The Transgender Reader*, pp.165–82. New York: Routledge.

Koh, Ben, Daryl Adair and Peter Sonksen. 2014. 'Testosterone, Sex and Gender Differentiation in Sport: Where Science and Sports Law Meet'. http://www.lawinsport.com/articles/item/testosterone-sex-and-gender-differentiation-in-sport-where-science-and-sports-law-meet (accessed 6 March 2015).

Mahajan, S. (ed.). 2003. 'Redefining Oppressions and Articulating Rights – Marginalised Sexualities and Genders in India', *Combat Law* (Mumbai) October.

Living Smile Vidya. 2007. *I am Vidya* (translated by V. Ramnarayan). Chennai: Oxygen Books.

Macur, Juliet. 2014. 'Fighting for the Body She Was Born With', *New York Times*, 6 October. http://www.nytimes.com/2014/10/07/sports/sprinter-dutee-chand-fights-ban-over-her-testosterone-level.html (accessed 6 March 2015).

Mahajan, S. 2008. 'Questioning norms and Bodies', *Seminar*. http://www.india-seminar.com/2008/583/583_shalini_mahajan.htm (accessed 12 October 2014).

Mehta, K. 2008. 'Women's Movements in India', *Seminar*. http://www.india-seminar.com/2008/583/583_kalpana_mehta.htm (accessed 12 October 2014).

Menon, N. (ed.). 2007. *Sexualities*. New Delhi: Women Unlimited.

Mohan, S. and S. Murthy. 2013. *Towards Gender Inclusivity: A Study on Contemporary Concerns Around Gender.* Bangalore: Alternative Law Forum and LesBiT.

Moten, F. and S. Harney. 2004. 'The University and the Undercommons: Seven Theses', *Social Text*, 22(22): 101–15.

Narrain, A. 2003. 'The Articulation of Queer Rights: The Emerging Right to Sexual Orientation and Gender Identity'. http://altlawforum.org/publications/the-articulation-of-queer-rights-the-emerging-right-to-sexual-orientation-and-gender-identity (accessed 12 October 2014).

———. 2004. *Queer: Law And Despised Sexualities in India.* Bangalore: Books for Change.

Narrain, A. and G. Bhan (eds). 2005. *Because I Have a Voice: Queer Politics in India.* New Delhi: Yoda Press.

Narrain, A. and M. Eldridge. 2009. *The Right that Dares to Speak Its Name: Decriminalising Sexual Orientation and Gender Identity in India.* Bangalore: Alternative Law Forum.

Narrain, A. and A. Gupta. (eds). 2011. *Law Like Love: Queer Perspectives on Law.* New Delhi: Yoda Press.

Orchids: My Intersex Adventure (documentary). 2010. Produced and directed by P. Hart. http://www.wmm.com/filmcatalog/pages/c802.shtml (accessed 6 March 2015).

Parker R. and P. Aggleton (eds). 1999. *Culture, Society, and Sexuality: A Reader.* London: UCL Press.

Reddy, G. 2006. *With Respect to Sex: Negotiating Hijra Identity in South India.* New Delhi: Yoda Press.

Reinharz, S. 1992. *Feminist Methods in Social Research.* New York: Oxford University Press.

Reis, E. 2009. *Bodies in Doubt: An American History of Intersex.* Baltimore: The Johns Hopkins University Press.

Rembis, M.A. 2010. 'Beyond the Binary: Rethinking the Social Model of Disability', *Sexuality and Disability*, 28(1): 51–60.

Revathi, A. 2010. *The Truth about Me: A Hijra Life Story* (translated by V. Geetha). New Delhi: Penguin Books.

Salomon, G. 2010. *Assuming a Body: Transgender and Rhetoric of Materiality.* New York: Columbia University Press.

Scott, J. 1998. *Seeing Like a State: How Certain Schemes to Improve the Human Condition Have Failed.* Yale: Yale University Press.

Serano, J. 2007. *Whipping Girl: A Transsexual Woman on Sexism and the Scapegoating of Femininity.* Emeryville: Seal Press.

Shah, C. 2005. 'The Roads that E/Merged: Feminist Activism and Queer Understanding', in A. Narrain and G. Bhan (eds), *Because I Have a Voice*, pp. 143–54. New Delhi: Yoda Press.

Shah, C., Raj, S. Mahajan and S. Nevatia. 2013. 'Breaking the Binary: Understanding Issues and Concerns of Queer Persons Assigned Gender Female at Birth Across a Spectrum of Lived Gender Realities'. Report by LABIA, Mumbai. https://sites.google.com/site/labiacollective/ (accessed 4 April 2015).

Shakespeare, T. 1997. 'Researching Disabled Sexuality', in C. Barne and G. Mercer (eds), *Doing Disability Research*, pp.177–89. Leeds: The Disability Press.

Sharma, M. 2006. *Loving Women: Being Lesbian in Unprivileged India.* New Delhi: Yoda Press.

Spade, D. 2006. 'Mutilating Gender', in S. Stryker and S. Whittle (eds), *The Transgender Reader*, pp.315–32. New York: Routledge.

Stryker, S. 2008. *Transgender History.* Berkeley: Seal Press.

Stryker, S. and S. Whittle (eds). 2006. *The Transgender Studies Reader.* New York: Routledge.

Vanita, R. 2005. *Gandhi's Tiger and Sita's Smile: Essays on Gender, Sexuality and Culture.* New Delhi: Yoda Press.

Vanita, R. and S. Kidwai (eds). 2000. *Same Sex Love in India: Readings from Literature and History.* New Delhi: Palgrave-Macmillan.

Willkins, Rikki Ann. 2006. 'What Does It Cost to Tell the Truth?', in S. Stryker and S. Whittle (eds). *The Transgender Reader*, pp. 547–51. New York: Routledge.